Active Directory Field Guide

Laura E. Hunter

Apress®

Active Directory Field Guide

Copyright © 2005 by Laura E. Hunter

ISBN (pbk): 1-59059-492-4

Printed and bound in the United States of America 9 8 7 6 5 4 3 2 1

Trademarked names may appear in this book. Rather than use a trademark symbol with every occurrence of a trademarked name, we use the names only in an editorial fashion and to the benefit of the trademark owner, with no intention of infringement of the trademark.

Lead Editor: Jim Sumser
Technical Reviewer: Alexander N. Nepomnjashiy
Editorial Board: Steve Anglin, Dan Appleman, Ewan Buckingham, Gary Cornell, Tony Davis, Jason Gilmore, Jonathan Hassell, Chris Mills, Dominic Shakeshaft, Jim Sumser
Assistant Publisher: Grace Wong
Project Manager: Beckie Stones
Copy Manager: Nicole LeClerc
Copy Editor: Ami Knox
Production Manager: Kari Brooks-Copony
Production Editor: Ellie Fountain
Compositor: Diana Van Winkle
Proofreader: Linda Marousek
Indexer: Kevin Broccoli
Artist: Diana Van Winkle
Cover Designer: Kurt Krames
Manufacturing Manager: Tom Debolski

Distributed to the book trade in the United States by Springer-Verlag New York, Inc., 233 Spring Street, 6th Floor, New York, NY 10013, and outside the United States by Springer-Verlag GmbH & Co. KG, Tiergartenstr. 17, 69112 Heidelberg, Germany.

In the United States: phone 1-800-SPRINGER, fax 201-348-4505, e-mail orders@springer-ny.com, or visit http://www.springer-ny.com. Outside the United States: fax +49 6221 345229, e-mail orders@springer.de, or visit http://www.springer.de.

For information on translations, please contact Apress directly at 2560 Ninth Street, Suite 219, Berkeley, CA 94710. Phone 510-549-5930, fax 510-549-5939, e-mail info@apress.com, or visit http://www.apress.com.

For Mom, Dad, and Bryan

Contents at a Glance

Contents

About the Author

Photo by Rebecca Vlastaridis, Philadelphia, PA.
Hair & Makeup by Strands, Philadelphia, PA

Laura E. Hunter (CISSP, MCSE: Security, MCDBA, Microsoft MVP) is a senior IT specialist with the University of Pennsylvania, where she provides network planning, implementation, and troubleshooting services for various business units and schools within the university. Her specialties include Microsoft Windows 2000 and 2003 design and implementation, troubleshooting, and security topics. Laura has over a decade of experience in the areas of Windows and Novell networking; her previous experience includes a position as the director of computer services for the Salvation Army and as the LAN administrator for a medical supply firm. She is a contributor to the TechTarget family of websites, and to *Redmond* magazine (formerly *Microsoft Certified Professional Magazine*).

Laura has previously contributed to the *Syngress Windows Server 2003 MCSE/MCSA DVD Guide & Training System* series for exams 70-291/292/293/ 294/296/297/298 as a DVD presenter, author, and technical reviewer. Laura is a two-time recipient of the prestigious Microsoft "Most Valued Professional" award in the area of Windows Server—Networking. Laura graduated with honors from the University of Pennsylvania and also works as a freelance writer, trainer, speaker, and consultant based in the Philadelphia area. You can reach Laura at laurahcomputing@gmail.com.

About the Technical Reviewer

Alexzander Nepomnjashiy is a Microsoft SQL Server database designer for NeoSystems NorthWest—a security services, consulting, and training company.

He has over ten years' experience in the IT field. Currently he is working on several projects that involve the deployment of Microsoft Windows NT Server/Microsoft SQL Server within an enterprise business/financial environment.

His typical role in these projects is extending and improving client's corporate ERP systems to manage retail sales data, predict market changes, and calculate trends for future market situations (using DSS and OLAP tools and techniques).

You can contact him at alexnep@onego.ru.

Acknowledgments

A project of this scope is never the work of just one individual, and I would like to thank the following people who have been indispensable in nurturing this book through to its final form:

- Everyone at Apress who took the time to make me feel like such a welcome addition to the family: Gary Cornell, Jim Sumser, Beckie Stones, Tina Nielsen, Ellie Fountain, Ami Knox, Julie Miller, Glenn Munlawin, and Jonathan Hassell, along with Alexzander Nepomnjashiy for his outstanding insights as a technical reviewer.

- The wonderful people at Microsoft whom I've engaged with as a part of the MVP program and otherwise: Emily Freet, John Buscher, Eddy Malik, Christopher Corbett, Joseph Davies, Sean O'Driscoll, Susan Leiter, Candice Pedersen, Jan Shanahan, Mark Mortimore, and Steve Riley.

- Members of the Microsoft MVP community who have impacted me both professionally and personally: Steve Friedl, Susan Bradley, Joe Richards, Don Wells, Jeremy Moskowitz, Mark Minasi, Mitch Ruebush, Roger Abell, Thomas Lee, Charles Clarke, Roger Seielstad, Tony Murray, Dèjì Akómöláfé, Robbie Allen, and Ron Chamberlin.

- And last but certainly not least, my family: Carol, Charles, John and Paula Hunter, Stephanie Adams, Wayne Collins, Joey Huff, and Bryan Hopkins.

Introduction

Active Directory Field Guide is predominantly targeted at network administrators and consultants who have some experience with the Windows client and server operating systems. These administrators may fall into one of two groups:

- Readers who have little or no Active Directory experience and who are ready to make the transition from Windows NT 4.0
- Readers who have gained some Active Directory exposure either on the job or through an AD tutorial, and who are seeking to expand their AD administration repertoire

This book does not assume that you have any grounding in VBScript, JScript, or any other language commonly used for administrative scripting, though a little background knowledge does no harm. You'll find several examples of these types of scripts throughout the book, as well as a scripting primer at the end of the final chapter.

What Does This Book Cover?

In structuring this book, I tried to organize things in a logical manner that kept similar tasks and concepts grouped closely together so that you could find them easily. The first two chapters of this book revolve around installing a brand-new Active Directory infrastructure, both installing AD itself as well as the network infrastructure underpinnings that AD needs to function well. From there, you'll move into a trio of chapters about the kinds of tasks that you'll deal with on a daily basis: administering and securing your Active Directory network. You can take these three chapters in particular as one big chunk—they'll cover most of the skills you'll need to run the day-to-day operations of Active Directory.

The remaining chapters examine different aspects of Active Directory deployment and planning, including managing larger installations and protecting your network against disasters. Over the course of these nine chapters, you'll learn how to install, deploy, configure, and troubleshoot all of the major aspects of Active Directory. Each chapter also closes with a list of resources, both print and online, that you can reference for more information on a particular topic.

Here's a summary of the contents of this book:

- Chapter 1 is an introduction to installing Active Directory on a Windows 2000 or Windows Server 2003 computer. This is where we take the "view from 30,000 feet" and look at design considerations such as how your domains and forests should be set up, what your physical and logical design should look like, and how to plan for the necessary hardware capacity for your Active Directory domain controllers. We'll then walk through the process of installing a brand new forest, a new domain tree in an existing forest, a new child domain, and an additional domain controller within an existing domain. We'll also look at ways to automate the installation process through the use of scripts and unattend.txt files.

- Chapter 2 focuses specifically on the network infrastructure components that make Active Directory tick. The most critical of these is DNS, since this is what AD relies on for client and server name resolution. I'll show you ways to configure DNS zones and servers to optimize name resolution performance on your Active Directory network. We'll then look at some other technologies that are not *required* for AD to function, but that you'll probably need to work with at some point nonetheless. This includes DHCP, which is used to automate TCP/IP addressing and configuration for client servers and workstations, as well as WINS, which is used to streamline name resolution for legacy clients and line-of-business applications that still rely on NetBIOS instead of pure DNS.

- Chapters 3 and 4 are all about the day-to-day tasks you'll perform as an Active Directory administrator. This includes creating user and group accounts, managing user profiles and data, and creating login scripts to improve the user experience. In particular, I'll show you ways to automate user creation so that you can create hundreds of Active Directory users at the command line using a simple text file. In Chapter 4, I'll focus specifically on Active Directory Group Policy Objects, which allow you to customize virtually every aspect of your server and client computers from your administrative workstation. This includes using security templates and software restriction policies to protect your network from malicious software or errant users, as well as using software installation settings to deploy line-of-business applications at the touch of a button.

- Chapter 5 focuses on Active Directory security, a topic that has become increasingly important as more and more organizations are acquiring always-on Internet connectivity. We'll look at ways to harden the Windows server operating system and the TCP/IP stack, as well as using IPSec to filter unwanted traffic away from your domain controllers, member servers, and workstations.

- In Chapter 6, we'll move away from day-to-day tasks and go back up to 30,000 feet to look at managing large-scale Active Directory deployments. In larger environments, you'll probably find yourself in a position where you want to allow local administrators or help desk personnel to take over some of the more common tasks like resetting passwords or unlocking user accounts, and Active Directory gives you much more flexibility in this regard than any of its predecessors. We'll also look at some tasks that are geared specifically towards multisite or multidomain environments, such as setting up trust relationships, site replication, and Global Catalog servers.

- Chapter 7 focuses specifically on performing migrations to Active Directory from earlier versions of the Windows server operating systems, particularly Windows NT 4.0. We'll again start at the high-level planning stages and discuss what you need to do to prepare for a successful (or even an unsuccessful) migration. You'll then get an in-depth look at the Active Directory Migration tool, a free utility that helps to streamline the process of moving users, computers, and other resources from Windows NT 4.0 or Windows 2000 into a new Windows Server 2003 Active Directory environment.

- In Chapter 8, you'll gain some insight into disaster recovery, a crucial topic for any Active Directory administrator. Too many network administrators put off creating a disaster recovery strategy or even a data backup plan until it's too late, after the server has already died (taking your data with it) and you have no good way to get your server's clients back online. To help make sure that this horrible eventuality doesn't happen to you, I'll show you ways to protect your Active Directory database using data backups, as well as ways to troubleshoot a failed server.

- I close out the Active Directory Consultant's Guide with a chapter that has a bit of a split personality: Chapter 9 covers two slightly more advanced topics that you can add to your administrative skillset. We start out by looking at the Active Directory schema, which is the structure that defines how AD objects and information are created, indexed, and organized throughout your network. This includes how to manage and protect the schema, as well as ways to programmatically extend the schema to customize Active Directory for your business needs. We close things out with a quick introduction to using scripting languages to improve your Active Directory administrative skills. While I don't imagine that I'll turn you into a scripting whiz kid in the space of 15 pages, the final section of this book should at least put you on the path toward scripting excellence.

—Laura E. Hunter

CHAPTER 1

■ ■ ■

Installing Active Directory

I'm going to start things off literally at the beginning, by looking at the tasks involved in installing Active Directory (AD). If you need to build a brand new network from the ground up, you'll find helpful advice on the Active Directory design process, as well as actual walk-throughs of the Active Directory Installation Wizard and ways to automate the installation process. Even if you're working with a network that's already been installed, you might still find some useful nuggets here as we talk about the overall structure of Active Directory forests, domain trees, and domains, and how to configure Global Catalog servers and Flexible Single Master Operations role holders.

In this chapter, you'll learn how to

- Plan an Active Directory deployment.
- Develop the logical and physical design of Active Directory.
- Plan for domain controller placement and capacity.
- Install a new Active Directory forest.
- Install a new Active Directory domain.
- Install additional domain controllers in an existing domain.
- Automate the installation process.
- Troubleshoot common installation issues.

Planning Your Active Directory Installation

I'm going to begin with an assumption here; namely, that you're concerned with something more in-depth than just logging on to a server's console and typing **dcpromo** to create a single domain controller (DC). So we'll start with a discussion of actually designing an Active Directory infrastructure, perhaps for a brand new network or a new branch office of an existing network. (We'll talk about migrating an existing NT 4.0 domain to Active Directory in Chapter 7.) Designing an Active Directory network will require you to define both the physical and logical structure of your network so that you can translate this into logical entities like forests and domains, and combine these with physical network items like sites and subnets.

Creating the Logical Structure

Because Active Directory allows you to treat your physical and logical network design as completely separate entities, you're not necessarily tied into creating an Active Directory network that maps directly to the way your physical network is set up. So an Active Directory infrastructure depends on both the physical and logical components being thought out and designed well. Because Active Directory is a distributed database that's replicated between each domain controller and Global Catalog server in a domain and forest, creating an efficient network design will simplify the administration and sharing of your network resources, and optimize how your network utilizes its available bandwidth.

You'll break up an Active Directory network into forests, followed by domains, followed by Organizational Units, or OUs. The top-level Active Directory container is the forest, and each forest can contain one or more domains. Each AD domain can likewise contain one or more OUs. This gives Active Directory a hierarchical organizational structure, as you can see in Figure 1-1. These components will make up the logical structure of Active Directory, which remains independent of the physical layout of your network.

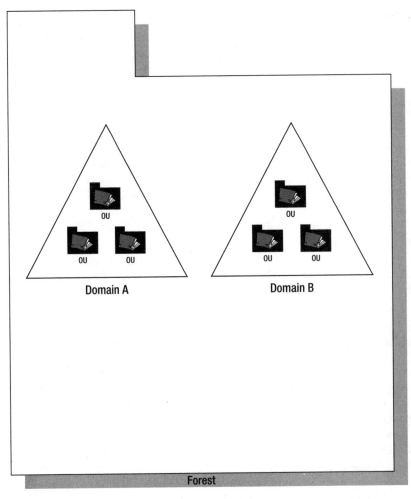

Figure 1-1. *The logical components of Active Directory*

Designing the Forest Structure

The *forest* is the topmost Active Directory container that you can create. Forests create a security boundary for AD, since no user outside of the forest can perform any kind of administration of the forest unless he is given explicit authority to do so. All domains and objects within a single forest will share a single schema and directory configuration, and will have two-way transitive trust relationships that are automatically created between domain trees within the forest. Each domain in an Active Directory forest also has one or more *Global Catalog servers* that replicate information between domains in the forest. Global Catalog servers allow for fast, efficient object searches that span an entire Active Directory forest. Every Global Catalog server in the forest, regardless of the domain to which it belongs, will hold an identical copy of the Global Catalog.

Probably the most important decision when creating your design is determining how many forests your organization needs. A single-forest design is the simplest to deploy and administer because there's no need to coordinate between multiple groups of IT administrators or enable synchronization between more than one forest. However, this not suitable for every situation since you may have resources and groups with differing administrative and security requirements. Determining the number of forests you require really comes down to a question of isolation versus autonomy. *Autonomy* refers to a situation where an administrator has independent control of a resource like an Organizational Unit, but other administrators can still exert control over the resource. So if you delegate control of an OU to a departmental administrator, that person will be able to control the resources in that area without turning to a domain administrator to perform, or even authorize, each administrative action. However, a member of the Domain Admins group would still be able to administer the OU in question, even though the day-to-day administration of it is being handled by the departmental administrator. This is probably the most common example of creating autonomy within Active Directory.

Having multiple domains in a single forest is another example of autonomy, since each domain has its own Domain Admins group, but the forest-wide Enterprise Admins group can still independently administer any domain in the forest. *Isolation*, on the other hand, refers to a situation where a group of administrators has exclusive control over a particular resource. So not only does an administrator need independent control over a resource to achieve isolation, but it also means that no other administrators can administer the resource in question, either overriding the local administrator's decisions or taking away her administrative rights. In the case of Active Directory, the only way to truly achieve isolation is by using separate forests, since there is no "higher authority" than the Enterprise Admins group in an AD forest that can interfere with or supersede the decisions of the forest administrators. The most common deployment scenarios you'll see for Active Directory forests are these:

- A *single-forest* model will consist of several different Active Directory domains contained in a single forest. This design option has the lowest amount of administrative overhead and is the simplest to administer.

- The *subscription-forest* design is useful for an organization with several autonomous divisions. It allows early adopters of Active Directory to deploy their own forests, while the majority of the organization will deploy AD as part of a single unified forest.

- A *multiple-forest* design will allow each division to deploy its own Active Directory forest, each of which will possess its own Global Catalog, schema, and administrative responsibility.

What it really boils down to is this: do you have groups and resources that need to be isolated from the remainder of your network, or will it be sufficient to simply delegate authority to different groups without needing to draw such a distinct "line" in the administrative "sand"? You may have different parts of your organization that require absolute isolation of their data and resources from the rest of your network: this is often the case when you're dealing with extremely high-security installations, like government organizations and companies dealing in sensitive research, or if you are dealing with legal or regulatory stipulations that require you to fully separate out different portions of your network. Conversely, your company may consist of a number of different departments that need to operate independently from one another, but are willing to be a part of a single shared infrastructure to decrease costs and administrative overhead.

▪**Note** Determining the number of forests you need can be a business or "political" decision as much as it is a technical one. While you may not see the need for a particular area of your company to have their own forest, management may see things differently. It's your job as an Active Directory consultant or administrator to point out the technical ramifications of deploying multiple forests.

Creating Multiple Domain Trees

One common area of confusion when designing an Active Directory forest is this: you don't need to deploy two separate forests solely to support two portions of a network that require separate namespaces. Each Active Directory domain requires a contiguous namespace, which means that the naming conventions of any child domains need to look like this:

- company.com
- east.company.com
- mktg.east.company.com
- west.company.com
- ad.west.company.com

Each of these child domains shares a contiguous namespace with the root domain, company.com. However, you can have a separate domain tree within the same forest that doesn't belong to the same namespace. So you could have a second domain tree within the same forest, with domain names as follows:

- airplanes.com
- finance.airplanes.com
- dev.airplanes.com
- research.airplanes.com
- sst.research.airplanes.com

In this case, you have a single Active Directory forest that contains two domain trees: the company.com domain tree and the airplanes.com domain tree. Even though the two domain trees don't share a namespace, they can still belong to the same forest. This will allow them to share the same schema, Global Catalogs, and directory configuration. (The argument against multiple domain trees is that, because the two domain trees are part of the same forest, they do not have the same level of isolation that multiple forests would create.) So when you're planning your Active Directory network, be sure that you're not deploying multiple forests in a situation where multiple domain trees would be more appropriate.

Deploying Multiple Forests

So let's say that you've decided that you simply must deploy multiple Active Directory forests. At this point, you need to determine how your resources are going to be organized within these different forests. In most cases, you'll group resources based on the organization of your company, so that users and objects in the department that requires isolation are all grouped into a single forest. You can use trust relationships between forests if you have users in one forest that need access to another one, so that administrators in each forest can grant access to their forest resources to users in other forests. In Windows 2000, you'll need to set up one-way trust relationships between each forest that requires trust access; Windows Server 2003 allows for two-way transitive trust relationships between forests. So let's say that you're administering a network that contains extremely sensitive Research & Development data that only a small percentage of employees should have access to. You can create the company.corp forest for day-to-day access to file and print resources, and then a company.dev forest that contains the sensitive R&D information. You can then create a one-way trust relationship between the two forests, so that a researcher with a user account in the company.corp forest will be able to access resources in the company.dev forest using a single user account, without allowing users in company.corp unnecessary access to information in the R&D forest.

For even better security, you can create a separate forest that doesn't have any trust relationships with the remainder of your network. For users to access resources in this restricted forest, they will need to have an account that was explicitly created for them within it. You can see where this can create administrative headaches, since your users will now have two separate usernames to juggle (with passwords that aren't synchronized and may have different complexity requirements and expiration settings); however, in extremely high-security environments, this type of protection is sometimes necessary. In our previous example, a researcher would require two user accounts: jdoe@company.corp to access the company's commonly accessible resources, and jdoe@company.dev to get into the R&D domain.

In case I haven't fully made the point yet, managing and maintaining multiple forests will create a great deal of administrative complexity for your organization. All in all, there are two specific scenarios in which multiple forests are a good idea; in all other cases, you should try to make a single forest model work. The two scenarios that are appropriate for a multiple forest model are as follows:

- You need to create a small number of domains that have limited trust relationships with each other, but are otherwise completely autonomous.

- You are working with two existing organizations that already have their own Active Directory forests in place.

Establishing Trust Relationships

Within Active Directory, you'll use trust relationships to allow users from one container to access resources in another container. You can set up trust relationships between domains, forests, and even non-Windows domains. In Windows NT 4.0, all trust relationships were one-way and nontransitive. A *one-way trust relationship* means that if you have two domains that need to trust each other, you need to set up one trust relationship going from Domain A to Domain B, and then a second trust relationship going from Domain B back to Domain A. A *nontransitive trust relationship* means that if you set up a trust going from Domain A to Domain B, and then another trust going from Domain B to Domain C, you don't automatically have a trust relationship between Domain A and Domain C—you'll need to set up a separate trust relationship directly between Domain A and Domain C. And each of these individual trust relationships needs to be managed separately, so you can see how this can get really complicated if you have a lot of domains. If you're working in a complete trust model where all of your domains needed to trust each other, you would need to create $n(n-1)$ separate trust relationships, where n is the number of domains you're working with. For example, if you have ten domains that all need to be able to trust each other in NT 4.0, you need to set up 10 * 9 or 90 separate trust relationships.

Active Directory in Windows 2000 and Windows Server 2003 makes this a lot easier by creating two-way transitive trust relationships by default between domains that are located in the same forest. So if you have three domains within the same forest, a two-way transitive trust relationship will be created automatically so that users in any domain will be able to access resources in any other domain (as long as they have the appropriate NTFS and share permissions, obviously). This two-way transitive trust relationship gets created automatically between a parent domain and a child domain, and between the root domains of two domain trees in the same forest—you'll probably see these default trust relationships referred to as *parent-child* and *tree-root*. You can also create a number of manual trust relationships within Active Directory:

- *External trusts* are created between an Active Directory domain and an NT 4.0 domain, or between Active Directory domains in two separate forests. External trusts are nontransitive, and you can configure them to be either one-way or two-way.

- *Realm trusts* are used to set up a trust relationship between Active Directory and a non-Windows Kerberos realm, typically a UNIX MIT Kerberos realm. Realm trusts can be transitive or nontransitive, and can be one-way or two-way.

- *Forest trusts* allow you to create one-way or two-way transitive trust relationships between Active Directory forests. This type of trust relationship is only available in a pure Windows Server 2003 environment.

In Windows 2000, trust relationships between forests can only be one-way and nontransitive.

Shortcut trusts require a bit more explanation, since they're more a matter of efficiency than security. They're used to shorten the amount of time that it takes a user in one domain to access resources in a separate, trusted domain. By default, trust relationships are verified along a trust path. Take as an example a forest with two domain trees, as shown in Figure 1-2. If a group of users in the sst.research.airplanes.com domain needs to access a file share that's located in the mktg.east.company.com domain, Active Directory will verify each trust relationship from sst.research.airplanes.com all the way up to the root of the domain tree. Then AD will verify the trust relationship between the two domain tree roots: airplanes.com and company.com. After that, the trust relationship will get verified down the company.com domain tree to mktg.east.company.com.

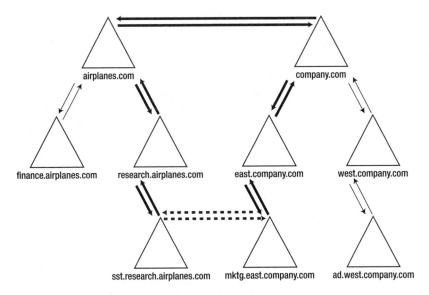

Figure 1-2. *Designing a shortcut trust*

■**Note** The lines in bold in Figure 1-2 indicate the default trust path.

If the users in question only need to access the domain in the other tree once in a while, or if every domain is linked using high-speed connections, the time it takes AD to go up and down the trust path will be negligible. But if any of these domains are connected using a slow or overburdened connection, or if the users need to access files frequently, navigating this trust path can create a noticeable time delay. You can use a shortcut trust to speed up the process by creating a direct trust relationship between the two subdomains, as indicated by the dashed line in Figure 1-2. Shortcut trusts are transitive, and can be one-way or two-way.

Designing a Domain Structure

Each Active Directory forest can contain one or more domains. A domain functions as a logical partition of the Active Directory forest, so that you can replicate a subset of the AD database only where it's needed. More importantly, Active Directory domains create a sign-on mechanism that allows users to log on and access resources with a single user account, even across multiple domains. When creating a domain design, your goal should be to maximize the efficiency of the Active Directory replication, so that your domain information gets distributed to where it needs to be without taking up too much of your available bandwidth. If you're situated in a single location or in multiple locations that are connected by reliable, high-speed connections, this creates a simple, easily administered environment, since the impact of replication traffic will be negligible. If you're working with slow or unreliable links, though, you can create multiple domains to control replication traffic. Your design decisions will primarily revolve around the available bandwidth on your network and the number of users you'll be supporting.

■**Note** You can also use sites within a single domain to control replication traffic, which we'll discuss in the "Creating the Physical Design" section later in the chapter.

In addition to the replication requirements I've already talked about, there are also certain features of Active Directory that are deployed on a per-domain basis. Each AD domain can only have a single password policy, account lockout policy, and Kerberos policy applied to machines belonging to the domain, in addition to a single Encrypted File System (EFS) and Public Key Infrastructure (PKI) configuration. So if you have a group of resources that require radically different configuration for any of these items, these resources will need to be separated out into their own domain. Just keep in mind that additional domains will create more work for you as an administrator; for example, if you have Group Policy settings that you want to apply forest-wide, you'll need to create a separate link to each Group Policy Object (GPO) for each domain.

You can also create multiple domains along regional or administrative lines. If you go this route, be sure to choose a domain structure that's not going to change over time so that you don't need to restructure your domain design after it's already in place. To do this, choose generic domain names that aren't likely to change over time, like ad.company.com or europe.company.com. Avoid naming domains after the operating system, since you don't want to be stuck with the win2k.airplanes.com domain five years from now when you've upgraded the network three times and it's now running "Son of Longhorn Part III." Some domain name changes or restructuring will be unavoidable in the long term, since companies merge and get bought out relatively frequently. But your job in the initial design phase is to create a domain structure that's flexible enough to last for a good long time.

Deploying Multiple Domains

Just like designing your forest structure, you'll also want to consider how many domains to deploy on your network. The simplest domain design you can deploy is a single domain model, where you deploy a single forest containing a single domain. This is the simplest configuration to administer because any domain controller can authenticate any user in the forest, so that you don't need to plan for Global Catalog placement. The largest disadvantage of a single domain model is that it creates the largest possible amount of replication traffic, since all Active Directory objects need to be replicated to domain controllers in any geographic location.

So a major consideration in figuring out how many domains you can deploy is the number of users that you'll be supporting. A well-connected network can easily support 100,000 users in a single domain; for domains that include slower links, you'll need to scale down that maximum accordingly. For example, a 28K connection can support a maximum of 40,000 users, though 10,000 would be a more manageable number. You should also estimate the number of users that you'll be adding to Active Directory so that you don't outgrow your initial design too quickly. And though it's possible to include any number of domains within a single AD forest, I'd recommend deploying no more than ten to maintain your sanity.

In addition to the number of users you'll be supporting, a number of other technical and business factors can influence your decision to deploy a single-domain versus a multiple-domain environment:

- *Deploying Active Directory in an international corporation*: Differences in languages and business practices might require you to deploy separate domains. In particular, American and European companies often have different security and privacy regulations that they need to comply with.

- *Unique security policies*: Since an Active Directory domain can only have one password policy, account lockout policy, and the like, you may need to deploy separate domains to meet differing security requirements for different locations or divisions in your company.

- *Managing an existing domain structure*: If you are migrating to Active Directory from an existing NT 4.0 network, you may need to maintain multiple networks for backwards connectivity. We'll cover Active Directory migrations in Chapter 7.

Deploying the Forest Root Domain

The first domain that you create becomes the *forest root domain*, which is the domain that contains the Enterprise Admins and Schema Admins groups. The domain that you designate as the forest root will remain in this role for the lifetime of the Active Directory deployment, so you'll want to choose this carefully. You can designate a domain that's in use on your network as the forest root, or configure an *empty root* to act as a dedicated forest root domain. Any other domains that you create underneath this empty root will be child domains of the forest root. Try to use an empty root wherever possible, since it gives you the flexibility to add and remove child domains as you need to. For example, say you configure an empty forest root called company.com, and two child domains for hr.company.com and training.company.com. Later, your company merges the Human Resources and Training departments into one. In an empty root configuration, you can use standard migration tools to merge the two child domains—if one of the domains had been configured as the forest root domain, your configuration options would be more limited. Using an empty root also allows you to safeguard the membership of the Enterprise Admins and Schema Admins group, since they will be in a separate domain from any new user accounts that you create. In this way, the empty root domain configuration also allows you to delegate authority over each child domain to a different group of administrators, while having a separate group that has authority over the entire forest.

Caution Choosing the appropriate domain name for the forest root domain is much more important than naming your other domains, since the forest root domain must remain in place for the life of the AD deployment.

Creating the Physical Design

Once you've determined the logical design of your Active Directory network, you then need to configure the physical components of your network. You'll use Active Directory *sites* to route client authentication requests and replication traffic, where a site represents a well-connected portion of your physical network topology. Remember that the physical and logical components of an

Active Directory design can be designed completely separately: you can have multiple sites within a single domain, or a single site that contains multiple domains within it. Active Directory domain controllers are *site-aware*, which means that they can use site information to control how and when they send replication information over slow or dial-up lines used to connect different sites. Most newer Windows applications and clients are also site-aware, so that a Windows XP client will attempt to locate a domain controller within the same site before it sends an authentication request across a slow WAN link to another site. Deploying sites effectively will help you to optimize replication traffic on your network, as well as improving your clients' response times in locating resources such as domain controllers and file shares located on Distributed File System (DFS) servers. Within each Active Directory site, you'll configure one or more *subnets* to specify which network addresses correspond to each site.

Note Active Directory–aware clients and applications use Service Resource Locator (SRV) records in the Domain Name System (DNS) to determine the site configuration of Active Directory resources.

Active Directory will perform replication differently, depending on whether the replication is occurring between domain controllers in the same site (intrasite replication), or between domain controllers in different sites (intersite replication). In intrasite replication, changes to the AD database are sent to all other domain controllers in nearly real time. When an administrator makes a change on a particular DC, the controller will wait for a configurable interval (the default is 5 minutes) before sending a notification to its replication partners. Replication partners within the site will then pull the changes to update their own copies of the AD database. If no changes occur for a configurable period (the default is 6 hours), then the DC will create a replication sequence anyway just to make sure that it didn't miss anything. Intrasite replication does not use any type of data compression.

Replication between sites happens on a "store-and-forward" basis, where one domain controller in each site stores up directory changes and then transmits them to DCs in other sites at predetermined intervals. Intersite replication uses data compression to reduce the CPU and network bandwidth usage during the replication process. Replication between sites can use one of two *transport mechanisms* to transmit information between sites:

- *RPC over IP*: This can be used for both intrasite and intersite replication, and allows for Kerberos authentication and data encryption during replication. For intersite replication, IP replication will occur every 15 minutes by default.

- *SMTP*: This can only be used for intersite replication, and should only be used if there isn't a reliable IP link between the two sites. SMTP replication requires the use of a Certificate Authority (CA), and is really limited in functionality compared to IP replication.

Intersite replication data is also compressed to minimize the impact of transmitting it over WAN links, whereas intrasite replication information is not. Basically, intrasite replication is designed for real-time transfer of data between computers on a single well-connected network, while intersite replication is designed to minimize network traffic.

Note So what does "well-connected" mean? The answer is, as always: "it depends." Microsoft defines a well-connected site as one where all machines in the site are connected by at least a 128K dedicated connection. But if you find that a 128K link is getting saturated by replication traffic, there's nothing stopping you from configuring the machines using that link as their own site.

Configuring Sites and Subnets

By default, each new domain controller and machine that you install in an Active Directory domain gets placed into a single site, called (imaginatively enough) "Default-First-Site-Name." You'll create a new site in the Active Directory Sites & Services MMC console by right-clicking the Sites folder and selecting **New Site**. You'll give the site a name, and select a site link that will connect the new site with any other sites already configured in the domain. Site links control the *cost* of a link; that is, which link will get used first if you have more than one configured. The preferred site link will be the one with the lower cost. So if you have Site Link A configured with a cost of 100 and Site Link B configured with a cost of 150, Active Directory will try to send replication information over Site Link A whenever possible, and only use Site Link B if the lower-cost link is unavailable. For IP site links, you can also configure the *frequency* of a link: how often it transmits replication information. Active Directory creates two site links by default, each with a link cost of 100 and a frequency of 15 minutes:

- DEFAULTIPSITELINK
- SMTPLINK

SITE LINK BRIDGING

By default, all site links in Active Directory are *bridged*, which means that the links are transitive. This means that two sites can communicate with each other even if they're not directly connected by a site link, so that if Site A is linked to Site B, and Site B is linked to Site C, Site A can communicate with Site C by way of Site B. This makes site link configurations easier to maintain because you don't need to create manual links between each and every site on your network. Site link bridging also means that the domain controllers from a single domain will automatically create a site link to any other site that houses a DC from that domain. If you have DCs spread out to a number of sites, this can create a fair number of connection objects.

A situation where you might want to disable automatic site link bridging is if your network is not fully routed, which means that some DCs on your network don't have a physical network path to the remainder of the network. You might also disable this feature if you want to prevent certain sites from communicating directly with each other for security reasons, or to exert more granular control over how replication traffic occurs.

You can disable automatic site link bridging by going into Active Directory Sites & Services and drilling down to **Intersite Transports** ➤ **IP**. In the **Properties** sheet for IP transports, simply clear the check mark next to the **Bridge All Site Links** option.

Once you've created a site, you'll configure one or more subnets that should be associated with that site. In the Active Directory Sites & Services console, you'll right-click the Subnets folder and select **New Subnet**. For each subnet you create, you'll need to supply the following information:

- *Address*: This is the network address of the subnet you're creating. So for a standard Class C subnet that contains IPs ranging from 192.168.1.1 to 192.168.1.254, the network address will be 192.168.1.

- *Mask*: This is the subnet mask. You can use standard Class A, B, or C subnet masks, or variable length subnet masks to further subnet your network.

- *Site object*: The site that this subnet should belong to. Each subnet can only be associated with a single site.

Preparing to Deploy Domain Controllers

So now you're finally in the homestretch. You've designed your forests and domains, and figured out how you're going to divide your physical network into sites. All that's left is to determine where your domain controllers are going to be located and how many you need. At a minimum, you should have two domain controllers in each domain as a fault tolerance measure, so that your users will still be able to authenticate and access resources even if one DC fails or needs to be taken offline for maintenance. Beyond that, a good rule of thumb is to deploy one additional domain controller for every 5,000 users that you're supporting. You'll also want to add DCs if you have a large number of sites configured, since handling a large number of replication connections will also place a strain on your DCs. At minimum, you should start adding additional domain controllers once you reach 15 sites or more, though you can obviously start adding domain controllers sooner for improved replication performance. Microsoft also offers the free **ADSizer** utility that allows you to play "what if?" scenarios to help in deciding how many domain controllers to deploy. **ADSizer** is questionnaire-based and will ask you a number of questions about your planned AD infrastructure, including

- Total number of users in the domain
- Percent of those users that will be connecting at the same time
- Number of groups that the average user will belong to
- How frequently passwords expire
- Number of computers and other Active Directory objects

▓**Note** You can download **ADSizer** from the Microsoft website at http://www.microsoft. com/windows2000/techinfo/reskit/tools/new/adsizer-0.asp.

Speaking of performance, you'll also want to give some thought to the hardware configuration that your domain controllers will be using. Your two biggest concerns will be disk space to store the Active Directory database and memory to improve how well the DC processes queries and replication. Your domain controllers will require enough disk space to store the Active Directory database and log files, the SYSVOL share, and the Windows operating system itself. Now, disk drives are already cheap and only becoming more so, so the simplest disk space recommendation I can make is "gobs and gobs." But if you find yourself running into a budget crunch, here are some guidelines to follow:

- Allocate 400MB of space for every 1,000 users in your domain. This is the amount of space that will be required by the actual AD database file: NTDS.DIT.
- Set aside 500MB of space for the transaction logs, and an additional 500MB for the SYSVOL share. For larger environments, you should consider placing the Active Directory log files on a separate disk controller or RAID channel from the NTDS.DIT file to improve performance.

- The operating system installation itself will require 1.5 or 2GB of disk space.

- Install a minimum of 1GB of RAM for less than 1,000 users, and 2GB for more than 1,000. (Though much like drive space, RAM is cheap and more is better.)

▓**Note** For the best performance, you should install the Active Directory components on a RAID-1 or RAID-5 disk array to provide fault tolerance.

Now that you've determined how many DCs you need, the next obvious question is where to place them. In most cases, you'll want to place your domain controllers in a single location so that they can be physically secured and centrally administered. In some cases, though, you might need to consider installing a domain controller at a remote site like a branch office, since you should place a domain controller in each site. This is usually necessary when you have an unreliable WAN link separating a central office from a branch office and the remote users need to be able to access domain resources 24 hours a day, or if logon times over a WAN link are simply too slow. But before placing a DC at a remote location, you need to ask yourself two crucial questions:

- Is the remote DC going to be physically secure at the remote site? Domain controllers are the "keys" to your network security "kingdom," so the personnel at the remote site need to understand that the domain controller is a sensitive piece of equipment to be kept in a controlled room under lock and key, not left in the middle of an open office space where anyone can access it. You should only deploy remote domain controllers to locations where you can be assured of their physical security.

- Will there be personnel onsite who can administer the server, or will you be able to do so remotely? Any Windows server is going to require ongoing maintenance to install security patches and updates, so you either need to have some type of remote control software in place like NetOp or VNC or a contract with a trustworthy local support provider who can provide for ongoing maintenance.

▓**Caution** Keep in mind that deploying a remote domain controller won't solve *all* of your traffic problems, since remote DCs will still need access to a WAN link to be able to replicate Active Directory information from other sites.

Placing Global Catalog Servers

Global Catalog servers are a special designation for domain controllers: Global Catalogs (GCs) not only store a full copy of the Active Directory data for their own domain, but also a partial replica of the domain data for all other domains in the forest. This allows applications to query any domain controller in a forest for Active Directory information from any domain. Global Catalogs are also where Universal group memberships are stored, which means that any user trying to log on to Active Directory needs to be able to access a Global Catalog server. Because Global Catalogs fulfill a special role within Active Directory, you need to give special consideration to how they're configured and placed on your network. You need to configure at least one domain controller in every domain as a Global Catalog server. Furthermore, you should place a GC in any remote location that houses an application that requires access to a GC, such as Microsoft Exchange. You should also deploy a Global Catalog if a remote site is supporting more than 100 users or a large number of roaming users, since roaming users will need to contact a GC the first time they log in at a new location.

Because Global Catalogs store partial copies of the NTDS.DIT file for other domains in the forest, you need to allocate additional disk space for domain controllers designated as GCs. You'll recall that you need to allocate 400MB of space for every 1,000 domain users on a domain controller. For Global Catalog servers, you'll need to set aside this amount, plus *half* of the database size for each additional domain in the forest. So if you have three domains in a forest, each containing 1,000 users, each domain controller will need 400MB of space to host the NTDS.DIT file for its own domain. Each Global Catalog server will require an additional 400MB (200MB * 2 other domains) to store the GC information for the entire forest.

Note If your network consists of only one domain, you can configure all of your domain controllers as Global Catalogs, since this won't create any additional replication traffic in a single domain forest.

Placing Operations Masters

One of the big reasons why Active Directory was such a huge improvement over earlier versions of Windows like NT 4.0 is that Active Directory allows for *multimaster* replication. This means that each DC has a read-write copy of the Active Directory database, and you can make changes from any domain controller in the domain. But some types of changes are sensitive or far-reaching enough that you really don't want them being performed from multiple locations, so you have five Flexible Single Master Operations (FSMO) roles available in Active Directory. They're called "Single Master" because only one DC can hold the role (and perform the associated task) at any given time. They're "Flexible" because you can transfer the role to different servers as your domain grows and changes, and a single server can hold more than one of the FSMO roles. In each Active Directory forest, you have two FSMO roles that are unique for the entire forest:

- *Schema Master* controls any changes made to the Active Directory schema.
- *Domain Naming Master* controls the addition or removal of any new domains in a forest.

There are three other FSMO roles that are unique to a single domain. So if you have a single domain forest, you'll have a total of five FSMO roles: one of each forest-wide FSMO role, and one of each domain-wide role. But if you have a forest that contains two domains, you'll have *eight* FSMO roles: one of each forest-wide FSMO, and *two* of each domain-wide role. The three domain-wide FSMO roles are as follows:

- *PDC Emulator* controls replication with NT 4.0 backup domain controllers and processes password changes for any non-AD-aware clients.
- *Relative Identifier (RID) Master* hands out unique RIDs to each domain controller so that each DC can create new objects that each have a unique Globally Unique Identifier, or GUID.
- *Infrastructure Master* keeps a list of any users in a remote domain that are members of groups within the domain.

All five FSMO roles are automatically installed on the first DC created in a forest, and the domain-wide FSMOs get placed on the first DC installed in any new domain. You should place the FSMO roles on servers that are reliable and highly available, especially the PDC Emulator and RID Master. Some recommendations for FSMO placement include the following:

- Place the RID Master and PDC Emulator roles on the same DC.
- The Schema Master and Domain Naming Master should be installed on a single server that is well secured and tightly controlled. Because you won't be performing tasks that require these roles as frequently as the three domain-wide FSMOs, your largest concern should be restricting access to the server.
- Place the Domain Naming Master on a server that is configured as a Global Catalog server.
- If you have more than one domain in your forest, the Infrastructure Master should be placed on a server that is *not* functioning as a Global Catalog server so that the FSMO role can replicate changes to the other

domain controllers properly. The exception to this is if *every* DC in your forest is a GC, at which point the Infrastructure Master becomes unnecessary.

To transfer the RID, PDC Emulator, or Infrastructure Master roles to another domain controller, follow these steps:

1. Open Active Directory Users & Computers.

2. Right-click the domain name, and select **Connect to Domain Controller**.

3. Select the name of the controller that you want to transfer the FSMO roles to, then click **OK**.

4. Right-click the domain name, and select **Operations Masters**.

5. Select the **RID**, **PDC**, or **Infrastructure** tab. Verify that the server you selected in step 3 is listed under the **Change** button, and then click **Change** to transfer the FSMO role.

You'll follow the same basic steps to transfer the other two FSMO roles. You'll transfer the Schema Master using the Active Directory Schema snap-in, and the Domain Naming Master using Active Directory Domains & Trusts.

Installing Active Directory

Now that we've tackled the big picture of designing an Active Directory network, it's time to get down to the nuts and bolts of actually installing AD on a Windows 2000 or Windows Server 2003 server. Before you start installing, though, you need to be sure that your network is prepared to support Active Directory. This centers primarily on the DNS service, since Active Directory lives and dies by DNS name resolution. Before you install AD, be sure that you're prepared with a DNS domain name that matches the name of your forest root domain. If your Windows machines are going to be publicly accessible via the Internet, this means selecting a unique Internet domain name and registering it with an Internet name registrar. If your AD installation is only going to be accessed by your internal network users, you can select any domain name you like, though it's a good idea to select a domain name that isn't going to interfere with any of your clients who access the Internet. For example, giving your private Active Directory domain the name of google.com will make for some interesting results the first time you try to perform a web search with the popular search engine. You should consider selecting a unique domain name even if you're not planning on making your network publicly accessible, since this will make it easier to do so later if you decide so. Alternatively, you can use a top-level domain (TLD) that isn't one of the Internet standards, using mycompany.local or mycompany.corp instead of mycompany.com.

If you have existing DNS servers on your network, you need to be certain that your DNS implementation supports the necessary features for Active Directory to function. At a minimum, this entails support for SRV records that AD uses to locate domain controllers, Global Catalog servers, and site information. Your DNS servers should preferably support the following advanced features as well:

- Incremental Zone Transfers (IXFR)
- Fast Zone Transfers
- Dynamic Updates

Windows 2000/2003 DNS servers support these advanced features, as do UNIX BIND servers running version 8.2.2 or later. If your existing DNS servers do not support these features, install DNS on the domain controller itself and delegate control of the Active Directory DNS zone from your legacy DNS servers.

■Caution Before installing a domain controller into an existing forest, be sure that the **_ldap._tcp.dc._mcdcs.** SRV record exists for the domain, the parent domain, or the forest root domain.

The simplest way to install Active Directory is by using the Active Directory Installation Wizard from the Run line of the server that you want to designate as a domain controller. The installation wizard will verify that DNS is configured to support Active Directory, and then either create a brand new Active Directory database or create a replica copy of an existing database. You can use **dcpromo** to create any of the following:

- A brand new domain in a brand new forest
- A new domain tree in an existing forest
- A new child domain
- An additional domain controller in an existing domain

To create a new forest using **dcpromo**, follow these steps:

1. Type **dcpromo** from the Run line and click **OK**. Click **Next** afterwards to bypass the initial **Welcome** screen.

2. On the **Domain Controller Type** screen, select **Domain controller for a new domain**, and then click **Next**.

3. On the **New Domain** screen, select **Domain in a new forest**, and then click **Next**.

4. Enter the full DNS name for the new domain, and click **Next**. On the **NetBIOS Domain Name** screen, you can accept the default NetBIOS domain name (used for backwards compatibility with NT 4.0 and Windows 95/98/ME clients), or enter a new one. Click **Next**.

5. Enter the location for the Active Directory database and log files. If possible, separate these files onto different disk drives to improve performance, as well as for disaster recovery purposes. Click **Next**, and specify the location for the files that make up the SYSVOL share.

6. The **DNS Registration Diagnostics** screen will test to see if a DNS server has been configured, and if it supports dynamic updates and SRV records. If it doesn't locate an appropriate DNS server, you can either allow the wizard to install DNS on the domain controller itself, or select **No** to install and configure DNS manually. You will need a functioning DNS server in order to install Active Directory, so you should allow the wizard to install one if one isn't installed elsewhere on your network. Having the DNS Server service installed on a domain controller will also allow you to take advantage of Active Directory–integrated DNS, which we'll discuss more in Chapter 2.

7. On the **Permissions** screen, select **Permissions compatible with pre-Windows 2000 server operating systems** if you are still supporting NT 4.0 BDCs or RAS Servers, since these servers require anonymous access to Active Directory to be able to authenticate clients. Otherwise, select **Permissions compatible with only Windows 2000 or Windows Server 2003 operating systems** to enable strong security for the Active Directory database.

8. The **Directory Services Restore Mode Administrator Password** screen will prompt you to enable a password that you'll use to get into Directory Services Restore Mode as well as the Recovery Console. Store this password in a safe location for when (not if) you need to use one of these disaster recovery options to troubleshoot an issue on your domain controller.

9. Your last stop is the **Summary** page, where you can verify that you configured the installation settings correctly. Click **Next** to begin the installation, and restart the computer when you're finished.

Creating a new domain tree in an existing forest is quite similar, except that you will select **Domain Controller for a new domain**, followed by **Domain tree in an existing forest**. At this point you'll be prompted for the username and password belonging to the Enterprise Admins group in the existing forest. Likewise, creating a new child domain will require you to select **Domain Controller for a new domain**, followed by **Child domain in an existing domain tree**, followed by Enterprise Admin credentials. To create an additional domain controller in an existing domain, you'll select **Additional domain controller for an existing domain** on the first selection screen, after which you'll be prompted for Domain Admin administrative credentials. After you've installed a new domain, you should verify that the _**msdcs.Domainname**_ record was created in DNS.

INSTALL FROM MEDIA

(Or "Where Has This Feature Been All My Life?")

One of the foremost annoyances of installing Active Directory in Windows 2000 was installing a domain controller at a remote site . . . and then waiting interminably for the contents of the NTDS.DIT file to replicate over a slow WAN link. In Windows Server 2003, you now have the **Install from Media** option, where you can install a new domain controller into an existing domain by using a System State backup of an existing domain controller in that domain. (You can only use this function to install additional domain controllers in an existing domain, not to create a new domain.) Using the **Install from Media** option is a three-step process:

1. Create a System State backup of an existing Windows Server 2003 domain controller using the **Windows Backup** utility—this must be a server running Windows Server 2003 and not Windows 2000. Copy the BKF file to a CD, DVD, or some other portable media.

2. Log on to the 2003 server that you want to configure as a domain controller. _Before_ you run **dcpromo**, open the **Windows Backup** utility and restore the BKF file. When restoring the System State from the source DC, select the **Restore Files to Alternate Location** option, and place the restored System State data in a temporary folder on the server's local hard drive. (Don't place it in the folder that will actually house the NTDS.DIT file when you run **dcpromo**, or all kinds of confusion will ensue.)

3. Run dcpromo /adv from the Run line of the new 2003 server. The /adv switch will take you past the initial **Welcome** screen to the **Additional Domain Controller for an existing domain** screen. The next screen is where the magic happens: on the **Copying Domain Information** screen, select **From these restored backup files:**, and point to the temp folder you created in step 2.

The remainder of the installation will proceed just like any other **dcpromo**. You'll still need network connectivity to verify DNS and to authenticate as a Domain Admin, but the bulk of the heavy lifting will be handled by the local source files, rather than going over the WAN.

Automating the Installation Process

If you're rolling out a large number of domain controllers or you need to roll out server installations on a regular basis, sitting at one console screen after another and clicking through the prompts in the Installation Wizard is probably going to get old really fast. Luckily, you have a number of options to automate your Active Directory installations. You can automate only the **dcpromo** process, or use technologies like Automated Deployment Services (ADS) that will bring up entire systems from bare metal with little or no intervention on your part. It's worth your while to set up an automated installation process even if you only need to set up two or three domain controllers, because your installation script can double as a disaster recovery plan if your company experiences some type of disaster and you need to quickly re-create your domain and forest environment from scratch.

Scripting the AD Installation

A scripted Active Directory installation begins with an *answer file*, which is nothing more than a text file you can create in Notepad that provides information to **dcpromo** without forcing you to sit and click **Next** until everything is finished—any question or prompt that you see in the Installation Wizard can be handled by the answer file. Installing AD with an answer file is as simple as using the following syntax on the Windows 2000/2003 machine:

```
dcpromo /answer:c:\filename.txt
```

A **dcpromo** answer file begins with [DCInstall] as a header, and then a number of fields to customize the way **dcpromo** behaves. Keep in mind that Windows 2000 and Windows Server 2003 have slightly different syntax for the answer files—but a Windows Server 2003 installation can use the Windows 2000 syntax, so that's mostly what I'll stick to in Table 1-1. Be sure to supply an entry in the answer file for anything that isn't marked as "optional," as well as any required entries that don't have a default value, since the Installation Wizard will stop and prompt for any required information that it doesn't find in the answer file.

Table 1-1. *dcpromo Answer File Fields*

Field Name	Default Value	Description
AdministratorPassword		When demoting a domain controller, this will set the local administrator's password after the server is no longer configured as a DC.
AllowAnonymousAccess		Used to specify whether the Everyone group should have anonymous access to Active Directory. Set this to **Yes** if you're still supporting NT 4.0 BDCs or Remote Access Servers. Set to **No** in all other cases.
AutoConfigDNS	**Yes**	Specifies whether the AD installation should install DNS on the local server if it can't find a functioning DNS server on the network.
ChildName		Creates the child domain name that's appended to the parent name when you're creating a child domain. So if you set `ChildName=east`, and `ParentDomainDNSName=company.com`, you'll be creating a child domain with the name of east.company.com. This is only used when installing a new child domain.
CreateOrJoin	**Join**	Set this to **Create** if you are creating a new forest. Set this to **Join** if you're creating a new domain tree in an existing forest. This is only used when installing a new forest or a new domain tree.
CriticalReplicationOnly		This optional parameter lets you stop the initial replication of **dcpromo** after critical information has been copied over. Any additional replication will take place during the normal replication schedule. This is useful if you're installing a Windows 2000 domain controller over a WAN link, since you don't have access to the **Install from Media** option. Set this to **Yes** to enable only critical replication during the initial install.
DatabasePath	**%systemroot%NTDS**	Specifies the drive letter and directory where you want the NTDS.DIT file stored. The folder that you specify here should be the fully qualified directory name of a directory on a fixed disk, not a UNC name. If the directory you specify already exists, it needs to be absolutely empty; if it doesn't exist, it will be created. Finally, free disk space on this logical drive needs to be at least 200MB, and the drive needs to be formatted with the NTFS file system.

Continued

Table 1-1. *Continued*

Field Name	Default Value	Description
DomainNetbiosName		Specifies the domain name used by downlevel clients on your network.
DNSOnNetwork	Yes	Use this entry when installing a new forest. Setting this to **Yes** will automatically configure DNS on your new server. Setting this to **No** will skip the process of auto-configuring DNS for your new domain.
LogPath	%systemroot%\NTDS	Specifies the drive letter and directory where you want the Active Directory log files stored.
IsLastDCInDomain	No	Used during demotion to specify that the DC being demoted is the last controller configured for a domain.
NewDomainDNSName		Use this to specify the DNS domain name of a new forest or a new domain tree in an existing forest.
Password		Use this along with the Username entry to specify necessary account credentials to create a domain tree, child domain, or DC in an existing domain.
ParentDomainDNSName	None	Use this in conjunction with Child. Specifies the name of the parent DNS domain name when installing a new child domain.
RebootOnSuccess	No	Specifies whether to reboot if the Installation Wizard completes successfully.
ReplicaDomainDNSName		Use this when adding a new domain controller to an existing domain for both BDC updates and replica domain controller installations. Specifies the DNS domain name of the domain you're joining.
ReplicaOrMember	Replica	Used when upgrading an NT 4.0 BDC. **Replica** will configure the upgraded server as a DC in Active Directory; **Member** will demote the BDC to member server status during the upgrade.

Table 1-1. *Continued*

Field Name	Default Value	Description
ReplicaOrNewDomain	**Replica**	Set this to **Domain** if you are creating a new forest, a new domain tree, or a new child domain. Set this to **Replica** if you're adding a new DC to an existing domain.
ReplicationSourceDC		Use this optional parameter when adding a new DC to an existing domain. Specifies a particular domain controller to replicate changes from. If this entry isn't included, the Installation Wizard will use the nearest domain controller based on site configuration.
SafeModeAdminPassword		Creates the local administrator password on a domain controller, used when you need to access Directory Services Restore Mode or the Recovery Console.
SiteName	**Default-First-Site-Name**	Use this when creating a new site, to specify a new site name. For all other installs, the Installation Wizard will automatically select a site based on the IP configuration of the new server.
SYSVOLPath	**%systemroot%SYSVOL**	Specifies the drive letter and directory where you want the SYSVOL share stored. Just like the DatabasePath option, the folder that you specify here should be the fully qualified directory name of a directory on a fixed disk, not a UNC name. If the directory you specify already exists, it needs to be absolutely empty; if it doesn't exist, it will be created. Finally, the drive needs to be formatted with the NTFS file system.
TreeOrChild	**Child**	Set this to **Tree** to create a new tree in an existing forest. Set this to **Child** to create a new child domain.
UserDomain		Used in conjunction with Username and Password. Specifies the domain name of the account being used to authorize the creation of a new domain tree, child domain, or domain controller. When creating a new tree, this defaults to the DNS name of the forest root. For a new child domain, this defaults to the parent domain.
UserName		Used in conjunction with Password and UserDomain. Specifies a user account with sufficient credentials to perform **dcpromo**. To create a new domain tree or child domain, this must be a member of the Enterprise Admins group. To create a new DC in an existing domain, this must be a Domain Admin within the domain.

■Caution As a security measure, if you hard-code the password of a Domain Admin or Enterprise Admin into an answer file, Windows will automatically remove the Password= entry after the installation has completed. This means that if you want to use the same answer file for a subsequent installation, you'll need to reenter the password.

So if you're creating a brand new forest, your answer file might look something like this:

```
[DCINSTALL]
ReplicaOrNewDomain=Domain
TreeOrChild=Tree
CreateOrJoin=Create
NewDomainDNSName=company.com
DNSOnNetwork=yes
DomainNetbiosName=COMPANY
AutoConfigDNS=yes
SiteName=NYC
AllowAnonymousAccess=no
DatabasePath=c:\ntds
LogPath=c:\ntds\logs
SYSVOLPath=c:\sysvol
SafeModeAdminPassword=Ant!d!$e$+abl!$hm3n+ar!ani$m
CriticalReplicationOnly=No
RebootOnSuccess=yes
```

To create a new domain tree in the company.com forest, you'll need to specify the username and password of a member of the Enterprise Admins group, so your answer file will use a slightly different syntax:

```
[DCINSTALL]
UserName=jsmith
Password=ireallyloveactivedirectoryautomation
UserDomain=company.com
ReplicaOrNewDomain=Domain
TreeOrChild=Tree
CreateOrJoin=Join
NewDomainDNSName=airplanes.com
DomainNetbiosName=AIRPLANES
```

You'll notice that we didn't specify a location for the database, log, or SYSVOL, so these will default to the values listed in Table 1-1. Next, to create a new child domain, you'll change the TreeOrChild entry to reflect the appropriate choice:

```
[DCINSTALL]
UserName=Enterprise Admin User
Password=Password
UserDomain=Domain of Enterprise Admin User
ReplicaOrNewDomain=Domain
TreeOrChild=Child
ParentDomainDNSName=company.com
ChildName=east
DomainNetbiosName=EAST
```

To add a new domain controller to east.company.com, you'll specify a username that belongs to the Domain Admins group in the east child domain, and change the ReplicaOrNewDomain entry accordingly:

```
[DCINSTALL]
UserName=fharrison
Password=ridingtheEAC
UserDomain=east.company.com
ReplicaOrNewDomain=Replica
ReplicaDomainDNSName=east.company.com
```

To use the **Install From Media** function in Windows Server 2003, you'll add two entries to your answer file:

- ReplicateFromMedia=yes
- ReplicationSourcePath=c:\NTDSTemplFiles

You'll also need to specify the /adv command-line switch when running **dcpromo**, so that the complete syntax will be

```
dcpromo /adv /answer:c:\answer.txt
```

Scripting a Bare Metal Install

So far we've only looked at automating the Active Directory Installation Wizard on a machine that already has Windows 2000 or Windows Server 2003 installed on it. But you can extend this automation process to configure a Windows server from the ground up. You can create an unattend.txt file to configure hardware and display settings, Internet browser and network configuration settings, and any other configurable item that you'd usually enable through the GUI setup sequence. Even beyond that, you can include additional commands that can be run after Windows setup completes, including the AD Installation Wizard.

The easiest way to create an answer file for a fully unattended Windows installation is to use the **Setup Manager** utility. This is included in the Windows Support Tools in Windows 2000/2003, and steps you through the process of creating an answer file. Once **Setup Manager** creates the answer file, you can either use it as-is, or manually edit sections of it in Notepad like we talked about in the previous section. You have the following configuration headers available in an unattend.txt answer file:

- [Unattended]
- [UserData]
- [Display]
- [GuiUnattended]
- [Networking]
- [NetAdapters]
- [NetClients]
- [NetProtocols]
- [Identification]
- [Components]
- [TapiLocation]
- [RegionalSettings]
- [FavoritesEx]
- [GuiRunOnce]
- [Commands]

The [GuiRunOnce] section allows you to specify commands that should run when the system first boots to the desktop. For a fully automated installation, you should add **dcpromo /answer:*dcanswerfile.txt*** here, since you won't be running it manually from the Windows Run line. Once you've created your answer file, you can distribute it on a bootable Windows setup CD, or using a service like RIS or Automated Deployment Services.

Troubleshooting Active Directory Installations

In most cases, installing a domain controller is as simple as running **dcpromo** and babysitting it until it's done. But once in a while it decides to be a bit grumpier than that, and then you need to go about troubleshooting what's gone amiss. By and large, any issues you encounter with Active Directory installations will fall into one of two areas: either network connectivity or DNS name resolution. And even though troubleshooting can consist of as much madness as method, there are certain steps you can take to figure out the root of most issues (hopefully without giving yourself an ulcer in the process!).

Troubleshooting Network Connectivity

Network connectivity issues will most commonly occur when you're adding onto an existing infrastructure, since you need to be physically able to contact a domain controller in the forest root domain to create a new domain tree, in the parent domain to create a child domain, or within the current domain to add another domain controller. To begin troubleshooting network issues, start at one end of the network "conversation," your system, and work your way to the other end of the network until you see where the failure is happening.

First, verify that the TCP/IP stack on the new server is functioning correctly. The quickest way to do this is to issue the following command from the command line:

```
ping 127.0.0.1
```

127.0.0.1 is the *loopback* address, which means that you're pinging yourself. If this step fails, then you're either having an issue with the physical hardware in the server or the TCP/IP stack has become corrupted. To rule out hardware failure as the issue, check the Device Manager from the Computer Management MMC snap-in. If any items (especially the NIC card) are listed with a red "X" or a yellow exclamation point, verify that the card is functioning and that the correct driver is installed.

■**Caution** You should also verify that all hardware in your server (not just the NIC card) appears on the Windows Catalog. While you might be able to get away with having unsupported hardware installed in your server on occasion, it generally creates more headaches than it's worth.

Once you've verified that your hardware is functioning, it's time to look at your network configuration. Go back to the command prompt and type **ipconfig /all**. You'll see a display similar to the following:

```
Ethernet adapter Local Area Connection:

      ...
    Autoconfiguration Enabled . . . . : Yes
    IP Address. . . . . . . : 192.168.1.100
    Subnet Mask . . . . . . : 255.255.255.0
    Default Gateway . . . . : 192.168.1.1
    DHCP Server .. . . . . .: 192.168.1.1
    DNS Servers . . . . . .: 10.197.0.38
                            10.197.0.39
Lease Obtained . . . . : Wednesday, January 05, 2005 9:12:54 PM
Lease Expires .. . . . . : Thursday, January 06, 2005 9:12:54 PM
```

Your next step is to ping your own IP address, followed by the IP address of another machine on the same network segment. If you can ping yourself but not another local machine, be sure that your subnet mask is configured correctly, since this is what TCP/IP uses to determine whether another machine is on the same subnet or on a remote subnet. If your subnet mask is configured correctly and you still can't communicate with other machines on your local segment, the problem is likely a faulty network cable, or a bad port on the hub or switch in your wiring closet. To finish verifying that network communications are working on your local segment, ping the IP address of your default gateway.

Now you can see if there's an issue somewhere between you and the remote host that you're trying to connect to. Use the **tracert** or **pathping** utility to view the path that IP packets are taking between your machine and the remote host to determine where traffic is getting lost. A successful **tracert** output will look something like this:

```
Tracing route to www.website.org [10.0.157.144] over a maximum
of 30 hops:
  1    17 ms    18 ms    17 ms   10.7.94.1
  2    21 ms    20 ms    21 ms   192.168.10.5
  3    22 ms    21 ms    21 ms   192.168.7.233
  4    22 ms    20 ms    21 ms   192.168.7.186
  5    25 ms    23 ms    24 ms   192.168.7.189
  6    23 ms    23 ms    28 ms   192.168.7.89
  7    24 ms    31 ms    26 ms   192.168.4.10
```

```
8    25 ms    26 ms    26 ms   64.200.88.54
9    28 ms    28 ms    29 ms   10.0.56.67
10   28 ms    28 ms    29 ms   www.website.org [10.0.157.144]
Trace complete.
```

The final entry in the **tracert** is the actual host you're trying to reach; the second-to-last entry is typically that host's default gateway. The 28ms portion of each entry refers to the response time of the intermediary router. If any portion of the route is down or overloaded, you'll see a * instead of a response time. You can use this information to figure out if the network outage is on a portion of the network that you control, or if it's some sort of transient Internet weirdness that warrants a call to your Internet service provider.

Troubleshooting Name Resolution

DNS errors tend to be the more common cause of Active Directory installation issues, and are also a bit trickier to nail down. Your first step is to be certain that your server's DNS settings are configured correctly. If you'll be installing the DNS Server service during **dcpromo**, the Installation Wizard will configure the server service and configure the server's TCP/IP properties automatically. If, on the other hand, you're installing a new server into a network with an existing DNS infrastructure, you'll need to verify that the new server is pointing to the correct DNS servers.

■**Note** A domain controller that's running the DNS Server service should point to itself for DNS name resolution so that it will be able to register its own DNS records.

Unless you're installing a brand new Active Directory forest, the machine you're promoting to DC status will need to be able to contact another domain controller in the forest: either in the same domain, the parent domain, or the forest root. In order for this to be successful, your DNS servers need to contain the appropriate DNS records for the domains and domain controllers in your forest. If your DNS servers don't contain the appropriate information, the AD Installation Wizard can fail with the following error message:

```
The wizard cannot gain access to the list of domains in the forest.
The error is: The specified domain either does not exist or could
not be contacted.
```

To troubleshoot this, verify that your DNS servers contain the necessary Active Directory DNS records. Table 1-2 lists the DNS records that need to be in place in a functional Active Directory forest.

Table 1-2. *Active Directory DNS Records*

Display Name	Record Type	Syntax
Dc	A	**FQDN of domain controller**
Location: One for each domain controller (multihomed DCs will have more than one)		
DsaCname	CNAME	***GUID._msdcs.ForestDNSName***
Location: One for each domain controller		
GC	SRV	**_ldap._tcp.gc._msdcs.*ForestDNSName***
Location: One or more per forest		
GcIPAddress	A	**_gc._msdcs.*ForestDNSName***
Location: One for each Global Catalog		
Kdc	SRV	**_kerberos._tcp.dc._msdcs.*DomainDNSName***
Location: One or more in each domain		
Pdc	SRV	**_ldap._tcp.pdc._msdcs.*DomainDNSName***
Location: One in each domain		

You can verify that these records are present using the DNS Management Console, or using the **nslookup** command-line utility. **nslookup** is a utility built into Windows 2000/XP/2003 that you can use to troubleshoot DNS from the command line. By typing **nslookup** from a command prompt, you'll enter **nslookup** *interactive mode*, where you can query for specific records, aim your queries at particular DNS servers, and filter your queries for only particular record types. When you first enter interactive mode, you'll see a prompt that lists your default DNS server's DNS name and IP address, like so:

```
c:\nslookup
Default server: ns1.company.com
Address: 10.0.1.100
>
```

To query your default DNS server for a particular record, just enter the name of the host you're looking for at the > prompt. **nslookup** will respond with the name of the DNS server that performed the query and the IP address it found, like this:

```
Default server: ns1.company.com
Address: 10.0.1.100
> www.airplanes.com
Server: ns1.company.com
Address: 10.0.1.100
Non-authoritative answer:
Name: www.airplanes.com
Addresses: 192.168.1.2, 192.168.1.3
```

Note A response will be marked as "nonauthoritative" for any query that's outside the zone hosted by your default DNS server.

In some cases, you may need to ensure that the results of a DNS query are consistent across multiple DNS servers. To query a particular DNS server, use the server command before issuing a query:

```
Default server: ns1.company.com
Address: 10.0.1.100
> server 10.0.1.101
Default server: ns2.company.com
Address: 10.0.1.101
> www.airplanes.com
Server: ns2.company.com
Address: 10.0.1.101
Non-authoritative answer:
Name: www.airplanes.com
Addresses: 192.168.1.2, 192.168.1.3
```

You can also use the ls command to return all records from a particular zone. ls -a will return only A and CNAME records, and ls -t will allow you to specify different record types, such as ls -t SRV to only query for SRV records. One thing to keep in mind about the ls command is that it's actually performing a zone transfer to return these multiple records. So if your DNS servers are configured to only allow zone transfers from particular hosts, you'll receive an error when you try to use the ls command from your workstation.

If you find that any DNS records are missing, you can either enter them manually or use the `ipconfig /registerdns` command to reregister them automatically. You should also stop and restart the Netlogon service on any domain controllers so that their SRV records will be repopulated correctly. You can also issue the following diagnostic commands from a domain controller to programmatically test your DNS configuration:

- `dcdiag /test:dcpromo /dnsdomain:FQDN /NewTree /ForestRoot: Forest_Root_Domain_DNS_Name/v`: This will test your DNS server to determine whether it can process the dynamic updates necessary to support Active Directory.

- `dcdiag /test:dcpromo /dnsdomain:FQDN /ChildDomain /v`: This will not only test your DNS servers to see if they will support dynamic updates, but it will also check for the presence of the DNS records for the parent domain.

- `dcdiag /test:dcpromo /dnsdomain:FQDN /ReplicaDC /v`: This will test your DNS server, and will look for DNS records for the domain that you're adding a new replica server for.

Summary

In this first chapter, we talked about the process of planning and performing an installation of the Active Directory directory service. Before you can install a new domain controller, you first need to have a good understanding of the overall structure of Active Directory, including how it logically organizes your network resources into forests, domain trees, and domains. This logical design is separate from the physical components of AD such as sites and subnets, which allows you to design your AD network to meet your business needs, rather than being tied into any limitations created by network connectivity or bandwidth. We also looked at ways to automate the Active Directory installation process by using answer files and scripts.

Now that we've seen how to implement the logical components of Active Directory, Chapter 2 will cover the network infrastructure that's necessary to allow AD to function. The majority of our focus will be on the Domain Naming System (DNS), but we'll also look at using DHCP for automated IP addressing for your Windows clients, and using WINS to provide NetBIOS name resolution.

Additional Resources

Windows Server 2003 Deployment Kit: http://www.microsoft.com/windowsserver2003/techinfo/reskit/deploykit.mspx (if this link has moved, just query for the title in your search engine of choice)—Chock full of background information and sample spreadsheets that you can use to help with your Active Directory deployment.

Microsoft public newsgroups: microsoft.public.windows.server.setup—Here you'll find any number of helpful network professionals (even me!) who can answer your Active Directory installation and deployment questions.

Microsoft Knowledge Base Article 265706, "DCDiag and NetDiag": http://support.microsoft.com/kb/265706—Detailed instructions for using the **DCDiag** and **NetDiag** command-line utilities to troubleshoot Active Directory errors relating to installation, replication, and name resolution. These are powerful tools with a plethora of command-line options, and are well worth becoming familiar with.

CHAPTER 2

■ ■ ■

Integrating the
Network Infrastructure

You may feel confused by the end of this chapter, when you realize that you haven't opened a single MMC snap-in that contains the words "Active Directory" in the title. That's because in this chapter we'll talk about the underlying network services that are necessary for AD to function and that will help it to work better and more efficiently. I'll start with the Domain Name System, or DNS. This is the default name resolution protocol for Windows 2000 and 2003, and is absolutely necessary for Active Directory to function. After that we'll look at the Dynamic Host Configuration Protocol, or DHCP, which is used for automatically assigning IP addresses to clients on your network. DHCP is one of those administrative life-savers through which you can deploy IP addressing and configuration options like a default gateway and DNS server settings to hundreds and even thousands of clients without the tedium of configuring everything manually. We'll close out with a look at the Windows Internet Naming Service, or WINS, which will let you configure centralized NetBIOS name resolution for your network. By configuring these underlying network services properly, you'll then be ready to install a healthy Active Directory network on top of them.

In this chapter, you'll learn how to do the following:

- Create a DNS infrastructure.
- Deploy DNS servers.
- Secure DNS.
- Integrate Active Directory with third-party DNS.
- Install and configure DHCP servers.
- Configure DHCP scopes, reservations, and optional settings.
- Integrate DHCP with DNS.
- Administer DHCP from the command line.
- Configure support for WINS servers and NetBIOS name resolution.

Deploying DNS

I'm sure I've already said it elsewhere in this guide, but it warrants repeating: Active Directory lives and dies by the Domain Name System. A well-designed and functioning DNS infrastructure is absolutely critical to the health and well-being of your Active Directory network; the latter simply can't exist without the former. Starting with Windows 2000, DNS has been the primary means of name resolution for Windows server and client operating systems, and that's not going to change anytime soon. And in an Active Directory network, you can integrate DNS directly with AD to create security and fault tolerance for your name resolution scheme.

Let's begin with the part where I can't help but give you a lightning-fast introduction to what DNS is and how it works—I'll try to keep it interesting, I promise. The simplest way to envision DNS is this: if you think of an IP address as a telephone number, then DNS is the phone book. This information is *distributed* geographically so that the people for whom the information is the most relevant can get to it the quickest. For example, you wouldn't open a Philadelphia telephone directory and expect to find a telephone number for someone living in Denver, and vice versa. (We're setting aside Internet sites like switchboard.com for the purpose of this example, obviously.) Just like local telephone books, DNS servers can be distributed across your network so that machines can find the information they need locally, rather than going across a Wide Area Network (WAN) link to locate a machine that's sitting five feet away from them.

DNS data is organized into zones, which correspond to different portions of the overall DNS namespace. Zones can be made up of one or more DNS domains, so long as those domains are contiguous to one another. So mycompany.com and east.mycompany.com could be managed as a single zone, but mycompany.com and airplanes.com could not. The DNS records that make up a zone are stored in a zone file, which is usually a simple text file that's being stored on one or more DNS servers, located by default in the *%systemroot%*\system32\dns directory of a Windows 2000 Server or Windows Server 2003 server. You can also delegate a portion of a DNS domain so that it becomes a separate zone—usually, you'll do this so that you can allow another administrator to have control over a portion of the directory structure. So you could delegate authority over the east.mycompany.com domain so that it becomes a separate zone file with its own administrator. At this point, the mycompany.com zone file will only contain records for the mycompany.com domain. The east.mycompany.com domain will have a zone all to itself. (An interesting thing to note here is that if you create a child domain called dev.mycompany.com, it will still be a part of the mycompany.com zone unless you delegate it to its own zone as well.)

The *fully qualified domain name* (FQDN) of any machine consists of its computer name, followed by the full name of the domain it's located in. So the web server in east.mycompany.com would have an FQDN of web-srv.east.mycompany.com, while the mycompany.com web server would be web-srv.mycompany.com. Notice how each FQDN is unique, even though the individual machine names (web-srv) are the same. This is because the main requirement of an FQDN is that it be able to uniquely identify any machine within DNS. There are two types of DNS zones: *forward lookup zones*, which match up IP addresses to DNS names, and *reverse lookup zones*, which allow you to find an FQDN if you know the IP address. In addition to allowing clients to be able to resolve FQDNs from IP addresses, reverse lookup zones are used extensively for troubleshooting, as you'll see later.

Individual DNS records are called *Resource Records* (RRs). A DNS Resource Record contains information relating to a host in a particular DNS domain. A DNS database will maintain this record so that DNS clients can retrieve and use the information to locate resources that are hosted by the corresponding computer. You can update Resource Records manually, or use dynamic updates. Dynamic updates allow Windows machines running 2000 or higher to contact a DNS server and register their own DNS information when they boot up, which saves an administrator the trouble of doing it. There are a number of different types of Resource Records, and these are listed in Table 2-1.

Table 2-1. *Types of Resource Records*

Resource Type Name	Description
A	An Address record is used to map a DNS hostname to a 32-bit IPv4 host address.
AAAA	This is similar to the A record, except that it maps to a 128-bit IPv6 address.
CNAME	This is short for Canonical Name, but it's easier (and accurate) to think of it as an *alias* for an A or AAAA record. For example, you may have a computer with an A record of web-serv.mycompany.com, for which you create a CNAME record of www.mycompany.com. This way, DNS clients can access the host using either DNS name.
MX	A Mail Exchanger record specifies a list of hosts for a particular domain that can receive e-mail addressed to that domain. You can have multiple MX records with different priorities to provide fault tolerance. MX records are critical if you are deploying Microsoft Exchange or any other type of SMTP-based e-mail service.
NS	A Name Server record specifies the IP addresses of DNS servers that are authoritative for a particular DNS zone.

Continued

Table 2-1. *Continued*

Resource Type Name	Description
PTR	PTR (short for PoinTeR) records are used for reverse DNS lookups, where you need to locate a domain name based on a known IP address. These are primarily used for DNS troubleshooting, and to allow reverse lookups of IP addresses to domain names.
SOA	The Start of Authority record indicates where a DNS zone starts—in other words, where one zone is separated from a parent or child zone. It contains the name of the server that is the primary source for information about that zone.
SRV	SRV (short for SeRVice locator) records advertise different *services* that are being hosted by a particular computer. In Active Directory, SRV records are crucial in allowing clients to locate domain controllers and Global Catalog servers.

DNS servers themselves can be either *primary* or *secondary* servers for any zone. A primary DNS server contains the only copy of the DNS zone file that can actually be updated; secondary servers contain read-only copies of zone files and are used to provide better performance and fault tolerance for a zone. Secondary zones can help to reduce network traffic on WAN links, as well as reduce the number of DNS queries that are handled by the primary server. Because of this distinction, a DNS server can house more than one DNS zone file: you'll often see a server acting as a primary server for one zone and as a secondary server for a few others as a fault tolerance measure. The *authoritative* DNS server for a zone is the server that holds the primary copy of a particular zone file; each zone can only have one authoritative server, but any number of secondary servers. Primary servers keep their secondary servers updated by using *zone transfers*, where the secondary servers request any changes that have been made to the zone file. A secondary server will contact its primary server at predetermined intervals to see whether there are any changes; if there are, the secondary server requests a zone transfer. Secondaries will also request a zone transfer every 24 hours even if no changes have been made, just to be sure that everything is up to date. In Windows Server 2003, primary servers can use *DNS Notify* to proactively inform secondaries that changes are available; however, the zone transfer still gets initiated by the secondary servers. A zone transfer can either be *full*, in which the entire zone file gets sent anytime there are changes, or *incremental*, in which only new or updated records get copied over. By default, a Windows 2000 or 2003 DNS server will use incremental zone transfers unless it's replicating to a DNS server that doesn't support them, such as NT 4.0 or older versions of UNIX BIND. If this is the case, 2000/2003 DNS will fall back to using a full zone transfer.

Note Most of what I've talked about in this introduction applies primarily to standard DNS. Active Directory–integrated DNS has its own terms and behavior that we'll talk about in a few minutes.

To close out this rapid-fire DNS overview, let's look at the actual process that takes place when a DNS client requests information from a DNS server. There are two types of DNS queries:

- Iterative queries
- Recursive queries

An *iterative* query is how DNS servers are able to translate a DNS name into an IP address. This type of query requests the best answer that a DNS server currently has for a particular DNS name. The DNS server will check its local cache and local zone files to see whether it's responded to a query for the same name recently. If so, it returns the cached information right away. If it doesn't have the information cached, the DNS server will check any zones that it hosts for an answer. But given how widely distributed DNS servers are, any DNS server is probably only going to find a *partial* answer from its local zone files. In cases where it only has a partial answer, the server will try to use it to identify the *next* DNS server to talk to and then *forward* the DNS query to that server.

You can think of this as a big game of whisper-down-the-lane. You need to find a web server at www.east.finance.example.com. So your client machine sends an iterative query to your ISP's DNS server. Now, your ISP's DNS server probably doesn't know exactly where this machine is. But it does know where the root server for the .com domains is. So it sends a query to the .com DNS server. The .com DNS server will responds back with "I don't know where that machine is, but I know where the DNS server for example.com is. Go ask it." The DNS server for example.com might know where this machine is, or it might not. If it doesn't know, it might return a response like "No, sorry, I don't know where that machine is. But here's the DNS server for the finance.example.com domain. Try there." And so on down the line until your ISP's DNS server finds the correct DNS server for east.finance.example.com. Once your ISP's DNS server knows where the www.east.finance.example.com machine is, it'll send a response back to the DNS client telling it where to go. You can see that it involves some pretty high overhead to process an iterative query, which is why they're used almost exclusively by DNS servers.

DNS clients (resolvers), on the other hand, will use *recursive* queries. A recursive query is basically looking for a "yes" or "no" answer. A client will ask its DNS server if it knows where a particular machine is. The DNS server either knows the answer and sends the client to the right place, or it doesn't know and returns some sort of "could not find host" error. Now, you can see how these two queries are combined: a DNS client sends a recursive query to a DNS server, expecting a "yes" or "no" answer. The client then sits and waits for the DNS server, which is off doing an iterative query to track down the machine with a bunch of different DNS servers. Once the DNS server has a definitive answer one way or the other, it answers the client's recursive query with a success or a failure.

■**Note** You can also configure a DNS server to use recursive queries. This is particularly common in the case of a server that's configured as a DNS *forwarder*, which we'll discuss in the "Configuring Forwarders" section.

Creating the DNS Infrastructure

You should plan your DNS infrastructure at the same time that you create your logical Active Directory design, since the two configurations should be as close to identical as possible. This is especially true of your Active Directory domain names, which need to match the DNS names deployed on your network. If you're going to connect your company to the Internet, you need to make sure that your domain name is unique and registered to your company. Even if you're not currently doing business on the Internet, you should consider registering a unique domain name anyway so that your DNS and AD structures won't need to be changed later if you don't get the Internet domain name that you wanted.

If you're upgrading an existing DNS infrastructure, you can consider leaving your existing DNS design intact and creating a dedicated Active Directory child domain to host your internal clients. Another option is to use a separate namespace for your internal machines, so that your Internet-connected machines use the company.com namespace and your internal machines use company.local. Regardless of which option you choose, your domain name should consist of only legal DNS characters: letters, numbers, and hyphens (-). The underscore character (_) used to be supported for backwards compatibility with NT 4.0, but it's not a legal DNS character and should be avoided.

Designing DNS Zones

Once you've taken care of the logical design of DNS and Active Directory, you can turn your attention to the physical layout of your network. In the case of DNS, this involves carving up your DNS namespace into manageable zones. You can maintain a single large zone that will be entirely centrally administered, or you can delegate DNS authority so that child domains are contained in their own zones with their own administrators.

Your first decision when designing DNS for Active Directory, though, is whether you're going to store your DNS data within the AD database itself. Creating *Active Directory–integrated zones* allows you to have DNS zone information that uses multimaster replication instead of relying on a single authoritative DNS server. Just like Active Directory itself removes the single point of failure of the NT 4.0 PDC, Active Directory–integrated zones remove the risk to your DNS implementation that's caused by having only one writable copy of your DNS data. AD-integrated zones also increase DNS security by allowing you to use secure dynamic updates, and improve on the zone transfer process by making DNS replication a part of Active Directory replication. You can even delegate a particular subdomain to be AD-integrated; you don't need to use AD-integrated zones for your entire network.

■**Note** Active Directory–integrated zones can only be installed on Windows 2000 or 2003 domain controllers.

Creating an Active Directory–Integrated Zone

To configure an Active Directory–integrated zone, follow these steps:

1. On a domain controller, install the DNS Server role from Add/Remove Windows Components in Windows 2000, or the Configure Your Server Wizard in Windows Server 2003. Remember that you can only install an Active Directory–integrated zone on a domain controller, not a member server.

2. Open the DNS Management Console MMC snap-in. Right-click the Forward Lookup Zones node and select **New Zone**. Click **Next** to bypass the initial **Welcome** screen.

3. On the next screen, shown in Figure 2-1, you'll select the zone type that you want to configure. Select the radio-button next to **Primary zone**, and place a check mark next to **Store the zone in Active Directory (available only if DNS server is a domain controller)**. Click **Next** to continue.

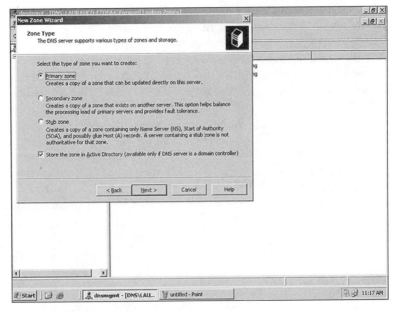

Figure 2-1. *Selecting a DNS zone type*

4. If you are working on a Windows Server 2003 computer, you will then be prompted to select the servers that you want this zone to be replicated to. You can choose from the three options listed here, which can help you control the amount of bandwidth that's used by DNS replication. Once you've made your selection, click **Next** to continue.

   - **To all DNS servers in your Active Directory forest**
   - **To all DNS servers in your Active Directory domain**
   - **To all domain controllers in your Active Directory domain**

5. Enter the name of the DNS zone that's being hosted on this server. Click **Next** to continue.

6. Choose whether to allow only secure dynamic updates, both secure and nonsecure dynamic updates, or not to allow dynamic updates at all. Unless you have a really good reason to do so, I recommend against allowing nonsecure dynamic updates, since it allows any machine to update DNS records within the zone. Click **Next** to continue.

Creating Primary Zones

If you're supporting third-party or legacy DNS servers, you may need to deploy a primary zone instead of an AD-integrated zone. As I've already mentioned, this creates a read-write copy of a DNS zone file on the server that's hosting the primary zone. You can then deploy secondary zones to provide fault tolerance and better performance for your DNS clients. The steps to create a primary zone are nearly identical to creating an Active Directory–integrated zone. Simply remove the check mark next to **Store the zone in Active Directory (available only if DNS server is a domain controller)** when you first create the zone.

Creating Secondary Zones

You'll deploy secondary zones to create fault tolerance and load balancing for standard primary zones. In the case of AD-integrated zones, you can also deploy secondary zones on machines that aren't domain controllers to improve response time for clients that might not be physically close to a domain controller. This is especially useful if you want to have DNS data available at a remote site that uses a WAN link. By placing a DNS server hosting a secondary zone at the remote site, you've enabled name resolution without forcing the remote clients to perform DNS queries across a slow connection. To configure a secondary zone, follow these steps:

1. Open the DNS Management MMC console. Select the server that should host the secondary zone. Right-click the Forward Lookup Zone node, then select **New Zone**. Click **Next** to skip over the first screen.

2. On the **Zone Type** screen, select **Secondary Zone**. (You'll notice that you don't have the option to integrate a secondary zone into Active Directory.) Click **Next**.

3. Enter the name of the DNS zone and click **Next**. Enter the IP address of the primary DNS server for the zone and click **Add**. You can include the IPs of more than one master server to create fault tolerance for your secondary zone. Click **Next** and **Finish** when you're done.

NEW TO 2003: STUB ZONES

One of the new features of Windows Server 2003 is a new type of DNS zone called a *stub zone*. A stub zone is essentially a placeholder for a child zone that's hosted by the parent zone. Here's an example:

You have two DNS domains that you've configured as two separate zones:

- mycompany.com

- child.mycompany.com

In order for clients in the mycompany.com domain to be able to find resources in child.mycompany.com, the DNS server in mycompany.com needs to know where the DNS servers are in child.mycompany.com. When you first delegate the child domain into its own zone, it creates Name Server records in the parent domain that list the DNS servers for the child domain. The problem here is that these NS records point to specific IP addresses; if those IPs change, mycompany.com could have a hard time resolving queries for child.mycompany.com

Stub zones are a new feature in Windows Server 2003 designed to address precisely this issue. The stub zone will be hosted on a DNS server in the parent domain, and maintains a list of all NS records for a child domain. The stub zone also contains the Start of Authority record for a zone, which lists the DNS name of the server that's authoritative for the zone, as well as "glue" records indicating the name servers for that zone. A stub zone will use this SOA record to be sure that its list of name servers gets periodically refreshed with any new information. This way, the stub zone always has the most current information about the configuration of the child zone's DNS servers. Stub zones are advantageous if you don't want to deal with the replication traffic necessary to host the full secondary zone for a child domain: it's called a "stub" zone because it contains just enough information to point your DNS server and clients to the right place. Another advantage over secondary zones is that you can integrate stub zones into Active Directory. In addition, using stub zones simplifies DNS administration for your Active Directory network. By using stub zones throughout your DNS infrastructure, you can distribute a list of the authoritative DNS servers for a zone without using secondary zones. Just remember that stub zones don't serve the same purpose as secondary zones, in that they do not provide redundancy, load balancing, or fault tolerance capabilities.

Integrating with WINS

If you still have WINS servers on your network, you may need to integrate WINS information into your DNS server to support NetBIOS name resolution requests from your clients. To do this, you can configure your DNS server to query a WINS server to resolve a query for a particular zone, by adding two records for a particular DNS zone: a *WINS lookup record* and a

WINS-R record for reverse lookups. This way, if the zone receives a query for a resource record that it can't resolve, it will check with the WINS server before giving up on the query; the WINS-R record is used in much the same manner as a PTR record in DNS. In this way, your DNS server will act as a go-between for the client and the WINS server: your DNS clients won't need to query the WINS server directly. You'll configure WINS lookups on the **WINS** tab on the **Properties** sheet of a DNS zone, as shown in Figure 2-2. You'll configure the IP address of one or more WINS servers that the DNS zone should query— DNS will query each of these servers in order, so place them accordingly. You can also choose whether or not to replicate the WINS lookup record to other DNS servers. If you're performing zone transfers with non-Microsoft DNS servers, you should not replicate the WINS lookup record since the third-party server won't know what to do with it.

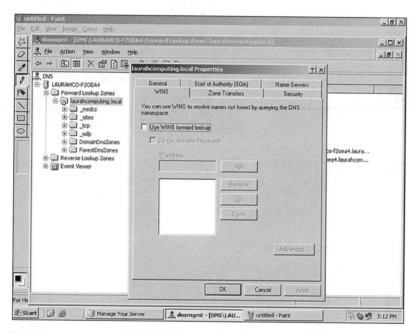

Figure 2-2. *Configuring WINS lookups*

Configuring Forwarders

Another key factor in designing a DNS infrastructure is deciding how you're going to configure DNS forwarding on your network. Anytime a DNS server doesn't have the answer to a query in its local cache or local zone data, it will forward that query to a DNS server that's been designated as a *forwarder*. In most cases, you'll use forwarding for Internet queries, or queries for hosts in a remote site. The trick is in deciding how you're going to configure forwarding. For example, you could configure your internal DNS server to forward any queries for Internet resources to the DNS server at your ISP, or you can have a DNS server at a remote office forward any nonlocal queries to the DNS server at a central office. In both of these cases, this allows DNS queries for local resources to *stay local*, without suffering the performance hit of sending unnecessary queries to an external network.

■**Note** Combining the use of DNS forwarders with a well-configured firewall can also improve the security of your network, since you can restrict Internet access to only your internal DNS server. You can further secure an internal DNS server by using IPSec policies to only allow DNS traffic from the external servers you've configured as forwarders. We'll talk more about IPSec in Chapter 5.

You'll configure forwarding for an entire DNS server by right-clicking the server name and going to the **Forwarders** tab on the server **Properties** sheet. As you can see in Figure 2-3, you can add the IP addresses of one or more DNS servers to forward queries to. For fault tolerance, you should always configure at least two forwarders; if the server doesn't get a response from the first forwarder it tries, it'll resend the query to the second forwarder on the list.

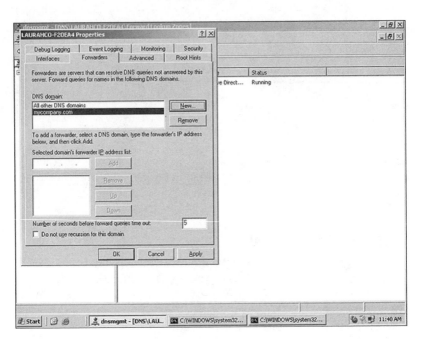

Figure 2-3. *Configuring DNS forwarding*

In Windows 2000, any forwarded queries would be sent to a single list of forwarders, regardless of the content of the query. In 2003, you can configure *conditional forwarding*, whereby you can create queries for particular domains to be routed to different forwarders, based on the specific domain names contained in the queries. Now, this doesn't buy you much if you're only worried about Internet name resolution, because you're not going to manually specify the IP address of the Google web server since it could change at any time. Where you see an improvement with conditional forwarding is if you're dealing with a large internal DNS namespace, particularly one that involves noncontiguous namespaces.

As an example, say that you're running DNS for the mycompany.com domain, and MyCompany decides to merge with one of its competitors, grayscale.com, which runs its own Active Directory. As far as the mycompany.com DNS servers are concerned, resources in grayscale.com are external resources, and so any requests for them will get forwarded out to the Internet to get resolved if you're using traditional forwarding. But with conditional forwarding, you can specify the IP address of the grayscale.com DNS server, so that any requests for resources in that domain will go straight to the correct DNS server. In this case, it's perfectly reasonable to configure the IP addresses for grayscale.com's DNS, since you have some control over the network and know where its resources are located. Using conditional forwarding this way will improve response time for your clients, since you're making the querying process much more efficient by effectively joining these two distinct namespaces.

Using Caching-Only Servers

You can even configure a DNS server as a *caching-only* server. This type of DNS server is not authoritative for any DNS domain; it only listens for client queries and forwards those queries on to DNS forwarders. When the caching-only server receives a response to a forwarder query, it stores the result in a local cache; if another client requests the same resource, the caching-only server will return the result from its local cache instead of forwarding the query. This is particularly useful for remote sites with limited connectivity or slow-speed links, especially if the machines in the remote site only need to locate a small number of resources. For example, you may have a warehouse containing machines that only run an order-entry application that needs to contact servers at your main office. Installing a caching-only server will improve response times for these machines, since the DNS names that it stores in its cache will probably not change very much over time. Conversely, a caching-only server becomes less useful if it's fielding requests that are all over the map, since it won't be able to build up a useful cache of information and will just need to keep forwarding new queries as they come along. In addition, caching-only servers do not perform any zone transfers, which will cut down on bandwidth usage in network-intensive WAN environments.

To create a caching-only DNS server, simply install the server service without configuring any zones on the server, and update the Root Hints on the caching server to point to authoritative DNS servers for the appropriate domain. You can then configure forwarders just like you did earlier in this section.

Managing Root Hints

Any DNS server that performs external or Internet name resolution requires a Root Hints file installed on the server. This is the file that points DNS at the root DNS servers for the whole of the Internet, which is necessary for performing iterative queries for unknown domains. The default Root Hints file is called cache.dns, and is located in the %*systemroot*%\System32\DNS folder on the DNS server. For an Internet-facing DNS server, you should leave this Root Hints file in place so that your server can resolve Internet queries. For DNS servers that are only going to be answering internal queries, you can edit the cache.dns file to point to DNS servers hosting your root domain, or else delete it entirely. For the best security, an internal DNS server shouldn't retain the default Root Hints, because you only want your external DNS server to perform queries on a public network such as the Internet.

Securing DNS

Just like any other part of your network, your DNS design plan should include some considerations for securing the DNS service. The trouble with securing DNS is that it's a really old protocol: it's been around since the very earliest days of the Internet. Back when the Internet first came into being, everyone using it was a scientist or a researcher. Nobody had really conceived of e-commerce yet, and if you'd told these guys that their cute little research idea was going to get as big as it's gotten, I'm not sure they would've believed you. What this means for DNS is that it really wasn't designed with security in mind; DNS, unfortunately, makes the assumption that everyone's a "good guy" until you configure it to be a little less trusting. Without taking some steps to secure the DNS service, your network will be open to any number of attacks, including the following:

- *Footprinting*: This type of attack happens when a malicious user grabs your DNS zone data to figure out where your critical servers, routers, and other network hosts are located, and how they're configured. This attack doesn't do any actual damage in and of itself, but it's usually the prelude to a more overt attack. For example, once an attacker can say, "Okay, I'm going to assume that www.mycompany.com is a web server, and now I have its IP address," she can launch an attack directly against the web server itself.

- *Denial of Service (DoS)*: This attack happens when your DNS servers get overwhelmed with fake queries by malicious users. When a DNS becomes flooded with more and more queries, it will eventually max out its CPU usage, and the DNS service will be unavailable to users on your network who want to perform legitimate queries. This can affect not only your internal users, but external customers who are trying to find your e-mail or web servers.

- *IP spoofing*: Once an attacker knows the IP addresses on your network (through a footprinting attack), he can manipulate malicious IP packets so that they look like they originated inside of your network. If this works, an attacker can use this to waltz past your routers and gain access to your internal network.

- *Redirection*: This occurs when an attacker is able to modify the contents of the cache on a DNS server. For example, a client sends a query for www.mycompany.com. The DNS server caches the result and sends the client on its merry way. Redirection happens when an attacker modifies that cached result so that it no longer points to www.mycompany.com, but to a different site entirely. The next client that queries the server for www.mycompany.com will be sent to the address that the DNS server has cached . . . only it won't be the result that anyone was expecting. This redirected address will usually be a site that's running malicious code or contains offensive material.

The best place to start protecting your DNS servers from attack is by isolating your private network resources as much as possible. The fewer DNS servers you have that are accessible from the Internet, the better your overall DNS security will be. If your DNS servers are only used to respond to internal clients, you can place them on a private network segment using nonroutable IP addresses. This will physically isolate them from public networks and limit their exposure to malicious outsiders. You should also configure separate DNS servers to host your private and public DNS records, so that anyone accessing your public DNS server will only be able to see things like your web server, mail server, and other publicly available resources. Use a second DNS server to host DNS records for private resources like SRV records and the names of internal machines.

To handle external queries, you can configure a single DNS server to act as a forwarder, and restrict Internet access to that server only. In this configuration, you would also disable Root Hints on your internal servers, or else modify the cache.dns file so that it points to your local network only. You can also configure a software- or hardware-based firewall to further restrict communications between your internal and external DNS servers, ideally only allowing traffic on TCP port 53. To protect against Denial of Service attacks, you can place a secondary DNS server on a separate subnet or an offsite location like your ISP, so that clients can still reach this secondary server even if your primary DNS server becomes overwhelmed by a DoS attack.

■**Note** A useful service for restricting traffic to and from a Windows 2000/2003 server is IPSec, which Chapter 5 covers.

If you have a multihomed server that's running DNS, you should restrict which network interfaces the server should use to listen for and respond to DNS queries. You may have a proxy server that contains two Network Interface Cards (NICs): one connected to your private network and one connected to your Internet service provider. If that server is also hosting your internal DNS server, you can configure the server so that it will only listen for DNS queries from the NIC attached to the private network; this will protect your DNS data from being queried by a malicious user on the Internet. To restrict DNS traffic to a particular NIC installed in a server, you'll do the following:

1. Go to the **Properties** sheet of the DNS server in the DNS Management Console.

2. On the **Interfaces** tab, change the enabled radio button option from **Listen on all IP interfaces** (which is the default) to **Listen on only the following IP addresses**.

3. Enter the IP address of the NIC or NICs connected to the private network, and then click **OK**.

As a final general security measure, you should configure DNS to allow only secure dynamic updates, rather than allowing both secure and nonsecure updates. (Remember that secure-only dynamic updates are available only with AD-integrated zones.) If you allow nonsecure dynamic updates, then anyone will be able to add, remove, and modify Resource Records in your DNS server: someone could set up a bogus machine with the same name as your web server, point it to your DNS server, and poof!—your DNS server would accept the new DNS registration and start pointing clients to this fake web server. Using secure-only dynamic updates prevents this by setting Active Directory permissions on your DNS records. This way, once a machine registers a DNS name, it becomes the "owner" of that record, and no other machine will be able to update it. This way, only authenticated users can update DNS information on your network, and you can even further restrict this so that only specific groups can make updates. To modify a DNS zone to only allow secure updates, go to the **General** tab on the zone's **Properties** sheet, and select **Secure Only** in the Dynamic Updates dropdown box.

■Note Windows Server 2003 defaults to **Secure Only** when you create an AD-integrated DNS zone.

Once you've configured secure-only dynamic updates, you can set permissions on an entire DNS zone, or just specific Resource Records—you may want to restrict the Resource Records for your critical servers so that they can only be updated by administrative users, for example. To change the Access Control List for an entire zone, go to the **Security** tab on the zone's **Properties** sheet. To modify the ACL for an individual record, go to the **Properties** sheet of the specific record within the zone.

Of course, the "best" way to secure dynamic updates on your DNS servers is to turn them off completely, so that any DNS records need to be manually created or updated by an administrator. Like most things, the dynamic update function is a trade-off between security and convenience: for internal DNS servers, allowing secure-only dynamic updates is probably worth doing since it saves you from repetitive data entry within the DNS console. But for Internet-facing DNS servers, I'd recommend turning off dynamic updates entirely to take away a potential avenue of attack for a malicious user.

Securing Zone Transfers

In order for a footprint attack to work, an attacker usually tries to initiate a zone transfer from one of your DNS servers, or else tries to intercept a zone transfer as it's being transmitted across the wire. The best way to secure the zone transfer process is to use Active Directory–integrated zones: all AD replication traffic is encrypted by default, and using AD-integrated DNS means that your DNS servers communicate through the same encrypted channel. Active Directory replication also uses Kerberos to perform *mutual authentication*, so that the identities of both servers are verified before any information gets exchanged. In addition, if you need to transmit DNS information over the Internet, you should use IPSec to encrypt the traffic, or set up VPN tunnels between sites.

If you're not using Active Directory–integrated zones, or you've configured secondary servers for better DNS availability, there are other steps that you can still take to secure the zone transfer process. On the **Zone Transfer** tab of a DNS zone's **Properties** sheet, you can control how a server will send DNS zone transfers. You can configure the following options:

- **Allow Zone Transfers to any server**
- **Allow Zone Transfers only to servers listed on the Name Servers tab**
- **Only to the following servers**

Allowing zone transfers to any server that requests one is the very definition of a Bad Idea; this setting is usually how footprint attacks happen. To secure the zone transfer process, you should restrict where your DNS server will send a zone transfer to. When you install a zone onto a DNS server, that server is listed in the **Name Servers** tab of that zone's **Properties** sheet. At a minimum, you should control zone transfers so that a DNS server will only accept transfer requests from the servers listed on this tab. You can even further control your DNS zone transfer traffic by restricting zone transfer traffic to only specific IP addresses.

■**Caution** If you are using only Active Directory–integrated DNS, you should disable zone transfers entirely. In AD-integrated DNS, the concept of the zone transfer goes away and is replaced by Active Directory replication. You should only enable zone transfers if you are supporting standard primary or secondary zones.

Integrating with Third-Party DNS

Everything we've talked about so far assumes that you're working in a pure Windows 2000/2003 DNS environment, but of course not everyone is that lucky. In larger environments, you'll often need to integrate Active Directory DNS with third-party DNS environments like UNIX BIND servers, or even Windows NT 4.0 DNS servers. Luckily, most of the features in Windows DNS are common to all DNS implementations; as long as you're running a recent version of the BIND software, it'll be a relatively simple matter to integrate with Windows 2000 or Windows Server 2003 DNS. At a minimum, Active Directory needs support for Service Locator or SRV Resource Records to be able to function. These records enable DNS clients to locate Active Directory resources like domain controllers and Global Catalog servers and access the services that are offered by these systems. SRV records are supported by the following common DNS server types:

- Windows NT 4.0 (Service Pack 4)
- BIND 9
- BIND 8.2.2
- BIND 8.2
- BIND 8.1.2
- BIND 4.9.7

Ideally, you also want any non-Windows 2000 or Windows Server 2003 DNS servers to support dynamic updates and incremental zone transfers as well. Support for dynamic updates will take quite a bit of administrative burden off of your hands, and incremental zone transfers will reduce the impact of DNS replication on your overall network bandwidth. The server types that support all three of these features are

- BIND 9
- BIND 8.2.2
- BIND 8.2

Keep in mind, though, that certain features are available only in Windows 2000 and 2003 DNS; these features won't be recognized by any other DNS implementation. These features include Active Directory–integrated zones, secure dynamic updates, and WINS integration. You may also find yourself in a situation where your organization's DNS infrastructure is able to support dynamic updates, but they've made the administrative decision to disable them. But at an absolute minimum, your DNS infrastructure *must* support SRV records: your clients and servers just won't be able to function without them. Though Active Directory without dynamic updates is a pain, I've seen it work. But what if you're using a DNS server that doesn't support SRV records and you want to deploy AD? Then it's time to upgrade or migrate to a solution that has SRV support. At minimum, you'll need to migrate any DNS zones that will be supporting Active Directory to an SRV-capable server. You can also delegate a separate domain to be used by your AD infrastructure and install 2000 or 2003 DNS servers in that domain. That way, the DNS servers that maintain the parent domain can stay in place.

Using DHCP

The Dynamic Host Configuration Protocol is a network service that's been supported by Windows Server operating systems for well over a decade. DHCP was created to simplify the lives of network administrators by allowing us to automatically configure TCP/IP information for our network clients, including their IP address, subnet mask, default gateway, and many optional settings like preferred DNS and WINS servers. In Windows 2000 and 2003, DHCP can integrate tightly with Active Directory and DNS to make for better security and manageability for your network clients.

The Microsoft implementation of DHCP is made up of three components: DHCP servers, DHCP clients, and (if necessary) DHCP Relay Agents. A DHCP server is simply a Windows server that's running the DHCP Server service, and that hosts one or more DHCP *scopes* to assign IP configuration information to DHCP clients. A DHCP server will provide an IP address and configuration to a client for a finite amount of time, called a *lease*. Once a client's lease on its IP configuration has expired, it needs to contact the DHCP server to renew its configuration. For a client to request an IP address from a DHCP server actually involves a four-step exchange known as the DORA process:

1. *DHCP Discover*: A DHCP client comes online and broadcasts a Discover packet onto the local segment. Basically, the workstation wakes up and shouts, "Hey! I need an IP address! Somebody help me out!"

2. *DHCP Offer*: A DHCP server responds to the Discover packet by broadcasting an Offer packet containing a valid IP configuration. The Offer packet needs to be broadcast because the client doesn't actually have an IP address yet. The DHCP server will also enter the MAC address of the requesting client into its database along with the IP address that was offered. At this point, the server is responding, "Hey client! Here's an IP configuration for you!"

3. *DHCP Request*: Once a client has received an Offer packet, the DHCP client will configure itself with the IP configuration contained in the offer. It will then respond directly to the DHCP server that sent the offer, confirming that it's going to use that server's offer. (This step is necessary if there are multiple DHCP servers and a client receives multiple Offer packets.) At this point the client and server can communicate directly, without using broadcasts. This is the "Okay, so I'm going to use this IP configuration. That's cool, right?" portion of the conversation.

4. *DHCP Acknowledge*: This is the final step in the lease process, where the client has requested a particular IP configuration, and the server sends final confirmation. Once the Acknowledge packet is sent, the DHCP transaction is complete.

The default lease length for a DHCP address is eight days. Once half of the lease has elapsed—four days, by default—the client will send another Request packet to the same DHCP server, requesting the same IP address. Assuming no changes have been made to the configuration of the scope, the server will probably respond with an Acknowledge packet to renew the same IP address. If the DHCP server isn't available when the client goes to renew its address, it keeps trying until its lease expires. If a client's DHCP lease expires, it starts all over again at the beginning of the DORA process, since at that point the client has lost its IP configuration.

Installing DHCP

You'll install the DHCP Server service through Add/Remove Windows Components under the Networking Components section, or through the Configure Your Server Wizard in Windows Server 2003. After you install the server service, you'll then need to *authorize* the new DHCP server within Active Directory. This is a security feature within Active Directory that helps to guard against *rogue* DHCP servers handing out invalid IP configurations. Basically, when a Windows 2000 or 2003 server starts the DHCP Server service, it checks in with Active Directory and says, "Hey, am I authorized to hand out IP addresses?" If the answer is "No," the DHCP service stops automatically. Unfortunately, this authorization trick only works with Windows 2000 and 2003; it doesn't prevent any NT 4.0 or third-party DHCP server from working without authorization. You need to be a member of the Enterprise Admins group to authorize a DHCP server in Active Directory. To authorize a new DHCP server, follow these steps:

1. Open the DHCP Manager MMC snap-in. If the server hasn't been authorized, you'll see a red down arrow on the icon next to the server name.

2. Right-click the server name, and select **Authorize**.

3. Hit F5 a few times until the red down arrow changes to a green up arrow to indicate that the server has been authorized within Active Directory.

■**Note** You can also use the **dhcploc.exe** utility to manually check for all active DHCP servers on a particular subnet. This is a good tool to help you track down any NT 4.0 or other rogue DHCP servers that aren't subject to the authorization process.

Configuring DHCP Scopes

Each DHCP server can host one or more DHCP scopes, which are made up of a contiguous block of IP addresses. You'll configure DHCP scopes within the DHCP Manager MMC snap-in. Scopes consist of three elements:

- *Exclusions*: These are IP addresses within the range of the DHCP scope that you don't want to be assigned to DHCP clients. Typically, this is a small block of IP addresses that you use to manually configure servers, network printers, or any other device for which you want to configure the IP stack manually. Remember that you need to set up all elements of the TCP/IP configuration when configuring a client or server manually.

- *Reservations*: You'll use reservations to ensure that a particular MAC address always receives the same IP address—you can think of it as a lease that never expires. The largest difference between exclusions and reservations is that, by using reservations, the client will still receive configuration info from the DHCP server. So a client will receive a single consistent IP address, but any other configuration information will still get configured automatically by the DHCP server.

- *Address pool*: Any IP addresses that you don't configure as reservations or exclusions will go into the pool of IPs that DHCP will hand out to clients making DHCP requests.

When you create a DHCP scope, you'll also need to configure the subnet mask of the scope, as well as any optional configuration items that you want to be pushed out to your DHCP clients. The most common of these options are the default gateway and DNS server information, but there are more than 30 different options you can set from your DHCP server. You can specify a global set of options at the server level, or you can configure different options for each scope on the server. You can even configure a special set of options for a particular client reservation. To configure a DHCP scope, follow these steps:

1. Right-click the DHCP server and select **New Scope**. Click **Next** to bypass the initial **Welcome** screen.

2. Type in a name and a description for the scope. This is the name that will appear in the DHCP Manager, so make it a recognizable one if you're hosting multiple scopes on a single server.

3. Enter the range of addresses for the scope. The subnet mask will be calculated automatically based on the IP addresses you enter; you can leave it at the default or enter a different one manually. Click **Next**.

4. Indicate any IP addresses that should be excluded from the scope. This can be either single IPs or a range that you want to exclude. Click **Next** when you're done.

5. Enter the lease duration for this scope—this setting defaults to eight days. You can lengthen the default lease duration if you have lots of IPs and client computers that don't move around that often, or you can shorten it if IP addresses are in short supply or you support a number of laptop computers that only log on to the network for a day or two. Click **Next** to continue.

6. Here you'll configure the more common options for a DHCP scope. Enter the default gateway for clients using the DHCP scope. Click **Add** to enter the gateway and click **Next**.

7. Enter your parent domain name, and the DNS name of your DNS servers. Click **Resolve** to ensure that the DHCP server can locate the DNS server. If the DNS server resolves successfully, click **Add** to include the server in the scope's DNS options. Repeat the process to add multiple DNS servers. Click **Next** when you're done.

8. Next you'll enter the NetBIOS name of your WINS server. Click **Resolve** to ensure that the DHCP server is able to resolve the name. If the WINS server resolves successfully, click **Add** to include the server, or else you can enter its IP address manually. You can repeat this process to add multiple WINS servers. Click **Next** when you're done.

9. If you're ready for this scope to start handing out IP addresses, click **Yes, I want to activate this scope now**. Otherwise, click **No**. Click **Next**, and then **Finish**.

■**Note** You can configure additional exclusion ranges after you've created the scope by going into the **Properties** sheet of the scope, as well as changing the lease duration, the name of the scope, and the starting and ending IP addresses.

Once you've created the scope, you can also create any client reservations you need. Expand the scope you just created, and then right-click the Reservations node and select **New Reservation**. You'll need to specify a name and description for the reservation, the IP address that the machine should receive, and the MAC address of the NIC that should receive the specified IP address. Keep in mind that since DHCP reservations are based on MAC address, you'll need to update this information if you replace the network card on a machine, since the MAC address will be different on the new NIC.

Configuring DHCP Options

You can specify a number of DHCP options in addition to the basic ones you set up when you created a new scope. Each DHCP option has a numeric identifier, along with a text string that actually specifies the optional setting.

So when you specify the DHCP option for a DNS server, for example, you'll double-click the **DNS Server** option within the DNS Management Console and then manually type in the IP address of the DNS server you want your DHCP clients to point to. You can see an example of this in Figure 2-4.

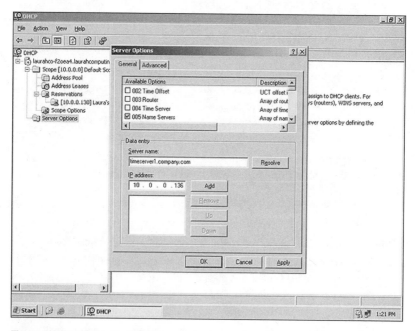

Figure 2-4. *Configuring DHCP options*

You can configure DHCP options at a number of different levels to control which machines should receive which options. *Server-level* DHCP options will apply to all clients who receive their IP configuration from a particular server, even when that server is hosting multiple scopes. In a larger network, you'll obviously want to be fairly cautious when configuring server-level options, since these will need to apply to a large number of clients. To configure DHCP options at the server level, follow these steps:

1. Open the DHCP Manager and expand the DHCP server that you want to configure.

2. Right-click Server Options and select **Configure Options**.

3. Select the option that you want to configure and enter the information in the Data Entry section. Table 2-2 lists some of the more DHCP common options that you'll configure for Windows clients.

Table 2-2. *Common DHCP Client Options*

Option Number	Option Name/Description
1	**Subnet Mask**
3	**Default Router**: This is the default gateway.
6	**DNS Server**: You can specify one or more DNS server IP addresses.
15	**Domain Name**: This is the default DNS suffix that's appended to each client's hostname.
44	**WINS Server**: The IP address of one or more WINS servers.
46	**NetBIOS Node Type**: Specifies the type of NetBIOS name resolution in use. Set this to 0x1 for B-Node, 0x2 for P-Node, 0x4 for M-Node, and 0x8 for H-Node. (More on Node Types in the "Supporting WINS and NetBIOS" section.)
47	**NetBIOS Scope ID**

If you're hosting multiple scopes on a single server, you'll use scope-level options for most of your configurations. This allows you to specify different parameters for machines on different scopes since computers on different subnets will likely require different default gateways and potentially different name servers. To configure DHCP options for a particular scope, you'll expand the scope in DHCP Manager, right-click Scope Options and select **Configure Options**. From here the process is identical to setting options at the server level.

You can even configure specific options for individual clients by setting DHCP options for a particular DHCP reservation. For example, you may have a reservation for your internal DNS server. The remainder of the clients in the scope point to the internal DNS, but the internal DNS requires the IP address of an external DNS server to forward Internet name resolution requests. So you can configure a reservation-level DHCP option so that only the internal DNS server will receive that particular DNS configuration. To configure DHCP options for a reserved client, you'll expand the Reservations node in the appropriate scope, right-click the individual reservation, and select **Configure Options**.

■Note If you have DHCP options set at multiple levels, scope-level options will override those set at the server level, and reservation options will take precedence over both server- and scope-level DHCP options.

Creating Fault Tolerance

Whenever possible, you should install a DHCP server on each subnet that has clients who require automatic IP configuration. This provides the best performance for your clients, and guards against a DHCP server being unavailable because of a WAN link or router failure. But even with a DHCP server on the local subnet, you should still create a plan for fault tolerance. For example, you can split a DHCP scope between a local DHCP server and one on a remote subnet, so that clients can still receive DHCP information even if their primary DHCP server goes offline or becomes unavailable. In order to do this, you'll create an identical scope on two DHCP servers, and exclude a portion of the IP address range on each one. If you're only using the remote DHCP server for fault tolerance, you can use an 80-20 or 70-30 split between the two. So you have two DHCP servers called DHCP1 and DHCP2. You'll configure scopes on the two servers like this:

- **Server**: DHCP1
- **Scope Name**: Local Scope
- **IP Address Range**: 192.168.1.1–192.168.1.254
- **Exclusions**: 192.168.1.201–192.168.1.254
- **Server**: DHCP2
- **Scope Name**: Remote Scope
- **IP Address Range**: 192.168.1.1–192.168.1.254
- **Exclusions**: 192.168.1.1–192.168.1.200

You can see that DHCP1 will be able to hand out addresses from 1 to 200, while DHCP2 will be able to hand out 201 to 254. This way, the two scopes won't trip over each other if they're both online at the same time: even if a client on DHCP1's subnet somehow acquires an IP address from DHCP2, there won't be any conflicts. This split configuration creates a bit of administrative overhead, since you need to maintain two separate DHCP scopes. Any changes that you make to the DHCP options on DHCP1 also need to be made on DHCP2, and you need to duplicate any reservations on each server so that both servers are aware of them. But this is still a good way to provide fault tolerance for your DHCP servers. As an alternative, you can configure the DHCP service on a Windows 2000 or Windows Server 2003 cluster. This will create a "virtual" DHCP server that's split between two physical servers; if one node of the cluster fails, the DHCP configuration will switch over to the other cluster node without skipping a beat.

USING SUPERSCOPES

So if you have DHCP servers serving up IPs on two different subnets, what happens when clients receive their address information from one server versus the other? Say you have a DHCP server on one subnet that's serving up IP addresses from 10.0.0.1 to 10.0.0.100. Then you add another DHCP server to a different subnet that uses the 10.0.0.101 to 10.0.0.254 range. If you have two separate DHCP servers handing out addresses in the 10.0.0.*x* subnet, they might hand out duplicate IP addresses since neither server knows which IPs the other one has dealt out.

You can solve these problems using superscopes. A *superscope* gives you a way to manage multiple DHCP servers without having the servers tripping over each other. On the first DHCP server in this example, you'd create a new scope with the range of 10.0.0.101 to 10.0.0.254. You'd then configure an exclusion range for *all* IP addresses in the other range: 10.0.0.101 to 10.0.0.254. You'll do the same thing on the second DHCP server: configure a scope that goes from 10.0.0.1 to 10.0.0.100, and then configure an exclusion for every IP in the scope. You'll then create a superscope on each server by adding both scopes to a single superscope. This way, each individual scope recognizes the IP addresses used by the other scope, but at the same time the servers will only hand out IP addresses from their own scope.

Using DHCP Relay Agents

If at all possible, you should configure a DHCP server on each subnet that has clients who require dynamic IP configuration. In some cases, though, this simply isn't practical: you may not have the money to deploy a DHCP server in every subnet of a complex network, or you may want to house your DHCP servers centrally for better security and control. If a client resides in one subnet and the DHCP server in another, most modern routers can simply forward the DHCP DORA packets as needed. (This is specified in RFC 1542 and 2131.) If you're using routers that don't have this capability, you'll install the DHCP Relay Agent service on a machine in the same subnet as the DHCP clients. The DHCP Relay Agent works by taking broadcast-based DHCP packets and wrapping them up inside of unicast packets. The Relay Agent will then send these unicast packets directly to the DHCP server on the remote subnet.

To run the DHCP Relay Agent on a Windows 2000 or 2003 server, you need to install the Routing and Remote Access Service. To configure the Relay Agent, open the RRAS MMC console and browse to **Routing and Remote Access ➤** *ServerName* **➤ IP Routing ➤ DHCP Relay Agent**. From the **Properties** sheet of the agent, you'll add the IP address of each DHCP server that you want to forward requests to.

Integrating DHCP with DNS

One of the most convenient features of DHCP is that it can integrate directly into your DNS infrastructure to support clients that can't handle dynamic DNS on their own. Windows 2000, XP, and 2003 machines can automatically register their own DNS information; however, downlevel clients such as Windows NT and 9x clients are unable to do this. (This is becoming less of a problem as support for NT and 9x goes away, but you may find yourself needing to do so at some point anyway.) If you're still supporting these legacy operating systems, you can configure the DHCP service on a Windows 2000 or 2003 server to register DNS records on behalf of clients that are unable to do so on their own. This takes away the need for you to do so manually whenever the IP address of an older client machine gets changed.

To enable your DHCP servers to perform dynamic updates, follow these steps:

1. Right-click the DHCP server you want to configure and select **Properties**.

2. Go to the DNS tab, and make sure that **Enable DNS dynamic updates according to the settings below** is selected (it should be on by default). From here, there are three ways you can configure dynamic updates:

   - Always update DNS and PTR records.

   - Only update records if the client requests it. By default, a 2000/XP machine will update its own A record, and the DHCP server will update the PTR record.

   - Dynamically update DNS A and PTR records for clients that do not request updates—this is useful for clients running Windows NT 4.0.

■**Note** You'll still need to manually register the DNS records for any legacy clients that don't receive their IP information through DHCP.

If you've enabled secure-only dynamic updates and you have multiple DHCP servers installed on your network, you need to add each of the DHCP servers to the DnsUpdateProxy security group so that all of your DHCP servers will be able to update records for any client. Otherwise, the DHCP server that first registers a client's information will be seen as the "owner" of that record, and no other DHCP server will be able to update it. This is necessary even if your clients are all running Windows 2000/XP, since the DHCP server will update each client's PTR record by default. You can also configure the credentials that DHCP will use to perform updates from the DHCP server's **Properties** sheet; click the **Advanced** tab, and then select **Credentials**.

■**Caution** Don't add your DHCP server to the DnsUpdateProxy group if the service is running on a domain controller, since this can leave your Active Directory database open to a potential attack. If you're running multiple DHCP servers and need to use this group to update legacy DNS settings, DHCP should only be installed on member servers.

ADMINISTERING DHCP FROM THE COMMAND LINE

Windows 2000, and especially Windows Server 2003, have a number of command-line utilities that you can use to migrate DHCP settings from one server to another, as well as perform a number of other DHCP administration tasks. This can save you hours of work if you're replacing an old DHCP server with new hardware or just trying to back up your DHCP configuration as a part of disaster recovery planning.

To import and export DHCP settings from an NT 4.0 or Windows 2000 DHCP server, you'll use the **dhcpexim.exe** tool that's available as a free download from the Microsoft website. The tool itself is pretty self-explanatory—you can either export your DHCP information to a .DAT file or import a file that you've exported from another machine. You have the option to disable the scopes you're exporting before you perform an export operation, and activate any new scopes after they've been imported. The only thing I find somewhat tricky about **dhcpexim** is that you don't get any sort of progress bar while it's running; you simply have to sit and be patient until you see the message "The operation completed successfully" pop up.

Once you've exported your DHCP settings from an NT 4.0 or 2000 DHCP server, you'll use the **netsh** command-line utility in 2003 to import the DHCP configuration. The syntax to import a DHCP database into a 2003 server is as follows:

```
netsh DHCP server import <path of export file> all
```

This will import the configuration settings for all of the scopes that were running on the old server. You can also use **netsh** to authorize a DHCP server in Active Directory, using this syntax:

```
netsh dhcp add server ServerDNSDomainName ServerIPAddress
```

Using **netsh**, you can manage your entire DHCP server from the command line, including creating scopes, adding exclusion ranges and options, and setting a scope to an active state. And the following simple line of code will export all of your 2003 DHCP settings for backups and disaster recovery, just like **dhcpexim.exe** did for Windows NT 4.0 and 2000:

```
netsh dhcp dump > filename.dat
```

Supporting WINS and NetBIOS

Though WINS and NetBIOS aren't quite as prevalent as they once were, you'll still probably run into a situation where you need to deploy and support them on an Active Directory network. As a quick refresher, NetBIOS is the name resolution service that was used by Microsoft operating systems prior to Windows 2000. NetBIOS differs significantly from DNS in that it's a flat naming scheme rather than a hierarchical one. On a DNS network, you can have two different machines that have the same hostname just as long as their FQDNs are different: server1.east.mycompany.com and server1.mycompany.com would be seen as unique hosts. On a NetBIOS network, this wouldn't work: there could only be one machine named SERVER1 across an entire network. NetBIOS also relies heavily on broadcast traffic to function. Without a WINS server in place, any client that needs to locate a NetBIOS resource will send a broadcast to their entire network segment in order to locate it. Not only can this become bandwidth-intensive, but it also becomes interesting to manage in a WAN environment since NetBIOS traffic (and broadcast traffic in general) doesn't travel beyond the router boundary by default. Sending NetBIOS traffic over a WAN also creates some security challenges, since the NetBIOS ports are well-known attack vectors for viruses, worms, and hackers.

Windows 9x and NT especially were heavily dependent on NetBIOS to locate computers and resources across a network, and continued support for those legacy operating systems means that a number of Active Directory deployments require some type of NetBIOS support. But even if you're running a purely 2000/2003/XP environment, you still might not be able to get away from WINS completely, since a number of business applications require NetBIOS name resolution to function. The most likely place where this is going to make its presence known is if you're supporting a Microsoft Exchange environment, since Exchange 5.5, 2000, and 2003 all depend on NetBIOS to some extent. So it's helpful to have this understanding of NetBIOS and WINS and how to support them, even as Windows administrators the world over wait for them to go away and not bother us anymore.

Deploying a WINS server helps to cut down on NetBIOS broadcasts by creating a centralized database of NetBIOS name registrations. Much like with dynamic DNS, a Windows machine configured with the address of a WINS server will register itself with that server when it boots up. Say you have a single WINS server, SERVER-A, on your network. You configure a machine called CLIENT-A, with the IP address of 192.168.1.100, to use SERVER-A as a WINS server. When the machine boots up, it will contact SERVER-A and register its name and IP address in the WINS database. If a machine called CLIENT-B needs to access a file share on CLIENT-A, then CLIENT-B will send a query to SERVER-A. SERVER-A will return CLIENT-A's

IP address to CLIENT-B, and then CLIENT-B can contact CLIENT-A directly without needing to resort to a NetBIOS broadcast.

Installing a WINS Server

You'll install WINS on a 2000 or 2003 server just like any other network service, using the Add/Remove Windows Components applet in Windows 2000 or the Configure Your Server Wizard in Windows 2003. Once you've installed the WINS server, the client registration process is basically automatic: just point your Windows machines to the IP address of the WINS server, and they'll register their IP address and NetBIOS name with the server when they boot up. If you need to modify the default behavior of a WINS server, there are a number of parameters that you can modify in the WINS MMC snap-in. Just like with DNS and DHCP, you'll configure server options by right-clicking the server name and selecting **Properties**. These parameters including the following:

- **Renew Interval:** This specifies how often a WINS client needs to renew their registration information in the WINS database to prevent stale or inaccurate records. This defaults to every 6 days, but you can make it as frequently as every 40 minutes or as infrequently as every 365 days. Decreasing the renew interval will increase NetBIOS traffic on your network, but will keep the WINS database current if you have roaming clients who connect and disconnect from the network frequently. Increasing the renew interval will reduce NetBIOS traffic, but will increase the likelihood that your WINS information will become inconsistent.

- **Extinction Interval:** When a WINS client shuts down, it *releases* its WINS registration with the local server. But because WINS information can be replicated between multiple servers, the local server will wait a certain amount of time before declaring a released record "extinct," so that the same client can easily renew the same record in the WINS database. If a released IP-to-NetBIOS-name mapping hasn't been renewed within the extinction interval, the local WINS server will mark the record as extinct and replicate that extinction to any other WINS servers. This interval defaults to 4 days, but can be configured anywhere from 1 to 365 days.

- **Extinction Timeout:** This specifies the amount of time between a record being flagged as extinct, and when it's actually removed (*scavenged*) from the WINS database. This extra time interval is necessary for the extinction can be replicated to any other WINS servers on the network, so that any replicated servers are in a consistent state. This defaults to 6 days, but can go anywhere from 1 to 365 days. The combination of the **Extinction Interval** and the **Extinction Timeout** parameters means that a released WINS record will remain in the WINS database for 10 days by default before the record is ultimately deleted.

- **Database Verification**: If you're replicating WINS information between multiple servers, you should verify the consistency of any replicated information on a regular basis. To enable automatic consistency checks, go to the **Database Verification** tab on the WINS server **Properties** sheet and place a check mark next to **Verify database consistency every X hours**. This setting defaults to every 24 hours, and you can specify the start time in the **Begin verifying at** window. This can be a resource-intensive process, so schedule verification to occur during off-hours.

- **Database Backup**: You'll configure WINS backups on the **General** tab of the server properties. The WINS database isn't backed up by default, but once you specify a folder to store the backups, they will run automatically every 3 hours. You can also configure additional backups to run every time the WINS service shuts down, such as when the server is rebooted.

- **Burst Handling**: If a large number of clients attempt to register their information at the same time, the WINS server can become overloaded. This can happen first thing in the morning in a 9-to-5 office, or if your office suffers a power outage and every machine suddenly comes back online at the same time. Burst handling will allow the WINS server to queue a certain number of registration requests before clients need to retry the registration request later. This is enabled by default and set to **Medium**, which creates a queue of 500 requests. You can change this setting to **Low** (300) or **High** (1000), or you can set a **Custom** queue length of anywhere from 50 to 5000 requests.

A WINS server installed on well-equipped server can handle the daily activities of about 10,000 clients, give or take a few hundred. Depending on the number of queries it needs to process, WINS can be more resource intensive than DNS or DHCP, so be sure to deploy it on a server that has a lot of RAM and available disk space, as well as a fast CPU. You should especially consider deploying additional WINS servers when your network spans multiple locations separated by WAN links, so that you don't have hundreds of machines trying to register with the WINS server when they all power on at 9 a.m. every day. To create fault tolerance, you can point your clients to a WINS server on their local subnet as the primary WINS server, and a server on a remote subnet as a backup in case the local WINS is unavailable.

RESTORING THE WINS DATABASE

In most cases, restoring a WINS database is as simple as following these steps:

1. Stop the WINS service, or right-click the server in the WINS console and select **All Tasks ➤ Stop**.

2. Right-clicking the server and select **Restore Database**.

3. Specify the folder containing the backup files and click **OK**.

4. Restart the WINS server once the backup is done.

If your WINS server still won't start after a restore, you may need to clear the entire WINS database and start from scratch. This will require your WINS clients to create new entries in a freshly created WINS database, either by rebooting the client or issuing the nbtstat -RR command to refresh their NetBIOS registrations. To clear out the WINS database and start over, you'll need to do the following:

1. Go to the **Advanced** tab on the server's **Properties** sheet. Make a note of the path listed in the **Database Path** entry, and click **OK**.

2. Stop the WINS service.

3. In Windows Explorer, go to the path containing the database files and manually delete all of the files you find.

4. Restart the WINS server. It will create a blank database to accept new client registrations.

Specifying Client Options for WINS

Once you've configured a WINS server, you should then configure the NetBIOS *node type* on your clients, which determines how your clients use a combination of WINS and broadcasts to locate NetBIOS resources or map a NetBIOS name to an IP address. Properly configuring the node type for your clients can go a long way toward cutting down on broadcast traffic. The good news is that NetBIOS node type is one of the options that you can configure and deploy as an option on a DHCP server. You can configure your clients to use one of four node types:

- *b-node*: This node type will use only broadcast packets to locate a NetBIOS resource. Use this one only if you don't have a WINS server configured on your network. (Actually, just configure a WINS server and don't use this one at all.)

- *p-node*: Uses only WINS communications to locate NetBIOS names. This is obviously less bandwidth intensive than b-node, but if you have any sort of issue with your WINS server, NetBIOS name resolution will start to fail.

- *m-node*: Uses a combination of b-node and p-node. This one will use broadcasts first, and then look for a WINS server if it can't find what it's looking for from the broadcast. I don't think this one's really any better than using b-node—skip it.

- *h-node*: Like m-node, this uses a combination of broadcast and WINS. This one's much smarter, though, since it'll query a WINS server first, and only resort to broadcast traffic if it can't locate the resource it needs from the WINS server. Unless you've got a really compelling reason to use one of the other three, h-node is your best bet for NetBIOS node type.

Each node type has a number associated with it when you're specifying it as a DHCP option. You'll use 1 for b-node, 2 for p-node, 4 for m-node, and 8 for h-node. If you're dealing with a multihomed computer, the node type will apply to every NIC installed in the machine.

■**Note** The one instance where I could make an argument for using b-node or m-node resolution would be if you had the majority of your resources situated on a local subnet, but your WINS server is located on a remote subnet. In that case, it might actually make for better bandwidth utilization to broadcast locally for a resource before looking to the WINS server, but you'd need to make that determination based on the specific traffic patterns on your network.

Configuring WINS Replication

You can deploy up to 12 WINS servers on your network to create fault tolerance and improve name resolution performance. Much like primary and secondary DNS servers, multiple WINS servers will replicate their databases between themselves, which will allow WINS clients to locate NetBIOS resources on different subnets. Depending on the speed of the links between your subnets, you can configure multiple WINS servers to use *push*, *pull*, or *push/pull* replication.

Let's look at configuring replication between two WINS servers: WINS-A and WINS-B. In pull replication, WINS-A will periodically send a request to WINS-B, asking WINS-B to return any changes that have been made to its database. Pull replication is primarily useful over lower-speed WAN connections, since replication will only occur at predetermined intervals. The default setting is every 30 minutes, starting at midnight. To add a replication partner to a WINS server and configure it to use pull replication, follow these steps:

1. Open the WINS MMC snap-in. Select the WINS server you want to manage and drill down to the Replication Partners folder.

2. Right-click the folder and select **New Replication Partner**. Enter the IP address or NetBIOS name of the server you want to replicate with, then click **OK**. This will create a push/pull replication schedule by default. To change this, go to the **Properties** sheet of the replication partner and select to the **Advanced** tab.

3. Change the **Replication Partner Type** to **Pull**. Configure when you want pull replication to start, and how frequently it should occur. Click **OK** when you're done.

By contrast, a push partner will use notifications to inform its replication partners about changes to the WINS database. You can specify the number of changes that are required before a push partner will send out a notification. This defaults to zero, which means that a push partner will send a notification every time it receives a change to its database. So in the previous example, WINS-B will notify WINS-A whenever WINS-B receives a new WINS registration, update, or release. This configuration is obviously more suitable for Local Area Network (LAN) or high-speed WAN connections that can accept more frequent WINS replication traffic.

Note As you can probably guess, push/pull replication uses a combination of both replication types. So WINS-B will send WINS-A its changes as it receives them, and WINS-A will query WINS-B for updates on a scheduled basis. This is the most effective way to ensure that all changes to the WINS database get replicated, but it's also the most bandwidth intensive.

If you're configuring replication for a large number of sites, each with its own WINS servers, you can configure a *hub-and-spoke* replication configuration to optimize WINS replication traffic. This means that you select one WINS server to be the central server, or "hub," and then you configure all other WINS servers to be replication partners of that one single server. This way, every site will receive the WINS updates from every other site when they replicate with the central hub server. But when you configure replication for a large environment, you need to be aware of possible delays in *convergence* time for WINS replication. This refers to the amount of time it takes a record in one "spoke" site to be replicated to all other spokes in the network. Let's say that you've designed a hub-and-spoke network that spans a number of cities: San Diego, Seattle, Austin, and Chicago. You designate the Chicago WINS server as the hub server, since it has the best connection to the other three sites. The San Diego WINS server pulls updates from the Chicago hub every 30 minutes, and the Seattle and Austin WINS servers pull updates from Chicago every 10 minutes, as shown in Figure 2-5. This means that it can take up to 40 minutes for a record in San Diego to be replicated to the WINS server in Seattle or Austin. If a client in Seattle tries to access a new server in San Diego and the WINS record hasn't replicated yet, for example, the WINS request will fail. You need to strike a balance between controlling how much bandwidth gets used by WINS versus how quickly your clients need to be able to access new resources: a 40-minute delay might be acceptable to some companies and unthinkable for others.

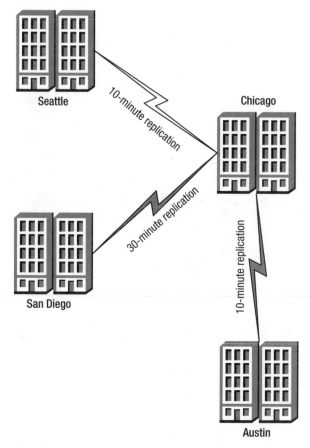

Figure 2-5. *Configuring hub-and-spoke WINS replication*

■**Caution** Though it should hopefully go without saying by now, be sure to encrypt any WINS replication traffic going across the Internet with an IPSec tunnel or a VPN connection. Otherwise, the names and IP addresses of your private network resources could be subject to a footprint attack similar to the vulnerability created by allowing unknown computers to request DNS zone transfers.

Summary

In this second chapter, you learned about the different technologies that form the underpinnings of an Active Directory network. Without a well-designed and fully functional DNS infrastructure, your AD deployment won't do anyone much good at all, so that's where we started out. Active Directory lives and dies by DNS, relying on it to advertise the necessary Service Locator (SRV) records for domain controllers, Global Catalogs, and site information. Without these SRV records, your network clients won't be able to locate the DNS records that they need to authenticate to Active Directory and browse resources. You can deploy standard DNS for interoperability with third-party DNS solutions, or use Active Directory–integrated DNS to take advantage of advanced features like fault tolerance, multimaster replication, and secure dynamic updates.

For backwards compatibility with Windows NT 4.0, you'll probably also need to deploy a WINS server for NetBIOS name resolution. Not only was NetBIOS the default name resolution standard for Windows operating systems prior to Windows 2000, but it's still required for certain applications such as Microsoft Exchange. You can even integrate your DNS and WINS deployments together to create a complete name resolution scheme for your clients. We also looked at the Dynamic Host Configuration Protocol, or DHCP. While DHCP isn't actually necessary for Active Directory to function, it does make your life as an administrator quite a bit easier by allowing you to automatically configure clients with TCP/IP configuration information. By integrating DHCP with dynamic DNS, you can create a nearly fully automated name resolution and IP addressing scheme for your clients that will allow them to easily access Active Directory resources.

In the next chapter, we'll turn our attention to some of the day-to-day tasks that you'll perform as an Active Directory administrator, including creating and managing user objects within the Active Directory database.

Additional Resources

"Using Netsh": http://www.microsoft.com/resources/documentation/ windows/xp/all/proddocs/en-us/netsh.mspx—**netsh** is one of those unbelievably handy tools that will let you configure just about anything relating to network interfaces, DHCP, and WINS. The number of command-line options is simply overwhelming, so it's good to know you can turn to this command-line reference for help.

"Deploying Network Services": http://www.microsoft.com/resources/ documentation/WindowsServ/2003/all/deployguide/en-us/dpgdns_ overview.asp—Provides an overview of deploying the network technologies we've discussed here in Windows Server 2003, as well as ISA Server, IPSec, Remote Access, and wireless connectivity.

Support WebCast: Microsoft Windows 2000 DNS and UNIX BIND DNS Interoperability: http://support.microsoft.com/default.aspx?scid=/ servicedesks/webcasts/wc022602/wcblurb022602.asp—(As usual, use Google to search for the title if the link has moved.) A Technet support webcast that talks about interoperating between UNIX and Microsoft DNS, including several specific KB articles about migration and delegation.

■ ■ ■

CHAPTER 3

Daily Administration

While it may not seem on the surface to be the most glamorous pursuit, creating and administering Active Directory user accounts is one of the most critical tasks you can perform as a Windows administrator. It's the like the "tree falling in a forest" question: if you've created a highly available and elegantly configured network that your users can't access, have you really accomplished anything at all? The user account is the heart of the entire Active Directory infrastructure, since it's the "jumping-off point" for all user access to your network. Because of this, you have several utilities at your disposal to streamline and automate the user account creation process, as well as tools to help you configure your users' logon scripts and group memberships.

In this chapter, I'll cover the following topics:

- Creating user accounts
- Configuring account attributes
- Creating logon scripts
- Managing schema attributes
- Bulk account creation
- Delegating administrative authority
- Configuring security groups
- Managing user profiles
- Encrypting user data
- Recovering encrypted data

Managing Users

Though troubleshooting hard-to-find DNS or replication issues might seem more impressive or "important" than managing user objects, the latter issue is probably one of the most critical aspects of managing an Active Directory environment. This is really quite logical if you think about it: the user object creates the entryway for your users to access the network resources and directory services that you've so painstakingly configured for them. However, it can certainly become tedious to manually create user objects and profile settings over and over again, especially in an organization that is expanding or experiencing high turnover. So in this section, I'll show you some simple ways to automate the user management process to save you time and effort. We'll also talk about ways to create user accounts in bulk, such as you might need to do during a company merger or migration, as well as creating logon scripts to configure user working environments by creating network connections and starting programs. I'll finish up with a look at delegating administration of your user accounts: this is useful for scenarios where you are in a larger IT organization with staff of varying levels of authority and expertise.

Creating Users

If you're only dealing with one or two users that need to be created, the simplest way to do so is still through the Active Directory Users & Computers GUI. Simply right-click the container or Organizational Unit (OU) where you want the new user object to be created, and then select **New ➤ User**. You'll then go through an extremely friendly wizard that will prompt you for the user's name (though only the first name is mandatory) and logon name for pre-Windows 2000 computers. You'll also need to specify the user's initial password and a few password attributes such as **User must change password at next logon**, **Password never expires**, and **Account is disabled**. Once you've configured this basic information, you can double-click the user object to configure additional settings such as group membership, Terminal Services settings, and address/telephone contact info.

   If you find that you're constantly creating new users that are configured in the same way (in a department with high turnover, for example), you can create a user object *template* that will save you time in creating new users. Just create a user object called "Call_Center_Template" or something similarly intuitive, and configure it with all of the settings that are common to users for that department or area. Then whenever you need to create a new user, you can simply copy the template and name the new user as necessary.

When you copy a user object template, the following default attributes will carry over to the newly created object:

- **User must change password at next logon**
- **User cannot change password**
- **Password never expires**
- **Account is disabled**
- **Logon hours**
- **Workstation restrictions**
- **All address information *except* the Street Address**
- **Account expiration date, if any**
- **User profile and home folder settings**
- **Title**
- **Security Group membership**

■**Caution** For security purposes, you should configure any template accounts to be disabled in order to prevent unauthorized access to your network using a template account.

Beginning with Windows Server 2003, you can also use the **dsadd.exe** command-line utility to create Active Directory objects. To add a single user to Active Directory, simply type **dsadd user *UserDN*** at the command line, where *UserDN* refers to the distinguished name of the user object, such as **cn=smith, dc=example, dc=com**. **dsadd** allows you to set a huge number of user attributes at the command line by using any of the following parameters:

- -samid *SAMName*: Specifies the SAM account name for backwards compatibility with Windows NT 4.0 and legacy applications.
- -upn *UPN*: Specifies the user principal name, like "smith@example.com".
- -fn *FirstName*
- -mi *MiddleInitial*
- -ln *LastName*
- -display *DisplayName*
- -empid *EmployeeID*
- -pwd *Password*: Specifies the password for the user to be set to. You can either enter the password when you issue the dsadd command, or type * to be prompted for a password when the user object is created.

- -desc *Description*
- -memberof *GroupDN*: Specifies the security groups that this user should belong to. Separates multiple group names using a comma.
- -office *Office*
- -tel *TelephoneNumber*
- -email *Email*
- -hometel *HomePhoneNumber*
- -pager *PagerNumber*
- -mobile *CellPhoneNumber*
- -fax *FaxNumber*
- -iptel *IPPhoneNumber*
- -webpg *WebPage*
- -title *Title*
- -dept *Department*
- -company *Company*
- -mgr *ManagerDN*: Specifies the distinguished name of the manager of the user account you're currently creating.
- -hmdir *HomeDirectory*: The user's home directory.
- -hmdrv *DriveLetter*: The drive letter that a user's home directory should be mapped to.
- -profile *ProfilePath*: Path to the user's profile.
- -loscr *ScriptPath*: Path to the user's logon script.
- -mustchpwd {yes | no}: Specifies whether the user needs to change his password the next (or first) time he logs on to Active Directory. This defaults to no if it isn't specified.
- -canchpwd {yes | no}: Specifies whether the user is allowed to change her password. This needs to be set to yes if -mustchpwd is set to yes. The value for -canchpwd defaults to yes.
- -reversiblepwd {yes | no}: Specifies whether the password should be stored using reversible encryption. This defaults to no if you don't specify a value.
- -pwdneverexpires {yes | no}: Specifies whether the user password expires (if set to yes) or not (if set to no). Defaults to no.
- -acctexpires *NumberOfDays*: Number of days from today when the account will expire.

- `-disabled {yes | no}`: Specifies whether the user account is disabled. Defaults to `no`.

- `{-s Server | -d Domain}`: Specifies whether the user account is configured on a member server or a domain controller. This defaults to a domain controller in the user's logon domain.

- `-u`: Specifies the user account that you'll use to connect to the remote server. This allows you to improve the security of your network by logging on to your workstation using an everyday user account, and using the `-u` option to specify an administrative account to create a new user.

- `-p`: Specifies the password that you'll use to connect to the remote server. You can enter the password manually, or enter an asterisk (*) to be prompted for a password when **dsadd** runs.

- `-uc | -uco | -uci`: Specifies that the input or output file is formatted using Unicode formatting. `-uc` specifies Unicode for both input and output files, `-uci` specifies that only the input file is Unicode, `-uco` specifies Unicode for only the output file.

- `-q`: Suppresses any output from **dsadd**; the command runs in "quiet" mode.

To create a single user object using the **dsadd** utility, you would use the following syntax:

```
dsadd user cn=smith, dc=mycompany, dc=com -samid smith -fn Bryan
 -ln Smith
```

■Note **dsadd.exe** is not available for Windows 2000 Active Directory, but there is a similar **addusers.exe** utility available as a part of the Windows 2000 Resource Kit. This is a free download, available at http://www.petri.co.il/download_free_reskit_tools.htm.

Performing Bulk Operations

If you need to import a large number of users into Active Directory, you can use the command-line tools already discussed in addition to two Microsoft utilities that were purposely built with this need in mind. Both **csvde.exe** and **ldifde.exe** will allow you to import and export Active Directory information: **csvde** into a comma-separated CSV file, **ldifde** into a more extensible LDAP Interchange Format (LDIF) file. The two commands use identical syntax; the only difference in this respect is the format of the input and output files, though **ldifde** is a more powerful tool in general, allowing you to create, delete, and modify Active Directory information and modify the Active Directory schema. The syntax of **csvde.exe** and **ldifde.exe**, as well as explanations of their parameters, is as follows:

```
csvde/ldifde [-i] [-f FileName] [-s ServerName]
      [-c String1 String2] [-v] [-j Path] [-t PortNumber]
      [-d BaseDN] [-r LDAPFilter] [-p Scope]
      [-l LDAPAttributeList] [-o LDAPAttributeList] [-g]
      [-m] [-n] [-k] [-a UserDistinguishedName Password]
      [-b UserName Domain Password] [-?]
```

- -i: Specifies that you're working in import mode. If this isn't specified, it defaults to export mode.

- -f: Specifies the name of the file that you're importing to or exporting from.

- -s: Indicates the domain controller that you want to use to perform the import or export operation.

- -c *String1 String2*: Replaces all instances of one string with another. This is particularly useful if you've exported a CSV file from one domain and now need to import the information into another, where information like the distinguished name of the domain or a UNC path needs to be changed.

- -v: Sets verbose mode for maximum details of the import or export operation.

- -t *PortNumber*: Specifies an LDAP port number to connect to the DC on, if you've changed it from the default of 389.

- -d *BaseDN*: Sets a particular distinguished name as the base for the export—if you only want to export information about a single OU, for example.

- -r *LDAPFilter*: Filters the information that gets exported. If you only want to export user objects, for example, you would use the following syntax:

  ```
  -r "(objectClass=User)"
  ```

- -l *LDAPAttributeList*: Returns only the attributes that you specify. If you leave this blank, all attributes will be returned.

- -o *LDAPAttributeList*: The opposite of -l, this specifies a list of attributes to omit from the export.

- -j *Path*: Sets the location of the log file created by the utility. This defaults to the directory that you run the command from.

- -p *Scope*: Specifies the scope of the import or export. You can specify Base, OneLevel, or SubTree.

- -m: Omits Active-Directory–specific attributes like the SID or GUID that's attached to the object that aren't typically included in an import or export operation.

- -n: Omits the export of any binary values.

- -k: Instructs the utility to ignore any errors that it encounters and to continue processing.

- -a *UserDistinguishedName Password*: Specifies the distinguished name and password that should be used to perform the import or export. This defaults to the credentials that you're currently logged on with.

- -b *Username Domain Password*: Specifies the credentials that should be used to perform the import or export, using the format of *Username Domain Password*. Like -a, this also defaults to your current credentials.

So at the most basic level, to export all domain information to a CSV file, you would issue the following command:

```
csvde -f output.csv
```

Or you could customize this command so that you are only exporting user objects from the Finance OU, and using the **LDIF** format:

```
ldifde -f output.csv -s dc1.example.com -d
 "ou=Finance,dc=example,dc=com"
-r "(objectClass=user)"
```

To create a CSV file for use in importing with **CSVDE**, the first line of the CSV file needs to contain the field names of each attribute that you're defining. For example, the administrator of a college computer lab may receive an Excel file at the beginning of each semester with the names of incoming students who require user logons for computers in labs and classrooms. The administrator could easily massage this data to create a file that could be used to automate the user creation process, like this:

```
Cn,FirstName,SurName,DistinguishedName
jsmith,John,Smith,"cn=jsmith, ou=Students, dc=example, dc=edu"
ehopkins,Evan,Hopkins, "cn=ehopkins, ou=Students, dc=example, dc=edu"
mbarnett,Maryane,Barnett, "cn=mbarnett, ou=Students, dc=example
 dc=edu"
```

At this point, creating the user accounts is as simple as issuing the following command:

```
csvde -i -f input.csv
```

Configuring User Accounts

Once you've created your user accounts, you can modify any needed settings from the GUI or the command line. We've already seen how to use the GUI to modify user account settings: simply double-click the user object within Active Directory Users & Computers, and manually enter the new value on the appropriate tab. From the command line, Windows Server 2003 provides the **dsmod** tool, which can modify the properties of many AD objects, including user accounts. You'll use the same parameters with **dsmod** as was just listed for **dsadd**, specifying the distinguished name of the user you want to modify and the new value of the attribute. For example, the following command will change the LastName attribute of the smith user account to smith-grainer:

```
dsmod user cn=smith, dc=example, dc=com -ln "smith-grainer"
```

Any other attributes of the modified user object will remain unchanged in the previous example. While the **dsmod** utility may not seem very useful for one-off situations like this, we'll be using it elsewhere in this guide to make any number of Active Directory modifications to user and computer objects, domain controllers, and Organizational Units. You can type **dsmod/?** at the command line to see a full listing of the many options available to you with this handy and flexible utility.

If you need to change attributes for a large number of users within your AD structure, you can create a quick VBScript to modify the user attributes directly. For example, say that your organization's Accounts Payable department has always been a part of the Operations department, but the organization has recently expanded and restructured the org chart so that Accounts Payable is now its own business entity. If you create a new Organizational Unit for the new department, you can easily run a script that runs **dsmod** for each object in the OU to change their Department attribute from Operations to Accounts Payable. You can see how this works in the following code sample:

```
set objContainer = GetObject("LDAP://dc=AccountsPayable,
    dc=example, dc=com")
objContainer.Filter = Array("user")
for each objUser in objContainer
    WScript.Echo "Modifying " & objUser.Get("SAMAccountName")
    objUser.Department = "Accounts Payable"
    objUser.SetInfo
next
```

USING VBSCRIPT—THE LEAST YOU NEED TO KNOW

While I haven't specifically discussed using VBScript yet, the code sample listed in this section is fairly easy to follow. First you create `objContainer`, which references the distinguished name of the OU that you're attempting to access. Then you set a filter so that you will only be looking at user objects. Finally, you loop through each user object within `objContainer` (in this case, the Accounts Payable OU) and set the `Department` attribute on each one. If you've never worked with VBScript before, you can run this script by doing the following:

1. Copy the code into Notepad, making any modifications to customize it to your environment.

2. Save the file as **modify.vbs**—be sure that Notepad doesn't tack on an extra .TXT extension on the end, or the script won't run.

3. From the command line, type **cscript.exe modify.vbs**.

You can use even a basic understanding of VBScript to enhance and automate your network administration duties, especially since sites like the Microsoft TechNet Scripting Center (http://www.microsoft.com/technet/scriptcenter/default.mspx) contain any number of premade scripts that you can copy and use right away. If you're someone who likes to learn by looking at code examples, go download the Scriptomatic tool from the Scripting Center. This tool automatically generates queries that detail every single element in the various WMI classes, and is a great way to learn WMI scripting by example. You can see an automatically generated Scriptomatic query in the following figure:

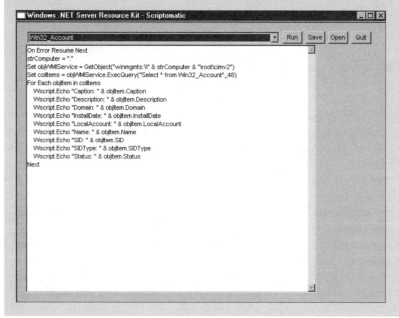

Creating Logon Scripts

Network admins have been using logon scripts to administer users and their environments since well before the advent of Windows Server 2003, and even before the release of Windows NT 4.0 over a decade ago. Though we'll discuss configuring Group Policy Objects in detail in Chapter 4, logon scripts still possess a number of advantages in automating day-to-day administrative tasks. (It's for this reason that you can assign scripts *within* a GPO—they're designed to work together.) For example, there are some tasks that Group Policy Objects are not well suited for, such as stopping and starting services or performing a hardware inventory. In addition, Group Policy isn't supported on machines running a pre-Windows 2000 operating system: if you are required to support a number of down-level clients, you'll almost certainly want to employ logon scripts as a part of your network administration process. Finally, logon scripts allow you to leverage certain Microsoft scripting technologies that are best suited for use on the local machine: the FileSystemObject, for example, is really designed to allow file and folder manipulation of the local hard drive, and is therefore well-suited to run under a logon script.

For Windows 2000, Windows XP, and Windows Server 2003 computers, you can create four types of scripts (Windows NT 4.0 and Windows 95/98/ME will only support scripts that run at user logon):

- User logon
- User logoff
- Computer startup
- Computer shutdown

You can assign a separate script to perform tasks during any one of these points. For example, you might create a script to run a hardware inventory on the computer when it starts up, or delete files from the C:\temp directory when a user logs off. When deciding how to configure your user administration scripts, you must consider a few key factors. First, user logon and logoff scripts will run in the *security context* of the logged-on user. This means that a script will only be able to perform those tasks that the users themselves would be able to do manually. If you need your logon script to stop a running service, for example, it will fail unless the logged-on user is a member of the local Administrators group or a domain group with appropriate permissions.

Computer startup and shutdown scripts, on the other hand, run in the security context of LocalSystem, which means that they have unlimited access to the system resources of the local computer. Creating a computer startup script to stop or disable a service would work just fine, even if the user of the system is only a member of the local Users group. The disadvantage to computer-centered scripts is that they run when no user is logged on to the machine, so you can't use them for conditional script actions based on a particular user's group membership, for example.

When planning and troubleshooting script behavior, it's helpful to understand in what order scripts are processed. From the time a computer is first powered on, here is the order in which scripts will run:

1. The computer is powered on.

2. Any startup script will run *before* the user logon screen appears.

3. The user presses Ctrl+Alt+Del and enters her username and password.

4. Any Group Policy login scripts will run next.

5. Any domain login scripts will run after the GPO-assigned scripts. (Domain logon scripts are those assigned manually to a user's object through Active Directory Users & Computers.)

6. Once all available login scripts have run, the user will reach her desktop and be able to work.

7. When the user logs off, any logoff scripts will run before the user is logged out of the machine.

8. After the user is logged out, computer shutdown scripts will run, and finally the machine will shut down.

While you may be tempted to cram as much as possible into your scripts, you should keep in mind that your scripts should not infringe on your users' productivity wherever possible. For example, if you create a login script that takes several minutes to complete, your users may incorrectly report that their machine is "malfunctioning," or simply complain about the wasted time. Likewise, a lengthy shutdown script may lead a user to believe that their computer has simply frozen. They may then decide to shut the machine down manually, interrupting your script.

■Caution If a user never logs off or never shuts off his computer, many of your scripts will obviously never run. If you need to perform critical administrative tasks through your scripts, you might need to consider forcibly shutting down or rebooting client worksta-tions through a scheduled task.

So what can you do within a logon script? Typically, you'll use a combina-tion of command-line tools and scripting commands, depending on what types of clients you're supporting. Windows 95, Windows 98, and Windows NT 4.0 clients, for example, don't natively support the advanced scripting capa-bilities recognized by Windows 2000 and more recent operating systems, but you can at least begin with simple batch file commands such as net use to map network drives. To take full advantage of scripting technologies, though, you'll want to make use of the following three technologies:

- Windows Scripting Host (WSH)
- Windows Management Instrumentation (WMI)
- Active Directory Service Interfaces (ADSI)

WSH, WMI, and ADSI will allow you to interact with almost every facet of the Windows operating system from the command line instead of relying on a GUI interface. These three software pieces are installed by default in Windows 2000, Windows XP, and Windows Server 2003, and can also be installed on machines running NT 4.0 and Windows 95/98/ME. In order to support scripts that can query and interact with Active Directory, your Windows 95/98/ME and NT 4.0 computers will also need the Active Directory Client Extensions installed, available from the Microsoft website at http://www.microsoft.com/windows2000/server/evaluation/news/bulletins/adextension.asp.

Note All of these products can be downloaded for free from the Microsoft website. Since URL locations tend to be moving targets, simply search the site for "ADSI," "WMI," or "Active Directory Client Extensions" to locate the current download location.

Assigning Logon Scripts

Once you've created your logon script, you should copy it to the NETLOGON share on one of your domain controllers so that it can be replicated throughout your Active Directory domain. Once this is complete, you can assign your scripts using Group Policy Objects, or use Active Directory Users & Computers to assign logon scripts for down-level computers that aren't compatible with Group Policy Objects.

To assign a script using Active Directory, follow these steps:

1. Open the Group Policy Object that you want to edit, using either ADUC or the Group Policy Management Console (discussed in Chapter 4).

2. Navigate to **Computer Configuration ➤ Windows Settings ➤ Scripts (Startup/Shutdown)** for startup and shutdown scripts, or **User Configuration ➤ Windows Settings ➤ Scripts (Logon/Logoff)** for logon and logoff scripts.

3. Double-click the script type that you want to add (startup, shutdown, logon, logoff) and click **Add**. You can either type in the file name in manually or browse to its current location in the NETLOGON share.

PROCESSING MULTIPLE LOGON SCRIPTS

So far I've only talked about having a single logon script run at any given point in the process: one startup script is followed by one logon script, and so on. But what happens if you've assigned multiple logon scripts through Active Directory Group Policy? What order will the scripts run in, and how will this affect the user? This depends on whether you've configured your login scripts to run *synchronously* or *asynchronously*. By default, Active Directory logon scripts run asynchronously: this means that the scripts are not guaranteed to run in any particular order, and can even try to run simultaneously. It also means that the user may reach the desktop before the logon scripts have completed, which may create an inconsistent interface configuration depending on which logon script ran first.

By configuring logon scripts to run synchronously, you are holding them to a specific processing order, which is from top to bottom in the Group Policy editing window. You're also ensuring that, if you have two scripts configured, the second script will not begin running until the first script has completed. This setting allows you to exert granular control over how your scripts are processed, but keep in mind that it can also create a lengthy logon time for your users if many scripts are forced to run one after the next after the next. You can configure logon scripts to run synchronously at the following location in a Group Policy Object: Computer Configuration\Administrative Templates\System\Scripts.

To configure a domain logon script for an individual user, you'll simply open the user object's **Properties** sheet in Active Directory Users & Computers, and enter the name of the script in the **Logon Script** field on the user's **Profile** tab. This assumes that the script resides in the root of the NETLOGON share; if it's in a subdirectory of NETLOGON or in an alternate location, you'll need to specify the full UNC or local directory path in addition to the file name.

■**Note** Scripts that are assigned through Group Policy Objects reside in the *%SYSTEMROOT%*\SYSVOL*domain_name*\scripts folder. The NETLOGON share is used for backwards compatibility with clients that aren't compatible with Group Policy.

Finally, you can even use scripting to assign a domain logon script to multiple users. Why would you go this route rather than using Group Policy? If you're supporting a diverse client base that includes a number of down-level clients, you may decide to use domain logon scripts across the board so that all of your users can receive the necessary script settings regardless of their client operating system. This way, if a user who typically logs on to an XP machine needs to switch to an NT 4.0 machine temporarily, she'll still receive all of her drive mappings and other necessary settings because she'll receive the domain logon script regardless of which client she logs in from. Much like the script we saw earlier in the chapter that changed the Department setting for each user in a particular OU, you can loop through each user object in an OU or an entire domain to enter its logon script information like this:

```
Set objOU = GetObject("LDAP://dc=example,dc=com")
objOU.Filter = Array("User")

For Each objUser In objOU
    objUser.Put "scriptPath", "logon.bat"
    objUser.SetInfo
Next
```

Caution Even though you can install support for WMI, WSH, and ADSI for NT 4.0 and Windows 95/98 clients, these machines will only support logon scripts with the .BAT or .CMD file extension, not .VBS or .JS like you can do in 2000/XP/2003. There is, however, a simple workaround: just call the VBScript or JScript file from within the initial .BAT file.

Managing Schema Attributes

When you are working with a multidomain environment, users have the ability to search for information across the entire Active Directory forest. The reason this is possible, even though domain controllers only hold the AD information relevant to their own domain, is because of *Global Catalogs*. The Global Catalog server, or GC server, is a special configuration of specific domain controllers across an AD forest. This feature allows users to search for information by storing a subset (referred to as a *partial replica*) of the most important AD information from every domain in the forest. So a GC server will not maintain a detailed description of every user object in the forest, for example, but it will maintain a copy of the user's last name, Universal group memberships, and other important details.

In most cases, the default GC attributes will be sufficient to allow users to search for pertinent information. But you may find, on occasion, that you need to add an additional attribute to the Global Catalog to customize your users' search abilities. This operation should not be taken lightly, since in many cases it will cause a full synchronization of all information stored in the Global Catalogs—this can create heavy network utilization, especially across slow links. However, if you need to do so, simply follow these steps:

1. Open the Active Directory Schema snap-in. This isn't one of the default Administrative Tools, so you'll need to open a blank MMC console in author mode (by entering **mmc /a** at the Run line) and add the snap-in manually.

▓**Note** If you don't see the Active Directory Schema snap-in, you need to manually register the appropriate DLL by typing **regsvr32 schmmgmt.dll** from the Windows command prompt.

---

2. Navigate to **Active Directory Schema ➤ Attributes**.

3. Choose the attribute that you want to add to the Global Catalog, like countryCode or employeeID.

4. Place a check mark next to **Replicate this attribute to the Global Catalog**.

5. Click **OK** until you're returned to the AD Schema MMC.

▓**Note** You probably also notice the **Attribute is copied when duplicating a user** option. You can use this to customize what information is copied from one user object to another, such as when you're using the user template we discussed in the previous section.

You may also find yourself in a situation where the default Active Directory attributes aren't sufficient for your purposes, and you need to add a new attribute to a user object or other object type within AD. *Extending the schema* in this manner is much like editing the Registry on a Windows machine: you should only attempt it if you know what you're doing, and if you have a tested and error-free backup of your Active Directory database before you start. Also, it's extremely advisable to test any such modifications in a test lab before applying them to your production network, since changes to the AD schema are largely permanent and cannot currently be completely undone. In Windows Server 2003, for example, you can deactivate an unneeded schema class or attribute, but you cannot delete it entirely. Even this is an improvement over Windows 2000, which doesn't even allow for deactivation of classes or attributes. For more information on creating new schema classes or attributes, consult the Active Directory Programmer's Guide on the Microsoft website at http://msdn.microsoft.com/library/default.asp?url=/library/en-us/ad/ad/using_active_directory.asp.

Delegating Administrative Authority

Perhaps you're working with a large corporation that wants to keep its IT management processes decentralized: the Chicago office has its own IT group, which handles support requests from Chicago users, the Seattle office has its IT group for Seattle users, and so on. Or maybe you're a one-person IT shop and you're being overwhelmed with too many simple yet time-consuming requests: resetting a forgotten password, creating user accounts for temporary employees, etc. In early versions of Windows such as NT 4.0, you didn't have many options for delegating authority in your domain. To give someone the authority to change passwords or unlock accounts, for example, you needed to make him an Account Operator for your entire domain, when you probably wanted to allow an administrative assistant the ability to reset passwords for the users in his department only.

In Active Directory, you now have much more granular control over how ordinary users can administer portions of the Active Directory tree. Using the Delegation of Control Wizard, you can grant a user or group of users the authority to perform only those tasks that you want them to perform. And you can grant this authority on only a portion of your Active Directory network, rather than giving someone *carte blanche* over your entire domain. In the example I gave you where each physical location has its own IT group, you can create a separate Organizational Unit for each office and move all users, groups, and printers into their respective containers. From there, you can create a ChicagoAdmins security group and delegate control of the OU to that group.

To configure delegated permissions for a portion of your Active Directory tree, follow these steps:

1. Open Active Directory Users & Computers. Right-click the domain or OU that you want, and then select **Delegate Control**. Click **Next** to bypass the initial **Welcome** screen.

2. The first step is to select the users and groups in question: *who* are you granting control to? Click **Add** to select the necessary users and groups. You can add multiple entries at once by separating them with a semicolon. Click **Next** when you've finished.

3. The Delegation of Control Wizard includes several preconfigured tasks which you can grant permissions to perform on an Organizational Unit or domain, or you can create a custom set of permissions to meet your needs. In Windows Server 2003, these preconfigured tasks consist of the following (Windows 2000 only includes a subset of these tasks):

- Create, delete, and manage user accounts.
- Reset user passwords and force password change at next logon.
- Read all user information.
- Create, delete, and manage groups.
- Modify the membership of a group.
- Manage Group Policy links.
- Generate Resultant Set of Policy (Planning) (Windows Server 2003 only).
- Generate Resultant Set of Policy (Logging) (Windows Server 2003 only).
- Create, delete, and manage **inetOrgPerson** accounts (Windows Server 2003 only).
- Reset **inetOrgPerson** passwords and force password change at next logon (Windows Server 2003 only).
- Read all **inetOrgPerson** information (Windows Server 2003 only).

4. Select the task or tasks that you want to delegate, and then click **Next** and **Finish** to effect the changes.

■**Note** The **inetOrgPerson** class is a new feature of Windows Server 2003 that allows for interoperability with non-Microsoft directory services.

If none of these preconfigured tasks is appropriate, you can instead choose **Create a custom task to delegate** in step 3 of the previous example. In this case, you can grant a specific set of permissions to the container, all objects currently in the container, and any new objects created in the container. Alternatively, you can restrict these permissions to specific objects within the container. This would allow you to delegate control over user objects within a given OU, for example, but no other resources. Once you've selected the object types, you'll finish by selecting the specific ACL permissions that should be delegated, ranging from full control down to permissions over specific attributes of different objects, as you can see in Figure 3-1.

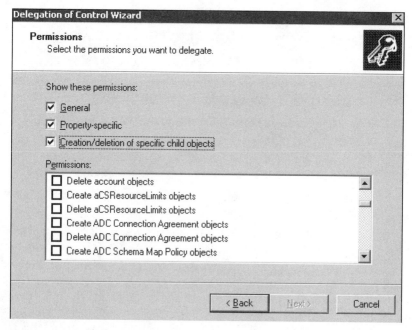

Figure 3-1. *Assigning NTFS permissions to Active Directory objects*

Managing Groups

The notion of organizing user accounts into groups has been around almost as long as computer networks themselves. The benefits of using groups to manage your users is obvious: rather than assigning a set of permissions to dozens or hundreds of individual users one at a time, you can assign those permissions one time to a group object and be done with it. This simplifies the administration process, and also improves the security of your network since there is less of a chance that you'll make configuration errors if you're only assigning a permission or right *once*. Windows 2000 and Windows Server 2003 have numerous options for group management within Active Directory that we'll be discussing in this section.

Configuring Groups

Within Active Directory you'll define groups based on two criteria: their *type*, and their *scope*. Group *type* in Active Directory refers to whether a group is a security group or a distribution group. Security groups are the group type that most of us are familiar with: you'll use them to group users together with similar security requirements. Security groups are what you'll use to assign permissions to a file or folder, or to grant or deny user rights such as "Log on locally" or "Access this computer from the network." Distribution groups, on the other hand, are new to Active Directory and are available in Windows 2000 and Windows Server 2003. You'll use them solely to create a mailing list for users' e-mail addresses, particularly if your network uses Microsoft Exchange 2000 or 2003. Since Exchange stores its user information right in Active Directory, you can create distribution lists in the same location as you would a security group.

Note Security groups can also be assigned an e-mail address, and so perform double-duty as a way of distributing e-mail like a distribution group. The difference is that security groups can be used for assigning permissions *and* receiving e-mail, while distribution groups cannot be assigned any rights or permissions and are *only* used for e-mail. You can convert a security group to a distribution group and vice versa, though converting a security group means that the group will lose any permissions that were assigned to it.

Group scope is not new to Active Directory, but AD networks introduce a new way of configuring groups to streamline administration, especially in a large network. In a Windows 2000 or Windows Server 2003 network, a group can have one of the following scopes:

- Domain Local
- Global
- Universal

A *Domain Local* group can contain users from any domain within the Active Directory forest, as well as Global groups and Universal groups from any domain. So why is it called a local group? Because you can only use Domain Local groups to grant permissions to objects that are in the same domain as the group. A *Global group* is effectively the opposite of a Domain Local group. It can only contain user objects from within the same domain, but you can use it to assign permissions anywhere in the Active Directory forest.

So far this is familiar territory to anyone coming from earlier Windows server operating systems: Windows NT 4.0 also had global and local groups. But Active Directory creates a third group type that, when used properly, can allow for extremely flexible user account administration. This is the *Universal group*. Universal groups can contain other Universal groups from anywhere in the forest and domain tree, Global groups from anywhere in the forest or domain tree, and user accounts from anywhere in the forest or domain tree. Furthermore, the Universal group itself can be used to assign permissions to any resource in the forest or domain tree.

So what's the downside here? In other words, why not use Universal groups all the time? The reason is that this level of flexibility comes at a price. Because Universal groups can be used to grant or deny permissions anywhere in the forest, each domain controller in the forest needs to be aware of a user's Universal group memberships before they can be allowed to log on to the domain. Active Directory accomplishes this by replicating Universal group memberships to every Global Catalog server in the forest. In the case of Domain Local and Global groups, only the group names are replicated to the Global Catalog. Universal groups have their entire membership roster replicated. This means that every time a Universal group has a user added or removed, that change needs to be replicated throughout the entire AD infrastructure. If you're using slow or overburdened WAN links, this can create an unacceptable level of traffic on your network, especially if your company experiences a high level of turnover that requires user accounts to be added, deleted, or moved on a regular basis. Table 3-1 illustrates the major functions and differences between the three available group scopes.

Table 3-1. *Active Directory Group Scopes*

Group Type	Can Contain	Can Be Used to Assign Permissions To
Domain Local	User accounts, Global groups, and user accounts from any domain, or Domain Local groups in the same domain	Resources in the same domain
Global	Groups and accounts from the same domain	Resources in any domain tree in the forest
Universal	Groups and accounts from any domain tree in the forest	Resources in any domain tree in the forest

---

■**Note** Windows Server 2003 improves on this somewhat by allowing for caching of Universal group membership information. You can configure this in the Active Directory Sites & Services MMC snap-in, by right-clicking the NTDS Site Settings of the site in question and placing a check mark next to **Enable Universal Group Membership Caching**. You can specify a particular site that the cached information should be retrieved from, or you can accept the default of the nearest site that contains a Global Catalog. Universal group caching allows you to deploy Active Directory sites that don't contain a GC, which wasn't recommended under Windows 2000.

Leveraging Group Nesting

Before your head starts to spin with all of these different group types, I'll give you a concrete example that should help to sort things out. Say you have a domain called example.com, and a child domain called sales.example.com. There is a file share in the sales.example.com domain called SalesFigures. Each domain contains a number of supervisors who require access to the documents in this folder. If you create a Supervisors Domain Local group in the sales.example.com domain, it can contain the supervisors' user accounts from both domains. However, you will only be able to assign permissions to the SalesFigures folder in the sales.example.com domain, since that's where the Domain Local group is located. Think of it this way: as far as the example.com domain is concerned, the Domain Local group in sales.example.com doesn't even exist.

If we decided to use Global groups instead, our previous example would be reversed: a Supervisors Global group created in the sales.example.com domain would be able to receive permissions to folders in both domains; however, the group could only contain the user objects from the sales.example.com domain.

In this case, the best solution is to use a combination of these two group scopes. Create a Global group in each domain that contains the user accounts from the respective domains. Then create a Domain Local group in sales.example.com, where the folder is located. Add the two Global groups to the Domain Local group in sales.example.com, and then grant permissions on the SalesFigures folder to the Domain Local group in sales.example.com.

So how do Universal groups fit into this plan? If you're going to use Universal groups, you should configure them so that they only contain other group objects, particularly Global groups. This way, the Universal group membership "roster" will remain almost entirely static. This is because you won't be adding or removing the Global group from the Universal group when you need to add or remove a user. Rather, you'll be changing the member listing of the Global group, which doesn't affect Global Catalog replication. In this way, using group nesting can help to reduce network traffic within your AD infrastructure, by reducing replication traffic because of unnecessary changes to Universal group memberships.

Note   Microsoft refers to this scheme as *AGUDLP*. You'll place A̲ccounts into G̲lobal groups. Then you'll place those Global groups into U̲niversal groups. The Universal groups will then go into a D̲omain L̲ocal group. Finally, the Domain Local group will receive the necessary P̲ermissions that will filter down the chain of group memberships, all the way back to the user accounts.

FUNCTIONAL LEVELS—
GETTING THE MOST OUT OF YOUR WINDOWS INSTALLATION

Depending on the types of domain controllers that are present in your network, you may find that you have different options available to you when you are creating new group objects. In Windows 2000, you could operate in either *mixed* or *native* mode: mixed mode if you were still supporting NT 4.0 domain controllers, native mode if you had transitioned all of your DCs to Windows 2000. The most visible limitation to mixed mode is that Universal groups aren't available to you, since an NT 4.0 domain controller wouldn't know how to handle them.

Windows Server 2003 provides two additional functional levels, in addition to the two offered by Windows 2000:

- Windows Server 2003 interim, for networks that are transitioning directly from NT 4.0 to 2003. This mode only supports NT 4.0 and 2003 domain controllers; Windows 2000 DCs aren't supported.

- Windows Server 2003 is the functionality level to choose if all of your DCs are running Windows Server 2003. Because the DCs no longer need to worry about backwards compatibility to Windows 2000 or NT 4.0 domain controllers, this mode provides the greatest level of functionality for your Active Directory domain.

Transitioning to at least the Windows 2000 native mode domain functionality level allows for several new features including full group nesting and converting groups between security and distribution types. Moving to the Windows Server 2003 mode also enables the use of the built-in Domain Rename feature.

Creating Groups

Just as we can use **dsadd** to create new user accounts within Active Directory, we can use the same utility to create groups. When used to create group objects, **dsadd** takes a slightly different syntax, as you can see here:

```
dsadd group GroupDN [-secgrp {yes | no}] [-scope {l | g | u}]
     [-samid SAMName] [-desc Description] [-memberof Group ...]
     [-members Member ...] [{-s Server | -d Domain}] [-u UserName]
     [-p {Password | *}] [-q]
```

- *GroupDN*: Specifies the distinguished name of the group you're creating.

- -secgrp {yes | no}: Specifies whether the group should be a security group (if set to yes) or a distribution group (set to no). By default, the group will be a security group (yes).

- -scope {l | g | u}: Specifies whether the scope of the group should be a domain local (l), global (g), or universal (u) group. If you don't specify this parameter, it defaults to creating a Global group.

- -desc *Description*: Specifies a description for the group.

- -memberof *Group* ...: Specifies any groups that this group should be a member of, allowing you to automate group nesting.

- -members *Member* ...: Specifies the distinguished name of any users and/or groups that should be a member of this group. This is possibly the most useful feature, since it allows you to add users to the group at the same time that you create it.

- -u *UserName*: Specifies the user name with which the user will log on to a remote server, if you need to connect using alternate credentials.

- -p {*Password* | *}: Specifies the password to use when connecting. If you enter a *, you'll be prompted to enter a password manually.

So to create a new global security group called TemporaryEmployees in the Seattle OU of your network, you can use the following syntax:

```
dsadd group "cn=Temporary Employees, ou=Seattle, dc=example, dc=com"
     -secgrp yes -scope g
```

■**Note** If you need to modify a group once it's already been created, you can use the dsmod group command. dsmod group takes the same parameters as dsadd group, allowing you to change any aspect of the group's behavior or properties.

Managing User Files

In the final section of this chapter, we'll talk about some ways to manage your users' day-to-day interactions with the network, especially the appearance of their desktops and files. By configuring roaming user profiles, you can ensure that your users will have the same files, shortcuts, and drive mappings available to them from anywhere on the network, regardless of which workstation they log in from. Offline files will help you to balance your users' need for remote access to files with the equally important need to keep critical documents centrally located for backup and maintenance purposes. Finally, we'll look at ways for your users to encrypt their confidential files, and how you can manage that process as an Active Directory administrator.

Configuring User Profiles

One of the major challenges for an administrator is trying to deal with files stored on users' local hard drives, especially when those files are lost due to a hardware failure on a local workstation. You can map all of the network drives that you want, and you can send out all of the "Please save your files to the network" e-mails you want, but someone somewhere on your network is still going to save his files to his local hard drive and complain when those files are lost. Active Directory allows you to centralize your user profiles onto a network server so that any information can be retrieved instantly if someone receives a new workstation, needs a hard drive replacement, or simply needs to log on to the network from a different workstation for any reason.

Before we look at configuring roaming profiles, we need to take a look at what a user's profile actually consists of. On a Windows 2000 or a Windows XP machine, you'll find a Documents and Settings folder in the root of the system drive (usually C:\). On a fresh installation, this folder contains a Default User profile, as well as an All Users profile. When a new user logs on to a machine for the first time, Windows will create a new folder with the same name as the user's logon ID, and will copy into that folder the contents of the Default User profile and the All Users profile. The Default User profile will include some or all of the following folders:

- *Application Data*: Application-specific data for user configuration of applications like Word, Outlook, etc.

- *Cookies*: Internet cookies accumulated during web browsing

- *Desktop*: Any shortcuts and files stored on the user's desktop

- *Favorites*: Contents of the Internet Explorer Favorites menu

- *Local Settings*: Other local application settings

- *My Documents*: Contents of the default Save location for word processing applications, spreadsheets, etc.

- *NetHood*: Contents of the Network Neighborhood or My Network Places

- *PrintHood*: Contents of the Printers folder
- *Start Menu*: Contents of the user's Start menu
- *SendTo*: Available options in the Send To context menu: floppy drive, CD drive, Notepad, etc.
- *Templates*: Default document templates for Microsoft Office documents

Using Roaming Profiles

By configuring roaming profiles, you can ensure that some or all of your users' profile information gets stored to a centralized location instead of on each individual workstation. If you're only working with one or two users, you can specify a profile location in the Active Directory Users & Computers GUI. Simply right-click the user object, and select the **Profile** tab from the account **Properties** sheet. Specify the UNC path to the user's profile, using the %USERNAME% placeholder if necessary. In this way, \\server\share\ hunter could be specified as \\server\share\%username% if you're modifying multiple accounts. If you need to modify many accounts, you can use the dsmod user command that we discussed earlier in the chapter; you'll remember that one user attribute you can modify is the location of the user's profile. And just like with anything else, you can use VBScript to programmatically change the profile path for an entire OU or even a whole domain.

When a user with a roaming profile logs on for the first time, Active Directory will check to see if she already has a profile stored on the file server. If she doesn't, the contents of her local profile will be copied up to the appropriate location on the file server. Since you're going to be storing these profiles on a network file share, you're obviously going to want to make sure that each user's profile information is as secure as possible. To prevent users from poking around in the Profiles share, consider sharing the parent folder with a dollar sign ($) at the end of the share name, which will prevent it from being displayed in Network Neighborhood or My Network Places. Also, if you're storing profiles in multiple locations, you should use security groups to further restrict access to the Profiles folders. Let's say that you've decided to create roaming profiles for the members of your Accounting Department, all of whom are members of the Accounting security group. You should assign the minimum necessary permissions to the parent folder, as follows:

- CreatorOwner should be assigned the **Full Control** permission to subfolders and files only.
- Accounting security group should be assigned **List Folder/Create Data, Create Subfolders/Append Data** for the parent folder only.
- LocalSystem should have **Full Control** for this folder, all subfolders, and files.

You should then remove either **Everyone** or **Authenticated Users** from the ACL of the parent folder so that only members of the Accounting security group will have access to the Profiles share. By configuring permissions in this way, you're allowing each user to be able to create their own profile when they log on to the network without giving them access to the parent folder or to other users' profile directories. Finally, you should assign the **Full Control** permission to the file share itself.

The previous paragraph assumes that you're going to allow users to create their own profiles as they log on to the network. But what if you want to create user profiles ahead of time in order to configure a consistent look-and-feel for new users coming into a department? In this case, you can make use of the account templates that I described in the "Creating Users" section earlier in the chapter. Configure the account template to use a roaming profile, then log on to a sample workstation using the template account, preferably from a workstation with similar hardware as the workstation the user will be using. Configure the desktop, printers, and drive mappings as you want them to appear for the new user, then log off of the workstation. (This is necessary so that your changes can be copied up to the file server.) At this point you'll log back on to the workstation with an administrative account. Open the System utility in Control Panel, then navigate to **User Profiles ➤ Settings**. (You can also simply right-click My Computer and select **Properties**.) Select the profile for the template account you just configured, and then click **Copy To**. You'll see the dialog box shown in Figure 3-2.

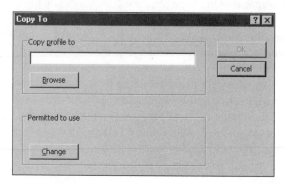

Figure 3-2. *Copying an existing user profile*

Under **Copy To**, enter the UNC path to the new user's profile directory. Under **Permitted to Use**, click **Change** and specify the new user account. This way, when the user logs on to the network for the first time, they will have a preexisting profile that will be pulled down to their local workstation. If you manually create the profile folder for a specific user, you should specify the following permissions on the folder:

- %USERNAME% should receive **Full Control**, and should be specified as the owner of the folder.

- LocalSystem should have **Full Control**.

- Finally, remove any entries for **Everyone** or any other security group so that only the individual user will have access to his profile.

■**Note** If you want all of your users to have the same default profile, copy the template account profile to the ~\NETLOGON\Default User profile of any domain controller in your network. (It will be automatically replicated to other DCs.) Select the **Everyone** group under **Permitted to Use**, and every user on your network will receive this profile as the basis for their roaming profile.

You can take this even further by configuring a mandatory profile for some or all of your users. In the profiles we've talked about so far, users have been able to make whatever changes they wanted in order to customize their environment, and those changes get copied up to the file server when the user logs off. In the case of a mandatory profile, users can still make changes to their environment while they're logged in, but those changes won't be saved to the roaming profile when they log off. So the next time they log in, they will see the same environment as before any changes were made. This is mostly useful for specific machines that are configured for shared use, like in a call center or on a manufacturing floor. You should use mandatory profiles with caution, though, because users may save files to their Desktop or My Documents folder, only to have those documents "disappear" when they log off. This can make for some unpleasant support calls, so be sure to use mandatory profiles only when it's appropriate.

Configuring a mandatory profile is very simple: just browse to the profile that you want to make mandatory, and rename the NTUSER.DAT file to NTUSER.MAN. The advantage to mandatory profiles is that you can configure a single profile folder for multiple user accounts, rather than relying on the %USERNAME% nomenclature to store multiple copies of identical profiles.

■**Note** If you have certain machines on your network for which you want to disable roaming profiles, configure the **Prevent Roaming Profile changes from propagating to the server** and **Only Allow Local User Profiles** settings in the Computer Configuration\Administrative Templates\System\User Profiles section of a Group Policy Object. You'll learn more about Group Policy in Chapter 4.

Setting Up Offline Files

Another challenge when maintaining user files is the need for remote users to be able to access network files when they might not be connected to the network with a decent connection, or even at all. To combat this, Windows 2000 and Windows Server 2003 offer an Offline Files feature, which allows a user to copy network files to her local hard drives for editing, and then upload them back to the network when she has reconnected. Any offline files are stored on the user's hard drive in a folder named (conveniently enough) Offline Files. Configuring Offline Files is a two-part process: you need to take steps to configure both the server and the client in order for the service to function.

■**Note** If you remember the Briefcase feature in Windows 95, this is pretty similar in concept . . . except that it actually works.

Configuring the Server

You'll configure Offline Files for your servers once for the entire server, and then on a folder-by-folder basis. To enable Offline Files for the entire server, follow these steps:

1. Open My Computer or Windows Explorer.

2. Select **Tools ➤ Folder Options**.

3. Place a check mark next to **Enable Offline Files** on the **Offline Files** tab.

Now you're ready to enable Offline Files for specific folders. Once you've shared a folder in Windows 2000, click **Caching** from the **Sharing** tab of the folder's **Properties** sheet. In Windows Server 2003, click **Offline Settings** from the **Sharing** tab. In Windows Server 2003, you can configure the availability of Offline Files in one of three ways:

- **Only the files and programs that users specify will be available offline**: This is the default, and it requires users to specify which files they need.

- **All files and programs that users open from the share will be automatically available offline**: All files that a user opens from this share will be automatically cached for offline use. If your users have sufficient hard drive space on their workstations or laptops, this might be an appealing option since it requires the least user intervention.

- **Files or programs from the share will not be available offline**: This will disable Offline Files for this particular share.

Windows 2000 offers three different options when configuring Offline Files:

- **Automatic caching for documents**
- **Automatic caching for programs**
- **Manual caching for programs**

■Note Both Windows 2000 and Windows Server 2003 also have an option available to cache remote .EXE files so that they run locally. This can be a great performance boost since it decreases network traffic, but requires testing to be sure that the application in question can run locally on the client workstation.

Configuring the XP/2000 Client

Once you've configured your server shares for offline availability, you need to configure your client workstations to manage Offline Files. On the client workstation, go to My Computer, and then select **Tools ➤ Folder Options ➤ Offline Files**. Offline File support is not enabled for Windows 2000, but is turned on in Windows XP. Once you've enabled it, you'll have a wide array of options, as shown in Figure 3-3.

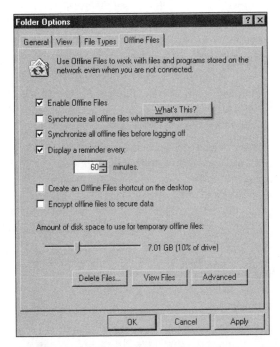

Figure 3-3. *Configuring Offline Files in Windows XP*

By default, you'll have the following options enabled on the client:

- **Synchronize all offline files before logging off**: Uploads any changes to the Offline Files before the workstation logs off, so that other users can have the most up-to-date version of a file on the network share

- **Display a reminder every [X] minutes**: (60 by default) Displays a pop-up window in the System Notification Area to remind users that they're working offline, and they should synchronize their files when they're done working.

■Caution Offline Files support is not available for Windows 95/98/ME client operating systems.

In addition, other configurable options are available that allow you to do the following:

- Configure the workstation to synchronize offline files when users log on to the network.

- Create a shortcut to the Offline Files folder on the user's desktop. (I highly recommend enabling this option.)

- Use EFS to encrypt offline files to secure data. (More on EFS in a minute.)

- Control how much drive space on the user's workstation or laptop should be dedicated to storing offline files, with 10% being the default. Offline Files storage operates on first-in-first-out basis: if a new offline file is copied down to the workstation and there isn't enough space allocated, the oldest unmodified offline file will be deleted to make room.

- Control how a workstation will behave if it suddenly loses its network connection. You can specify that the workstation should immediately go into Offline Mode and begin working on any cached copies of documents it already has. Alternatively, you can configure the workstation to never go into Offline Mode, so that any network files will be unavailable until the network connection is restored. You can even specify this behavior on a per-server basis: by clicking **Exceptions List** or **Advanced** (in Windows 2000 and Windows XP, respectively), you can specify different behavior depending on which server the client loses its connection to.

Using Group Policy

Like many client-side settings, you can configure how your workstations and laptops deal with Offline Files through a Group Policy Object, rather than configuring each workstation individually. (We'll talk more about Group Policy in Chapter 4.) Using a GPO, you can specify all of the options that you can configure manually, as well as some additional options:

- **Disable user configuration of Offline Files**: This prevents users from changing any settings that you've specified in Group Policy.

- **Synchronize all Offline Files when logging on**: This option is only available in Windows Server 2003.

- **Synchronize all Offline Files before logging off**

- **Synchronize Offline Files before suspend**: This is particularly useful for laptops, as you can imagine.

- **Action on server disconnect:** Specifies how offline files will behave if they lose their connection to a server.

- **Non-default server disconnect actions**: This specifies actions in the Exception List discussed previously.

- **Remove "Make Available Offline"**: Prevents users from specifying that new folders should be made available offline.

- **Prevent use of Offline Files folder**

- **Administratively assigned offline files**: Allows you to specify folders that will always be available offline.

- **Turn off reminder balloons**

- **Reminder balloon frequency**

- **Initial reminder balloon lifetime**

- **Reminder balloon lifetime**

- **Event logging level**: The Offline Files feature will record an event in the workstation Application log if the contents of the Offline Files folder have become corrupted. However, you can use this option to specify additional events that should be recorded to the Application log.

- **Prohibit "Make Available Offline" for these files and folders**: Prevents specific files from being made available offline. This doesn't affect any folders that are configured for automatic caching, only the user's ability to manually cache documents.

- **Do not automatically make redirected folders available offline**: By default, a user's roaming profile folders (My Documents, Start Menu, Desktop, Application Data, etc.) will be cached locally for improved performance. This setting allows you to turn this feature off. Bear in mind, however, that turning this setting off will prevent users from reaching their Start menu and Desktop shortcuts in the event of a network outage; I'd recommend leaving this at the default setting unless you have a really pressing need to do otherwise.

- **Default cache size**: This is set as a percentage of the user's hard drive.

- **Files not cached**: Certain file types, such as Access .MDB files, will never be cached by the Offline Files feature. This setting allows you to specify additional file types in addition to the defaults. This is useful if you have an in-house application that uses its own file types, and you don't want those files to be cached locally.

- **At logoff, delete local copy of users offline files**: Use this to save drive space on the user's local drive. Be aware, though, that files won't be synchronized before they're deleted. So if a user is offline when he logs off from his workstation, any changes he's made will be lost. I generally try to steer clear of this one unless it's absolutely necessary.

- **Subfolders always available offline**

- **Encrypt the Offline Files cache**

Configuring EFS

Beginning with Windows 2000, users have had the ability to apply encryption to any file or folder stored on an NTFS volume, providing an added layer of security for confidential information. You can either encrypt single files one at a time, or you can encrypt an entire file folder—encrypting a folder will ensure that any new files created in the folder will also be encrypted. (Because of this, it's usually a best practice to deploy encryption at the folder level. That way you don't have to remember to encrypt new files as you create them: if a file is in an encrypted folder, the file will be encrypted as well.) Once a file has been encrypted, only the user who encrypted the file will be able to open it; anyone else attempting to do so will either receive an error message or else only see a bunch of gobbledygook on her screen. The encryption isn't even application-specific, so you can encrypt a Word document and feel secure that no one else will be able to read the file, regardless of whether they try to open it using Word, Wordpad, Notepad, or any other program. File encryption is an NTFS attribute that is retained even when the file is backed up and restored. When moving or copying an encrypted folder, EFS encryption will adhere to the following rules:

- If you copy or move a file that's unencrypted into a folder that has encryption enabled, the file will become encrypted.

- If you copy or move an encrypted file into a folder that doesn't have encryption enabled, the file will remain encrypted.

- Copying or moving an encrypted file to a FAT or FAT32 partition will cause it to become unencrypted, since encryption is dependent on NTFS to function.

Configuring encryption is child's play from the user's perspective: simply go to the file or folder's **Properties** sheet, click **Advanced**, and place a check mark next to **Encrypt contents to secure data**. Hit **OK** a few times and poof! Your file is now encrypted, and only you will be able to access it. Sounds great, right? Not necessarily. From an administrator's standpoint, I'm not willing to admit that the ease of the encryption process is necessarily the greatest thing since sliced bread. Yes, the user's files are now secure and encrypted. But I think that Windows allows users to encrypt their files *too* easily, without really explaining to them the full ramifications of file encryption.

When you encrypt a file for the first time, Windows creates a private *certificate* for you, which allows you to encrypt and decrypt this and any subsequent files. This certificate is stored on your local hard drive, and you can view it using the Certificates MMC snap-in under **Certificates ➤ Personal**. This certificate is what makes the encryption process so transparent: anytime a user tries to open an encrypted file, Windows automatically checks the certificates in his personal certificate store. If the certificate is a match, the file opens as though nothing were any different. But what happens if a user's hard drive crashes and you, the administrator, restore his files from a backup without knowing that the user had encryption configured? If you don't (or as is more likely in this scenario, *can't*) restore the user's encryption certificate, he will lose access to his own files. And unless you've configured a Recovery Agent (more on this in a minute), those files are pretty much gone for good, which won't make for a happy user as I'm sure you can imagine. What's worse, if a Windows XP user forgets his logon password and needs to have it reset, this will also remove his access to any encrypted files.

Recovering Encrypted Files

So how do you configure the EFS process so that your users don't end up shooting themselves in the foot? One way is to instruct your users to export a copy of their private key to a floppy disk. That way if their hard drive is ever lost, they can use the exported private key to retain access to their encrypted files. This is a wizard-driven task that the user can launch from the Certificates MMC snap-in, just by right-clicking the certificate and selecting **Export**.

■**Caution** For increased security, you can delete the certificate from the hard drive once you've exported it. Otherwise, anyone who can gain administrative access to the workstation can circumvent the encryption process.

So that's one way to go about it, but it's really not my favorite. Call me paranoid, but I prefer to look after the security of my network for myself, rather than sending out instructions that someone else may or may not follow. In an Active Directory environment, it becomes fairly simple to manage the EFS. By configuring a Certificate Authority in your domain, users will receive their private certificates from Active Directory rather than from their local workstations. This allows you to configure Domain Admins or other users to serve as Data Recovery Agents, meaning that Domain Admins can open an encrypted file as if they had been the ones who encrypted it. Or, if the owner of a file has left the organization or her private keys have become corrupted, the Data Recovery Agent can *remove* encryption on the file so that the owner of the file can access them normally.

Note   If this seems like more trouble than it's worth, you can disable EFS entirely using a Group Policy Object. In Windows Server 2003, just navigate to Computer Configuration\Windows Settings\Security Settings\Public Key Policies\Encrypting File Systems, and remove the check mark next to **Allow Users to Encrypt Files Using Encrypting File System (EFS)**. In Windows 2000, go to the Computer Configuration\Windows Settings\Security Settings\Public Key Policies\Encrypted Data Recovery Agents node of the Default Domain Policy, right-click **Encrypted Data Recovery Agents**, and select **Delete Policy** followed by **Initialize Empty Policy**.

But if you decide to deploy EFS to your organization, your first step should be to create a Recovery Policy in order to avoid situations like the ones described previously. The simplest way to do this is to edit a GPO that's linked to your domain, and navigate to the following setting: Computer Configuration\Windows Settings\Security Settings\Public Key Policies. Then right-click the Encrypted File System folder and select **Add Data Recovery Agent**. A wizard will launch that will take you step-by-step through the process of configuring one or more users as Data Recovery Agents for your network.

Summary

In this chapter, we looked at the process of creating user and group accounts within an Active Directory network. AD includes the Active Directory Users & Computers graphical utility to step you through creating one object at a time, or you can use command-line utilities and scripts to automate the process of creating multiple objects. We also talked about modifying the properties of user and group objects, including configuring logon scripts and other account attributes, as well as managing user profiles on an Active Directory network. In the next chapter, we'll delve more deeply into the use of Group Policy Objects (GPOs) to centrally manage users and computers in Active Directory.

Additional Resources

Microsoft Script Center: http://www.microsoft.com/technet/scriptcenter/default.mspx—Online tutorials, on-demand webcasts, and a repository of sample scripts to get you started with VBScript and WMI.

Active Directory Cookbook for Windows Server 2003 and Windows 2000, by Robbie Allen. O'Reilly Publishing. ISBN 0-596-00464-8—This is one of those books that needs to go into the Geek Time Capsule—I've bought something like four or five copies because I keep loaning it out and not getting it back. The author's made the code samples used in the book available from his homepage, at http://www.rallenhome.com.

joeware.net: http://www.joeware.net—Maintained by Joe Richards, a Microsoft MVP for Active Directory Services, this is a treasure-trove of handy command-line utilities to help with daily administration of an AD network.

■ ■ ■

CHAPTER 4

Deploying Group Policy
Or How to Run the Whole Thing from Your Desk and Still Leave for Home by 5

I sometimes feel like a used car salesman when I start espousing the virtues of Group Policy, but I really can't help it; it's such a useful and complex tool that there seems to be very little that you can't do with it. (Okay, making au gratin potatoes might be a bit beyond its reach, but give the Redmond developers some time and I'm sure they'll figure it out.) Although it may sound overzealous of me to say, Group Policy might be one of the most useful tools that you can use as an Active Directory administrator. Group Policy integrates directly into Active Directory and allows you to manage and configure your servers and workstations from one single point. You can use Group Policy Objects (GPOs) to control almost every aspect of your computing environment, from creating a consistent desktop configuration, to securing your systems, to deploying and managing software across anything from a home office to a large enterprise. In this chapter I'll show you some of the more useful features of this technology, starting with a new tool that makes enterprise Group Policy management a snap. I'll then present some common scenarios that you might encounter as a consultant: using GPOs to create a consistent configuration for your desktop computers, and deploying software to the client desktop. I'll finish up with some advanced tips and techniques to use with Group Policy, including creating customized administrative templates and ways to exert granular control over how Group Policy Objects are deployed across your network.

In this chapter, we'll cover the following topics and tasks:

- Using the Group Policy Management Console
- Backing up, restoring, and migrating Group Policy Objects
- Creating Group Policy Modeling and Planning reports
- Using Group Policy to control client desktop configurations

- Implementing Software Restriction Policies
- Customizing security settings for your clients and workstations
- Using Group Policy to deploy software
- Controlling Group Policy deployment
- Advanced Group Policy tips and tricks

Group Policy Management Console

One of the reasons Group Policy doesn't get leveraged as much as it should is, I think, that the tools for managing it were a bit kludgy under Windows 2000, and even in the initial release of Windows Server 2003. Not anymore, though, since the Group Policy Management Console (GPMC) is *not* the same old clunky thing that you've been living with. But this tool has managed to fly under some people's radar because it wasn't released as part of the 2003 operating system. GPMC is an out-of-band product that you can download from the Microsoft website to manage Group Policies on 2003 networks. (You can even use GPMC on a 2000 AD domain, but some of the more advanced features won't be available to you.) GPMC can be installed on any Windows Server 2003 machine or XP workstation with Service Pack 1 or higher. Windows XP computers will also need the .NET Framework installed. (The GPMC will not run on 64-bit versions of Windows.) GPMC offers you the following key features to simplify Group Policy management:

- A simplified user interface that makes Group Policy much easier to use, manage, configure, and secure
- The ability to back up and restore individual Group Policy Objects, as well as all GPOs in a domain
- HTML reporting of the settings in an individual GPO
- Import/export and copy/paste functions for GPOs and Windows Management Instrumentation (WMI) filters

---

■**Note** If you're on XP Service Pack 1, you'll need to have the Q326469 hotfix installed. But don't worry; the installer will let you know if it's not, and even install it for you automatically.

The installer itself is pretty straightforward: as long as you're on an XP or 2003 machine, you just double-click the .MSI file and click **Next** until you're done. The console will launch, attach to the domain that your computer is a member of, and provide a graphical view of your forest as you can see in Figure 4-1.

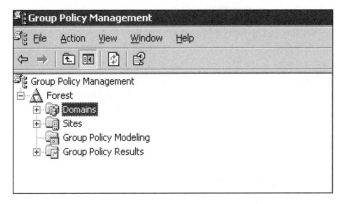

Figure 4-1. *The Group Policy Management Console*

Once you expand the Domains node, you'll see an entry for each Organizational Unit (OU) in your domain, and each GPO that's linked to a particular OU. Additionally, you'll see a list of every GPO that you've created, whether it's currently linked to a container or not. When you click an individual GPO, you can see a graphical summary of the settings it includes, like the one shown in Figure 4-2. You can view individual GPOs by drilling down in the following order:

1. Domains

2. *Your Domain Name*

3. Group Policy Objects

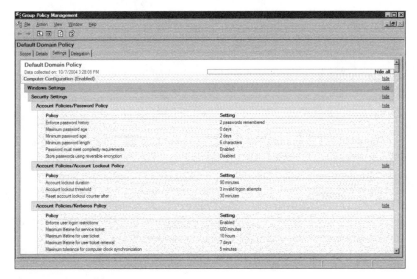

Figure 4-2. *GPMC settings report*

As you can see, this gives you an easy-to-read overview of your Group Policy settings. In addition, the **Scope** tab spells out precisely which domains, sites, and OUs are affected by this GPO and what Access Control Lists (ACLs) have been applied on it. Having this information right at your fingertips can save you a lot of time in troubleshooting, especially if you're taking over a network from someone else who may not have documented his GPO configurations very well.

■**Note** While you're looking at the pretty reports that GPMC generates for you, why don't you take a second to right-click the GPO and click **Save Report**. This will save the information to an HTML file that you can use as a part of your network documentation, so that the person who takes over from *you* doesn't have the same complaint.

Another great feature of GPMC, and one that's firmly embedded in the "Why didn't they let us do this before?" column, is the ability to back up and restore your Group Policy Objects, and even copy GPOs between different domains and forests. Prior to the release of the GPMC, your only option for backing up a GPO before making a change was to manually create a copy of the object, which quickly became time-consuming and a waste of resources if you wanted to maintain multiple copies that you could roll back to. Now it's easy: just right-click the GPO that you want to back up and click **Back Up**. (Or click the top-level Group Policy node and click **Back Up All** to take care of all of them at once.) This will create a series of file folders in the location you specify, all with rather ugly-looking GUID names like this:

- C:\{03230347-3CC1-46BA-996C-2B4937757EEC}
- C:\{21B22D32-DA2F-40FF-AD12-4DB9F62271F5}
- C:\{41153A47-CB86-4090-8786-88EB9D110560}
- C:\{4C5857F4-4D78-4A26-902D-1038A3AE55AF}
- C:\{549ED06F-D275-473E-B944-5952DC354DC1}

Once you've created the backups, you can store them to tape as a part of your usual backup schedule. But it gets even better than that: the GPMC installation includes a Scripts folder (installed to C:\Program Files\GPMC\ Scripts by default) with a number of predefined scripts that you can use to automate your administration tasks. BackupAllGPOs.wsf allows you to back up all of your GPOs within a given domain from the command line as a one-time or scheduled task, using the following syntax:

```
BackupAllGPOs.wsf BackupLocation [/Comment:value] [/Domain:value]
```

So a scheduled task to back up all of your GPOs to a file folder on your C:\ drive would look like this:

```
BackupAllGPOs.wsf c:\GPO-Backups /comment:"Back Up All Domain GPOs"
```

More than a dozen other predefined scripts are provided with the GPMC, including scripts that allow you to

- Back up all GPOs in your domain.
- Back up a single GPO.
- Find any disabled GPOs.
- Find GPOs with duplicate names.
- Get summary reports for all GPOs.

There's also a useful help file (found in the C:\Program Files\GPMC directory by default), called gpmc.chm, to get you started with these if you're unfamiliar with scripting. I'll admit that even *I* used to be immensely script-o-phobic, but getting past the script fear will make you a much better network manager. So say it with me, if you haven't already: "Scripting is my friend." We'll be talking about various other scripting solutions throughout this guide; it's a deceptively simple technology that will allow you to do pretty complex things with a relatively low learning curve.

Migrating Group Policy Settings

If you've ever wished that you could quickly move the settings from one Group Policy Object to another, the GPMC will also make that task immensely simple. As long as you have sufficient rights to both the source and destination domains and forests, copying a GPO is as simple as right-clicking a GPO and selecting **Copy** or **Import** within the console window. This is especially useful if you maintain a separate Active Directory forest for testing purposes; once you've perfected policy settings in the test area, you can simply copy the finished GPO into your production domain.

■**Note** In a *copy* operation, a new GPO is created in the destination domain or forest. During an *import*, GPMC requires that the destination object already exist; the imported settings will overwrite any existing information in the destination GPO.

You'll also have access to a Migration Table during the copy process. This will let you map any domain-specific settings like usernames, SIDs, and UNC paths from the source domain into the target so that the copied information will match up correctly. For example, you may have a test server called \\TEST-01 that contains the user directories for your test environment. But when you copy your GPO into production, you want \\TEST-01\HOME\%*username*% to change to \\APP1\HOME\%*username*%; the Migration Table will allow you to do this without needing to make the change manually anywhere that it occurs within the Group Policy Object. To use the Migration Table, follow these steps:

1. Run **mtedit.exe** from the GPMC installation folder. This will create a blank Migration Table.

2. To automatically populate the Migration Table, click **Tools ➤ Populate from GPO** or **Tools ➤ Populate from Backup**.

3. By default, each source value will assume that its destination name is the same as the value listed for source name. It's up to you to manually edit the Destination Name column to include the appropriate values, as you can see in Figure 4-3.

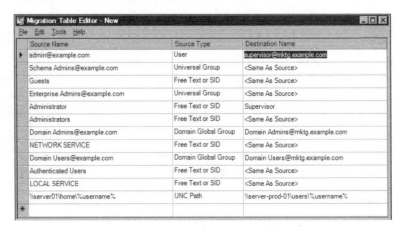

Figure 4-3. *Creating a Migration Table*

■**Note** You can either type in the mapped entries manually, or right-click the Destination field and select **Browse**.

---

4. When you've finished, click **Tools ➤ Validate Table**, which verifies that any security principals and UNC paths in the Destination column actually exist.

Modeling Group Policy

The Group Policy Management Console also assists you in planning and troubleshooting your Group Policy strategy by allowing you to play out "What if?" scenarios using a modeling tool. Like the rest of the GPMC, Group Policy Modeling is fairly intuitive and wizard-driven; in fact, if you've used the Resultant Set of Policy (RSoP) Wizard or **gpresult.exe** from the Windows 2000 Resource Kit, you're probably already familiar with the available options. To create a Group Policy Modeling report, follow these steps:

1. Open the Group Policy Management Console. Right-click Group Policy Modeling and select **Group Policy Modeling Wizard**. Click **Next** to bypass the initial **Welcome** screen.

2. Select the domain and domain controller that you want to use to perform the test. The DC needs to be a 2003 DC: you can either select a specific DC or allow the wizard to pick any available 2003 box. Click **Next** when you're done.

3. Select 1) the user or user container, and 2) the computer or computer container that you want to analyze. You can mix-and-match these as well: you can pick a single user object and an OU that contains your computer accounts, a single user and computer object, etc.

4. At this point you've given the wizard all the information it needs to create a basic report. So you can place a check mark next to **Skip to the final page of this wizard without collecting additional data**, or click **Next** to fine-tune the results of the report.

5. On the **Advanced Simulation Options** page, you can choose to modify the Group Policy behavior in any of the following ways:

   - Simulate a slow link.

   - Simulate loopback processing, using either the **Replace** or **Merge** setting. (We'll talk more about loopback processing in a minute.)

   - Specify which site to process, if you have GPOs attached to your Active Directory sites, and then click **Next**.

   - Specify which user and computer security groups you want to analyze. You can use security groups to do advanced filtering of GPO settings, which we'll talk about in the "Applying Security Filtering" section later in the chapter.

   - Specify which user and computer WMI filters you'd like to simulate.

   - At this point you'll be taken to a final screen that will list all of the settings you've selected. As with most wizards, you can click **Back** to make any changes, or click **Next** and then **Finish** to run the Modeling report.

Once you've completed the wizard, GPMC will create its now-familiar HTML report that will detail which GPO settings would be in effect in the situation you created. Perhaps most useful is that, if there are multiple Group Policy Objects present, the Modeling report will inform you which GPO "won." This is invaluable as an aid to troubleshooting, especially if your GPO structure is a complex one with multiple levels of inheritance.

Monitoring Group Policy Results

The Group Policy Results Wizard is quite similar to Group Policy Modeling, except that it provides the *actual* GPO settings that are being applied to a specific user/computer combination. Like the Modeling Wizard, it creates an HTML report detailing the GPO settings in place, and which GPO is enforcing those settings.

Caution You can't run the Group Policy Results Wizard for computers running Windows 2000. However, you can use Group Policy Modeling to basically mimic the same report. Yeah, I don't get it either; but there it is.

Who Gets What? Deploying Group Policies

Once you've customized your Group Policy Objects, you need to incorporate them into Active Directory so that your users can receive the appropriate settings. You accomplish this by *linking* Group Policy Objects to various containers within Active Directory: sites, domains, and Organizational Units. Once you've linked a GPO to a container, every object within that container will receive the GPO settings by default. In this section we'll look at how to link GPOs throughout your AD infrastructure, and how GPOs interact with one another if you have multiple objects linked to different points in your AD tree. We'll close with a look at some more advanced deployment topics such as controlling GPO inheritance and using security groups to fine-tune GPO deployment.

Using Organizational Units

The most common scenario for Group Policy deployment is to place the users and computers that require similar settings into a separate Organizational Unit, and then link a GPO to the OU to create a consistent configuration for all the members of that OU. You can link a GPO at the same time that you create it, or create an *unlinked* GPO and manually create a link once you've tested and finalized all of its settings.

- To create and link a GPO to an OU, open the Group Policy Management Console. Right-click the OU and select **Create and Link a GPO Here**.
- To link an existing GPO to an OU, open the GPMC. Right-click the OU and select **Link an Existing GPO**.

Note You can link a single GPO to multiple sites, domains, or OUs within Active Directory. However, it's a best practice not to link a GPO from one domain to a container in another, since this can create performance issues.

Configuring Policy Inheritance

In a complex network, you may find yourself with numerous GPOs deployed at various points throughout the infrastructure. It's important to understand how these different policies will interact with each other and ultimately affect your users. Much like NTFS permissions in the Windows file structure, Group Policy settings adhere to specific rules of *inheritance*. When a user logs onto your network, policy objects will be applied in the following order:

1. First, the Local Group Policy Object will be applied.
2. Second are any GPOs applied to the site the user and computer belongs to.
3. This is followed by any GPOs applied to the user's domain.
4. Finally, any GPOs linked to Organizational Units will be applied. If you have a nested OU structure, the GPO linked to the topmost OU will be applied first, and then the GPOs of any child OUs.

GPO inheritance is a cumulative process: this means that settings applied by later GPOs will be added to any earlier settings, rather than overwriting any previous settings. So if the domain GPO sets a minimum password length of eight characters, and then an OU GPO is applied that mandates a uniform screen-saver setting, the user will receive *both* settings.

So what happens if these additive settings conflict with each other? Say the domain GPO in your domain has a linked policy that blocks access to Registry editing tools, but you have created a Development OU that houses programming staff who require access to the Windows Registry. You create a GPO and link it to the Development OU, and explicitly grant access to Registry editing tools. Will this work? It will, because Group Policy Objects that are applied later have precedence over those that are applied earlier. (Think of it as having an argument where the person who gets in the last word is the one who wins.) So in this case, the Registry editing tools setting that was applied by the Development GPO "wins" over the setting applied in the domain GPO. So users in your Development OU will have access to the Registry editor, but other users in the domain (provided they don't have other GPOs applied elsewhere) will not be able to access them.

■**Caution** These inheritance rules do not apply to those settings that can only be set at the domain level: account policies, account lockout policies, and Kerberos policies. Even if you set different values for these items at an OU level, your domain users will still be held to the settings configured for the domain.

Customizing Policy Inheritance

What we've just described is the default behavior of Group Policy inheritance. But like anything else within Active Directory, you can customize these rules to finely control the way that Group Policies are deployed throughout your network. You can do this using security filtering with Active Directory security groups and Windows Management Instrumentation WMI filters, and by changing the default inheritance behavior for certain Organizational Units within your AD structure.

Blocking GPO Inheritance

If you have an OU that requires a very specific configuration, you may decide that you only want a single GPO to apply to it, so as to avoid interactions with other policy objects. You can accomplish this by right-clicking the OU within the Group Policy Management Console and selecting **Block Inheritance**. As the name suggests, this will prevent any GPO settings elsewhere in Active Directory from being applied within this particular OU; it will only receive settings from GPOs linked directly to the OU itself.

But in this case, even the exceptions can have exceptions: you can right-click a particular GPO *link* (not the GPO object itself) within the GPMC and select the **Enforced** option. This will ensure that the settings applied by this particular link cannot be blocked by any containers further down the GPO processing line.

■**Note** In Windows 2000, you'll enable the **No Override** option on the **Properties** sheet of the GPO itself.

As you can imagine, overuse of these two options can wreak havoc on your network and make troubleshooting quite a challenge. What happens if you have a GPO attached to a parent OU that has the **Enforced** option enabled, and then a child OU with a *different* GPO that has the **Enforced** setting enabled? If there is a setting conflict, which "enforced" GPO will win? In this case, the rules of inheritance will be reversed, and the *first* GPO applied with the **Enforced** setting enabled will take precedence. Tough to follow? I certainly think so: try to keep things simple and avoid convoluted scenarios like this one wherever possible.

Applying Security Filtering

Just like files and folders stored on NTFS volumes, you can create Access Control Lists for Group Policy Objects to control which Windows users and groups have access to them. In order for a GPO to be applied to a user or computer object, that object needs to have the **Read** and **Apply Group Policy** NTFS permissions to the GPO object. If both of these permissions are not present, the user or computer will not apply the settings within that particular GPO; in effect, it won't exist as far as that user/computer is concerned. When you create a new GPO in Windows Server 2003, for example, the following permissions are created by default:

- *Authenticated Users*: **Read**, **Apply Group Policy**
- *Enterprise Domain Controllers*: **Read**
- *Domain Admins/Enterprise Admins/SYSTEM*: **Read**, **Write**, **Create All Child Objects**, **Delete All Child Objects**

You can modify these permissions to ensure that specific GPOs will be applied to certain users or groups within a site, a domain, or an OU, and likewise prevent them from being applied to others. Notice that Domain Admins and Enterprise Admins do not receive the **Apply Group Policy** permission by default. This is to ensure that administrators do not become "locked out" of operating system functions when they need to perform troubleshooting or make modifications.

A scenario that is particularly conducive to using security filtering is software installation, since you may have one application that needs to be installed for specific users located across several Organizational Units, but not for your entire domain or even the entire population of an OU. Rather than creating multiple GPOs for each OU that requires the software, or managing multiple links to a single GPO, you can deploy the software within the domain GPO, and then use security filtering to specify which users and groups should receive the software. Depending on your specific needs, you can adopt one of two strategies:

- Remove the **Read/Apply Group Policy** entry for the Authenticated Users group. Then manually add the specific users and groups who should receive the GPO settings, and grant each one **Read** and **Apply Group Policy** permissions.

- Leave the default permissions for Authenticated Users in place, and then explicitly deny the **Read/Apply Group Policy** permissions to groups who should *not* receive the GPO. Setting explicit **Deny** permissions to a specific group will override the default Authenticated Users permission, and those specific groups will not receive the GPO settings.

Either of these procedures will be effective, you simply need to decide which is more appropriate for your organization. As a general rule, adopt the strategy that will result in the most straightforward permission assignment for the GPO, since this will simplify any changes you need to make later, as well as any troubleshooting you need to do.

Using WMI Filtering

For Windows XP and Windows Server 2003 machines, you can also control which machines receive particular GPO settings through the use of a WMI filter. WMI allows you to query a computer about its specific hardware and software settings, such as which service pack is installed, how much free space is available on the C:\ drive, and whether a specific service is installed or running. You can then create filters, which consist of one or more queries based on this type of data, to control whether or not the GPO gets applied. If the result of the WMI filter (such as "Is Service Pack 2 installed?" or "Does the machine have 350MB free drive space?") is true, then the GPO is applied to that destination computer. If not, then the GPO is ignored.

Caution On a machine running Windows 2000, any WMI filters will be ignored and the GPO will always applied.

To create a WMI filter, follow these steps:

1. Open the GPMC console tree, right-click the WMI Filters node, and click **New**.

2. Enter a name and description for the WMI filter, and then click **Add**.

3. In the WMI Query dialog box, enter the text of the query that you want to run, such as

```
Select * from Win32_OperatingSystem where
Caption = " Microsoft Windows XP Professional"
```

4. Click **OK** after you've entered your query. If you want to filter on more than one query, you can click **Add** to enter additional query information. When you're finished, click **Save**.

5. Select the GPO that you want to link this WMI filter to, and select the name of the filter in the WMI Filtering drop-down box near the bottom of the right-hand pane of the GPMC console.

Just as you can link a single GPO to multiple sites, domains, and OUs, so you can link a single WMI filter to multiple Group Policy Objects. However, you can only link a single WMI filter to a GPO at any one time. This is because processing a WMI filter, especially a complicated one involving multiple queries, can be resource-intensive for the target computer and can increase a user's logon time.

Controlling the Desktop

Perhaps the most visible effect of Group Policy Object is your ability to control the desktop environment for your end users' workstations. It can, however, create one of those tricky balancing acts between being in control of your desktops and being a control *freak* about them. Now, from an administrative standpoint, we all know that consistency is good: if everyone's desktop is configured the same way, it makes it that much easier to troubleshoot file incompatibilities or to make large-scale changes as applications need installing or upgrading. On the other hand, there's also a school of thought that says that too rigid of an environment makes for unhappy users (which can thus make for unhappy administrators). In most corporate environments, for example, you're not going to want to allow people to install games or other personal software on their business workstations, but is there really any harm in allowing some flexibility to customize their wallpaper, their screensaver, and the like? There *are* situations where such tight control is warranted, of course, such as a public kiosk in a library or an airport, or in a 24×7 customer service center where users share workstations over multiple shifts. Like anything else, it's a compromise; you need to decide where your organization's computers need to live on the "lockdown scale." Luckily, Group Policy allows you to grant varying levels of autonomy to different groups of users and computers, as we'll discuss in this section.

Configuring Lockdown (Kiosk) Workstations

In some cases, you'll want to lock down a workstation as much as possible, especially if it's in a public area like a library or a retail store. In many cases, such a machine will be used solely for accessing a specific web page to look up prices, check reservations, and the like. When configuring a GPO for this type of machine, you want to be as stringent as possible in controlling what the user is able to access and change. Some of the settings that you might want to enable (either from the GPMC or the **Group Policy** tab in Active Directory Users & Computers) include the following:

- Computer Configuration\Windows Components\Internet Explorer:
  - **Disable Automatic Install of Internet Explorer components**— Enabled
  - **Disable Periodic Check for Internet Explorer software updates**— Enabled
  - **Security Zones: Do not allow users to add/delete sites**—Enabled
  - **Security Zones: Do not allow users to change policies**—Enabled
  - **Security Zones: Use only machine settings**—Enabled
- Computer Configuration\Windows Components\Control Panel\Display:
  - **Hide Appearance and Themes tab**—Enabled
  - **Hide Desktop tab**—Enabled
  - **Hide Screen Saver tab**—Enabled
  - **Hide Settings tab**—Enabled
  - **Prevent changing wallpaper**—Enabled
  - **Remove display in Control Panel**—Enabled
- Computer Configuration\Windows Components\Desktop:
  - **Do not add shares of recently opened documents to My Network Places**—Enabled
  - **Don't save settings at exit**—Enabled
  - **Hide and disable all items on the desktop**—Disabled
  - **Hide Internet Explorer icon on desktop**—Enabled
  - **Hide My Network Places icon on desktop**—Enabled

- **Prevent adding, dragging, dropping, and closing the Taskbar's toolbars**—Enabled
- **Prohibit adjusting desktop toolbars**—Enabled
- **Prohibit user from changing My Documents path**—Enabled
- **Remove My Computer icon on the desktop**—Enabled
- **Remove My Documents icon on the desktop**—Enabled
- **Remove Recycle Bin icon from desktop**—Enabled
- **Remove the Desktop Cleanup Wizard**—Enabled

As you can see, these settings are quite rigid and designed for machines that are installed in public areas. You can certainly modify these settings to create a more relaxed desktop environment for machines that are "owned" by one particular individual. But the most powerful lockdown mechanism that you can (and should) employ involves controlling the applications that a user can launch from her client workstation; we'll discuss this in detail in the next section.

Using Software Restriction Policies

High on the wish list of most administrators is the ability to restrict what kind of software can run on the workstations on their network. Windows NT and 2000 offered a certain amount of control in this area, but it ranged from "hit-or-miss" to "darn near impossible to configure." You could disallow **freecell.exe**, for example, and a savvy client could simply rename the file to **notepad.exe** or another application on the permitted list. Once he did that, the blocked application would open as if you'd put no restrictions in place at all.

Windows Server 2003 has made significant advances in this area, providing nearly foolproof options for controlling how software is used on your network. This can be useful not only for restricting the use of games and other nonbusiness software on your client workstations, but also as a way to restrict viruses and malware. How is this possible? Imagine a virus that executes a VBScript to launch a Denial of Service attack. If you've configured software restrictions so that no VBScripts can run on your network, then the virus will be stopped even if someone accidentally opens an infected e-mail attachment. And even non-malicious software can create issues for an enterprise network if it hasn't been tested and approved: system files can be overwritten and can create the dreaded DLL Hell that makes Windows troubleshooting such a joy.

SOAPBOX: BLAME THE USER?

Wouldn't our lives all get a whole lot simpler if we could make those pesky users go away and stop bothering us? I mean, they're *horrible!* Always clicking on attachments and needing more disk space and generally making a mess of our nice, orderly networks!

But despite our occasional frustrations, part of what separates good network admins from great ones is the ability to secure a network without driving their clients to open revolt. It's very easy to say "We wouldn't need antivirus scanners if people would just stop clicking on things they're not supposed to." But that's also a bit of an oversimplification, since it assumes that every client on your network is just as technically savvy as you are. And this, as we all know, is hardly ever the case. If your network security strategy is "Get users to stop doing things they shouldn't," then it's a plan that's doomed to failure. And that's because it *only takes one—one* person who was in a rush, or forgot, or got fooled by a forged e-mail header, or any number of things that could happen to any of us. The reason I'm a big advocate of technologies like Group Policy and Software Restriction Policies is that they help to protect your clients from themselves. And if your clients are protected, then so, by extension, is your network.

Software Restriction Policies begin with one of two configurations whereby you decide how applications should be treated on your network, called **Unrestricted** and **Disallowed**. The difference between the two is pretty obvious: you need to make a choice between "Run everything except the stuff I tell you is bad" versus "Don't run *anything* except what I explicitly tell you is allowed." Once you've made this initial decision, there are four rules that Windows Server 2003 can use to restrict software usage on your network: Path, Hash, Certificate, and Zone.

■**Caution** If you don't use a test environment for anything else, I *strongly* urge you to create one before you deploy Software Restriction Policies. Imagine a worst-case scenario: if you create a policy, set the default to **Disallowed**, and then don't specify any programs that are allowed to run, you've just created a policy that won't allow *anything* to run. You wouldn't even be able to log on to a workstation or server that's been configured this way. Even in less extreme situations, this is a powerful tool that warrants thorough testing before implementing it on a production network.

Creating a Software Restriction Policy

Rather than drown you in details, I'll first walk through creating a basic Software Restriction Policy using some default options. Once you've got the big picture at that point, you can get into the nitty-gritty of each rule type and some of the other advanced options that you can set within the policy. To create a Software Restriction Policy, follow these steps:

1. Open the target GPO in the Group Policy Management Console. (Right-click the object and click **Edit**.)

2. Navigate to **User Configuration ➤ Windows Settings ➤ Security Settings ➤ Software Restriction Policies**.

3. Right-click the Software Restriction Policies folder and select **New Software Restriction Policy**.

4. Your first step is to decide whether your overall software policy will be **Unrestricted** or **Disallowed**. By default, a new policy will use the **Unrestricted** setting. To change this, right-click **Disallowed** and select **Set as default**. (But you really should configure rules for what programs *are* allowed to run before you do this.) For our purposes, we'll assume that you're leaving the default **Unrestricted** setting, and want to disallow specific programs instead.

5. Next, configure a Path rule to disallow a specific application. Let's say that you've been instructed to restrict use of the AOL Instant Messenger application on your network. Right-click the Additional Rules folder and select **New Path Rule**. You'll see the dialog box shown in Figure 4-4. Enter the path to the AIM executable, and set the security level to **Disallowed**. This change will take effect the next time that the GPO is refreshed, or when a user logs out and logs back in.

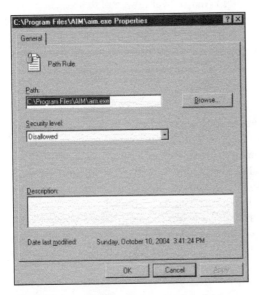

Figure 4-4. *Configuring a new Path rule*

■Caution If you support Windows XP workstations, Software Restriction Policies will take two (I've even heard anecdotal reports of *three*) reboots to take effect. This is because of the Fast Logon Optimization feature, in which Windows XP doesn't wait for a network connection to come all the way up before applying Group Policies. Check out Knowledge Base Article 305293 for the full explanation, available at http://support.microsoft.com/?id=305293.

Configuring Zone Rules

A Zone rule allows you to restrict software based on the Internet Explorer zone that it was downloaded from: Internet, Local Intranet, Restricted Sites, Trusted Sites, or Local Computer. This would be useful if you use an intranet site to make software applications available to your users: they could install and run software downloaded from the Local Intranet zone, but not anything they downloaded from an untrusted game server.

■Note Why are you using an intranet site to deploy software? Group Policy can do that for you! Never mind, we'll get there in a minute.

Before you break into a happy dance over how cool this feature is, though, you can only use it to regulate MSI installers, not .EXE files or other downloadable files. This makes it perhaps the *least* useful of the software restriction rules, unfortunately. Maybe it'll be improved in a future Group Policy or Windows operating system release, because it really is a great idea.

Configuring Hash Rules

One of the largest challenges of software restriction in Windows NT and Windows 2000 was the fact that restrictions were keyed to the file name of the executable that you were trying to allow or disallow. So you could disallow **sol.exe** or **kazaa.exe** all you wanted to, but all a crafty user needed to do was rename the executable to **notepad.exe** or a similarly innocuous name, and any software restrictions would be circumvented.

In Windows Server 2003, you can use a Hash rule to increase the effectiveness of your software restrictions. A *hash* refers to a kind of mathematical fingerprint that will uniquely identify a file regardless of where it lives within the file system, and even regardless of whether it's been renamed. This fingerprint remains unchanged when the file is copied, moved, or even renamed. This means that our intrepid user's "rename the file" strategy would be foiled if Hash rules were in effect. Creating a Hash rule is nearly identical to the way we created the Path rule, except that you'll select only the file name rather than the full path.

■**Note** Most antivirus companies will make the hash values of known virus files available to the public. You can then paste this hash into a Software Restriction rule to prevent the virus from running on your network.

Another great use for Hash rules is to prevent damage caused by viruses and Trojans that attempt to overwrite operating system files with malicious copies. So if your policy were configured to only allow the applications that you name, even if a virus could overwrite **WINWORD.EXE** with a malicious Trojan, it still wouldn't be able to launch because the hash value would not match the one specified in the Hash rule.

Configuring Certificate Path Rules

You can also configure Software Restriction Policies to use certificates to determine whether software can run or not. For example, you can use Certificate rules to automatically trust software from a third-party vendor or from within your organization. Certificates used in a Certificate rule can come from a commercial CA like Thawte or VeriSign, a Windows 2000/Windows Server 2003 PKI server, or a self-signed certificate. This is a really useful way to prevent users from downloaded unauthorized ActiveX controls from untrusted websites.

Configuring Path Rules

As you saw in the sample policy we created, Path rules can specify the fully qualified path to a program. You can also use wildcards and folder names to create less-specific Path rules. When a Path rule specifies a folder, it will apply to any program that's contained in that folder, as well as any programs contained within any subfolders. You can use both local and UNC paths to create a Path rule, as well as environmental path variables like %WINDIR%.

▦**Caution** Use system variables with caution since they are client-specific. If a user can modify her local environment variables, it can affect the results of any Path rules that rely on those variables.

You can also use the familiar * and ? wildcards to increase the flexibility and effectiveness of your Path rules. For example, *\Windows will apply to C:\Windows, D:\Windows, and E:\Windows, in case your clients have their OS installed to a nondefault logical drive. You can also use wildcards for such familiar tricks as *.exe, *.vbs, and the like.

If you need even more flexibility than wildcards offer, you can control your Path rules using Registry paths. This is especially useful if you need to restrict the contents of an application that may not be installed in a consistent location, but that stores its installation directory within a Registry key. So a Registry Path rule could look up the value in a Registry key such as this:

```
%HKEY_LOCAL_MACHINE\SOFTWARE\VendorName\AppName\
Directories\Install Dir%.
```

When creating a Registry Path rule, you'll use the following format:

```
%[Registry Hive]\[Registry Key Name]\[Value Name]%
```

Path Rule Precedence

There's a specific order in which multiple Path rules will be enforced, depending on how specific the policy is. What does this mean? Essentially, a Path rule that is defined on a specific file (a more restrictive rule) will take precedence over policies applied to a file folder, or to policies involving wildcards (less restrictive rules). Any conflicts between Path rules will be resolved using the following precedence:

1. *Drive*:*Folder1*\ will be applied first and has the lowest precedence.

2. *Drive*:*Folder1**Folder2*\.

3. **.Extension*.

4. *Drive*:*Folder1**Folder2**.Extension*.

5. *Drive*:*Folder1**Folder2**FileName.Extension* will be applied last and has the highest precedence.

Software Restriction Rule Precedence

In addition to resolving conflicts between Path rules, you'll need to understand how the different restriction types interact with each other as well. If multiple rule types are in effect, policies will be applied in the following order:

1. The Internet Zone rule has the lowest precedence of all Software Restriction Policies.

2. Path rules, in the following order:
   - *Drive:\Folder1*
   - *Drive:\Folder1\Folder2*
   - **.Extension*
   - *Drive:\Folder1\Folder2*.Extension*
   - *Drive:\Folder1\Folder2\FileName.Extension*

3. The Certificate rule.

4. The Hash rule has the highest precedence of all Software Restriction Policies, and will be applied last so that its settings "win."

Much like Group Policies, the last policy that applies is the one that takes precedence. So if you create a Hash rule that allows **Unrestricted** access to **iexplorer.exe**, but define a Path rule that disallows it, the program will be allowed to run.

If after all of this you *still* have two identical rules that are applying differing security levels to the same executable, the more stringent rule will take precedence. For example, if two Hash rules—one with a security level of **Disallowed** and one with a security level of **Unrestricted**—are applied to the same software program, the **Disallowed** rule will take effect and the program will not run.

▊Note As with any configuration policies on your network, I'm going to tell you that your best bet is to keep it simple. Applying multiple policies and worrying about precedence rules is mostly going to add to troubleshooting difficulties and not much else.

Securing Client Operating Systems

Another useful item in the Group Policy bag of tricks is that you can use it to create a standard security configuration across your entire network, without needing to visit individual machines to repeatedly perform the same configuration. (We all know how tedious that is, not to mention error-prone.) By using *security templates*, you can create a security policy for your entire network or for a smaller group of similarly configured computers. You can do this using one of the predefined security templates included in the Windows 2000 or 2003 OS, or you can modify one of these templates or even create a brand new one containing the specific security settings that you need. Security templates can be used to define the following components:

- Account policies
- Password policies
- Account lockout policies
- Kerberos policies
- Local policies
- Audit policies
- User rights assignments
- Security options
- Event log settings
- Restricted groups settings
- System services: startup modes and permissions
- Registry key permissions
- File and folder permissions

In this section, we'll look at the steps for implementing security templates on an Active Directory network. The process begins with analyzing the current security settings on various machines on your network, creating or modifying a security template containing your desired settings, and then importing that template into Group Policy so that it can be rolled out to your entire network.

Analyzing Current Security

You can analyze the security settings on any machine in one of two ways: either by using the MMC, or through the **secedit** command-line utility. The Security Configuration and Analysis console (which I'll refer to as SCA from this point on) isn't one of the default consoles installed in your Administrative

Tools folder; you'll need to open a blank MMC console in author mode (enter **mmc /a** from the Run line) and use the **File ➤ Add/Remove Snap-in** menu command.

Note Since you'll probably be using this tool fairly often, I'd recommend that you save a custom console to your Administrative Tools folder for easy access.

Using SCA is pretty intuitive since the opening screen provides you with instructions to get started. In order to work with SCA, you'll need to create a database that will store the security template values that you're comparing or applying. If you have an existing database, simply right-click the SCA node and select **Open**, and then browse to the database file you need. If you're creating a new database, you'll need to do the following:

1. Right-click the SCA node and select **Open Database**. (I know it seems counterintuitive to open a database that doesn't exist yet. Trust me, it works.)
2. Enter the path and name of the SCA database that you want to create, and then click **Open**.
3. You'll then need to select the template that you want to compare your current settings against. We'll go into detail about what the different templates do in a later section, but for now the file names should look fairly intuitive:
    - *compatws.inf*: Used for workstations that need backwards compatibility with legacy applications or networks.
    - *dcsecurity.inf*: This is created by the operating system when a member server is promoted to domain controller status.
    - *iesacls.inf*: Allows you to lock down Internet Explorer settings.
    - *hisec*.inf*: Used for a high-security configuration; hisecdc.inf corresponds to a domain controller, hisecws.inf is for a secure workstation.
    - *notssid.inf*: Used to remove the Terminal Server user SID from a server that isn't being used for Terminal Services connections.
    - *rootsec.inf, setup security.inf*: Ignore these for now, we'll discuss them in the "Using Security Templates" section in a moment.
    - *secure*.inf*: Used for situations where you want a secure configuration, but the settings in the hisec*.inf templates are a bit over-the-top. Sufficient for most environments.

4. Once you've selected a template, you'll then *analyze* your computer's security settings compared to those within the template. (The instructions that you see in the SCA GUI at this point describe the steps to *configure* your computer before the steps needed to analyze it: please, oh please, don't take this literally. You always want to analyze a computer's settings before blindly applying a new template.)

5. Right-click the SCA node again and select **Analyze Computer Now**. You'll be prompted for a location to store the analysis results as a .LOG file. Select a location, and then click **OK** to begin the analysis.

Once you've analyzed your computer's settings, you can browse through the SCA console to see where your settings differ from those within the template. You'll see a screen similar to Figure 4-5 with three columns: Policy, Database Setting, and Computer Setting. A red X will be displayed if a defined setting doesn't match the setting specified in the template, versus a green check mark if your settings are consistent.

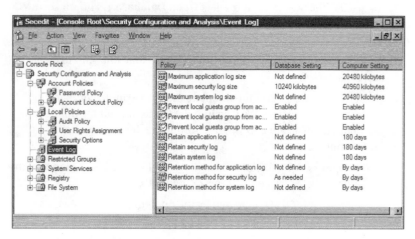

Figure 4-5. *Browsing the secedit database*

You can also perform a security analysis from the command line, using the `secedit` command with the following syntax:

```
secedit /analyze /db FileName.sdb [/cfg FileName] [/overwrite]
        [/log FileName] [/quiet]
Command-line arguments:
/db FileName specifies the database file used
        to perform the analysis
```

/cfg *FileName* specifies the security template to
      import into the database prior to performing
      the analysis. Security templates are created
      using the Security Templates snap-in.
/log FileName Specifies a file in which to log the
      status of the configuration process. If not
      specified, configuration data is logged in
      Scesrv.log, which is located in the
      %windir%\Security\Logs folder.
/quiet Specifies that the analysis process should
      take place without further comments.

■**Note** The /quiet option comes in quite handy if you want to perform a security analysis on all of the workstations in your network: simply add a command like secedit /analyze /db hisecws.sdb to a batch file or login script, and you can collect information from your client workstations with very little effort.

Using Security Templates

So you've already seen a glimpse of security templates in action, but what are they really about? Just as a template for a word processor can help you create a document according to certain standards, a security template is simply a premade file that simplifies the process of comparing your computer's existing security settings against a predefined list. There are dozens (if not hundreds) of options available to you when securing a server, and the number of possible combinations is enough to make even a security expert's head spin. Templates allow you to quickly create a secure baseline for your network clients and servers and make it easier to control how configuration changes occur.

Windows 2000 and 2003 both come with a number of default security templates installed in the %SystemRoot%\Security\Templates folder. Nine default templates are installed with the operating system, and numerous others can be downloaded from the Microsoft website. Each of the default templates has specific characteristics, described as follows:

- *compatws.inf:* Provides the ability for members of the local Users group to run software that typically requires Power User or local Administrator access. This relaxes the permissions that are normally assigned to the Users group so that you don't need to add your users to these more powerful security groups.

- *DC security.inf:* This template is applied when a 2003 server is promoted to domain controller status. The template contains modifications specific to domain controller security, including file system rights and registry permissions.

- *securedc.inf:* Designed to increase security for domain controllers, including settings for passwords, account lockout, and auditing policies. This template also increases restrictions for anonymous users.

- *securews.inf:* Similar to the settings in securedc.inf, but designed for workstations and member servers.

- *hisecdc.inf:* Provides additional security (over and above that provided by the securedc.inf template) for domain controllers.

- *hisecws.inf:* Increases security for member servers and workstations.

- *iesacls.inf:* Increases the default security configuration for Internet Explorer.

- *notssid.inf:* By default, Windows 2000 and 2003 add file system permissions and user rights for Terminal Services users on each server. If you know for certain that the server you're installing will not be used as a Terminal Server, you can apply this template to remove the unnecessary entries.

- *rootsec.inf:* Defines permissions for the root of the system drive; you can use it to reapply the root directory permissions if they are inadvertently changed. You can also modify this template to apply a specific set of permissions to the root of different volumes. This template doesn't overwrite any permissions that you've explicitly defined on any child objects below the system root; it merely propagates the permissions that are configured to be inherited by child objects.

- *Setup security.inf:* This template is actually created individually whenever you install a new Windows 2000 or 2003 computer; it allows you to revert the configuration of the machine back to its original settings at any time. This should obviously be used with extreme caution, since you'll be overwriting any configuration changes that you've made since the machine was initially installed.

Creating or Customizing a Security Template

If one of these preexisting templates meets your needs, you can apply it directly to your servers and workstations. You can also modify some of the settings to customize the template to address the specific requirements of your organization; however, it's a good idea to make a *copy* of the default template before making any changes to it. This way if you make a mistake or change your mind, it's easy to roll back to the default settings. To create a copy of a default template, do the following:

1. Open an MMC console in Author Mode (**mmc /a** from the Run line), and add the Security Templates snap-in.

2. Drill down to **Security Templates ➤ C:\Windows\security\templates**.

3. Right-click the template you want to copy, click **Save As**, and enter a new name for the copy.

■Note To create a blank template from scratch, right-click the C:\Windows\security\ templates node and select **New Template**.

Once you have the new template in place, you can manually edit its settings by browsing through the various nodes in the Security Templates console. Alternatively, you can copy a specific group of settings from one template to another. For example, to copy the account policies settings from the hisecws.inf template into a blank one, follow these steps:

1. Navigate to **C:\Windows\security\templates ➤ hisecws.inf**.

2. Right-click the Account Policies node and select **Copy**.

3. Navigate to the Account Policies node in your new policy, right-click, and select **Paste**. This will add the account policies from the hisecws.inf template while leaving the other nodes undefined.

Importing a Template into Group Policy

Once you've created a template containing the security settings you need, you'll import the template's settings into a Group Policy Object in order to propagate those changes to the machines on your network.

UNDERSTANDING DOMAIN-LEVEL POLICIES

It's important to keep in mind that certain Windows security policies can be set only at the domain level. These include the settings in the Account Policies node: account policies, account lockout policies, and Kerberos policies. This means that an Active Directory domain can have only *one* of these policies in effect at any given time: all users within a single domain will be bound to a single policy for things like password length and complexity, frequency of password changes, PKI policies, and Kerberos settings. The only exception to this is if you create a separate account policy on an Organizational Unit (OU) containing member servers. In this case, the *local* user accounts on machines within a given OU can have a different account policy apply to them. However, any *domain* accounts, even within a separate OU, will adhere to the domain account policy. If you have a significant portion of your user base that requires very different policies for account passwords, lockouts, etc., then you should consider creating a separate domain. Because of the transitive trusts created by Windows 2000 and Windows Server 2003, managing multiple domains isn't nearly as tedious as it was under Windows NT. However, maintaining separate domains will still add a level of complexity to your Active Directory environment; be sure when planning your AD infrastructure that you carefully consider these domain-level policies before creating an unworkable Active Directory structure.

To import a security template into a Group Policy, you'll need to do the following:

1. Open the GPO you wish to edit from the Group Policy MMC or the GPMC console.

2. Navigate to **Computer Configuration ➤ Windows Settings ➤ Security Settings**.

3. Right-click the Security Settings node and select **Import Policy**. You'll be prompted to browse to the .INF file that you want to import.

▬**Caution** A bit of Group Policy weirdness: importing a security template does not register as a "change" to a GPO. This means that the new settings won't be detected by your clients or servers when they query Active Directory for any changes to the GPOs. In order to resolve this, you should manually change a setting within the GPO, even if it's one you intend to change back later. This will ensure that your new security settings will be transmitted to your network machines in a timely fashion.

Configuring Software Deployment

You can also use Group Policy to deploy line-of-business applications throughout your Active Directory network. This installation can take place silently, without the need for user intervention or assigning elevated privileges to your users at the desktop level. Software that's installed via Group Policy is *self-healing*, which means that any application files that become corrupted or deleted will be replaced automatically by the Group Policy Object. Depending on the needs of your environment, Group Policy software deployment can allow a user's applications to follow him no matter where he logs on to the network from, or ensure that a specific set of tools is available on a particular machine no matter who logs on to it. In this section, we'll look at some of the most useful options available to you in using Group Policy to deploy software.

Creating an Installation Package

As long as you have an .MSI installer for the application you want to deploy, doing so through Group Policy is pretty much a snap. If your application does not have an .MSI file associated with it, though, you are still not entirely out of luck. You can create a .ZAP file that will still allow you to deploy the software, with the following caveats:

- The installation process can't take advantage of elevated privileges for installation. So if your users are only members of the Users group and they need Administrator access to perform the installation, the deployment will fail.

- The program can't be installed on the first use of the software—we'll talk about how .MSI does this in a moment.

- You won't be able to install a feature on the first use of the feature, similar to how Microsoft Word can leave the Thesaurus function uninstalled, but you can copy it to the user's workstation the first time she tries to use it.

- Most problematic of all, you can't roll back an unsuccessful installation, modification, repair, or removal of a .ZAP file the way you can with .MSI.

■Note With more and more applications complying with the Microsoft Logo Program, this is a much smaller concern now than it was even when Windows 2000 was first released.

To create a software installation package for an .MSI installer, follow these steps:

1. Open the GPO that you want to use from the GPMC console.

2. Navigate to **User Configuration ➤ Software Settings ➤ Software Installation** from either the Computer Configuration or User Configuration node. (You can also deploy software to computers instead of users; we'll talk about that in the "Understanding Deployment Options" section next.)

3. Right-click the Software Installation node and select **New ➤ Package**. Browse to the location of the .MSI file and click **OK**.

■**Caution** Since your network clients will need to access the .MSI file in order to perform the installation, be sure that it's located on a shared network drive and assigned the appropriate NTFS permissions.

---

4. The next screen gives you a choice of how you want to deploy the software: **Published**, **Assigned**, or **Advanced**. We'll go over the differences between these options next; for now select **Published**, which will install the application the first time a user clicks a file associated with it. (Double-clicking a .DOC file would launch the Microsoft Word installer, for example.)

5. Click **OK** to finish. The GPO Editor will take a moment to refresh itself, and then you'll see your software package listed in the Software Installation window. From here you can right-click the package and select **Properties** to change any deployment options.

Understanding Deployment Options

When deploying software, you need to make two major decisions:

- Do I want to publish this software package, or assign it?
- Do I want to deploy this software to a user object or a computer object?

In this section we'll look at the differences between these choices, as well as some more advanced options available for software deployments.

Publishing Applications

Publishing an application will make that application available to your users at their next login. Once you've published an application, a user can install or uninstall it by using the Add/Remove Programs applet in Control Panel.

The installer will also launch through *document invocation*, that is, when the user tries to view or edit a file that requires the published application to open. This is a good way to roll out applications that might not be used consistently across your network, since you won't be performing the actual installation unless (and until) the user actively requires the software. Using Group Policy will still ease the installation process for your users since they won't need to remember share names or instructions for manually installing software.

■Note You can deploy *published* applications only to user objects, not computers. It makes a lot of sense since, after all, what are the odds that your workstation will decide of its own volition that it needs to install Microsoft Word one day?

You have a few additional options available to you when publishing a software package. When you right-click the package and go to **Properties**, you'll see the screen shown in Figure 4-6 by clicking the **Deployment** tab.

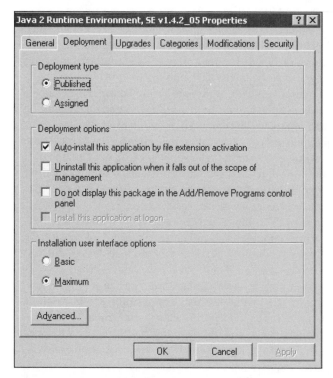

Figure 4-6. *Configuring software deployment options*

As you can see, the option to install the app when a user double-clicks the appropriate file extension is enabled by default. Two other options that you can enable are

- **Uninstall this application when it falls out of the scope of management**: Let's say that user JSmith is contained in the Accounting OU of your domain and has the PeachTree accounting package installed via Group Policy. If JSmith moves to Marketing, and the Marketing OU does not have the accounting software published to it, then the application will be uninstalled from JSmith's workstation. This is useful in ensuring that sensitive applications do not remain installed on a workstation if the user no longer has a need for them.

- **Do not display this package in the Add/Remove Programs control panel**: Just like it sounds, this ensures that a published application will *only* be installed through document invocation. You may enable this option to prevent applications from being installed unnecessarily by curious users.

Assigning Software

In addition to publishing an application, you can also *assign* it to either a computer or a user object. By assigning an application to a computer object, the application will be automatically installed the next time the computer boots up: this requires no document invocation or user intervention of any kind. Once the program has been installed, only an administrator will be able to uninstall it (either manually or through Group Policy). Like a published application, an assigned application is *self-healing* so that it can automatically repair or replace any damaged or erased program files.

Assigning an application to a user takes one of two forms. In the default scenario, the user will see a shortcut to the application on her Desktop or Start menu. However, the app won't actually be installed until the first time she double-clicks the shortcut or uses document invocation. And since the installation takes place silently, a user can easily be confused when he tries to launch the program and nothing seems to happen. It's important to be aware of this fact, since "I double-clicked the Excel icon and my machine has been hung up for like two minutes" can be a common help desk phone call in this situation.

While this was the only way of assigning software to a user in Windows 2000, Windows Server 2003 provides the **Install application at logon** option, which will perform an install as soon as the user logs on. Similar to the help desk calls you might experience from the default scenario, though, this option may greatly increase your users' logon times while the installation process is running. As with anything else, good communication with your users and support staff will help to make this operation as smooth as possible.

You'll typically assign software to computer objects for critical applications that need to be present on any computer on your network: antivirus software is a favorite use of this feature. Simply add the antivirus software's .MSI file to the Default Domain policy, and every machine in your network will receive the installation the next time they reboot.

Caution Installing applications with large source files can create congestion in your network traffic, especially if a large number of users request the installation at the same time. (At 9 a.m. when they arrive at the office, for example.) Be sure to take this into account when deciding which programs to assign to your users and computers.

Deploying Custom Applications and Upgrades

For applications with many different parts, such as Microsoft Office, you can even configure the installation file so that it only installs the components you want. The remaining components can be left out entirely, or you can allow them to be installed on their first use: the first time a user requests the Word spell-checker, for example. To customize your applications in this way, you'll use a *transform* file with the .MST extension. You'll specify these .MST files on the **Modifications** tab of the software package's **Properties** sheet, which you saw in Figure 4-6.

Finally, once you've deployed a software package through a GPO, you can use a newer installer to *upgrade* that package using the **Upgrades** tab of the **Properties** sheet. An upgrade package can either be optional or mandatory, and the upgrade will take place the next time the user logs on or the machine boots up.

Note Unlike other Group Policy settings that will refresh in the background every 90 minutes by default, software installation policies will only take effect at startup or logon. This is to prevent such catastrophes as a GPO trying to upgrade or uninstall a user's copy of Outlook while she's still trying to use it, for example.

Using Advanced Techniques

We'll close out the chapter with a few other Group Policy tricks that should be in any administrator's arsenal. This includes the ability to centrally configure permissions for all of your client workstations, as well as how to control membership to sensitive local and domain groups. At the end of the chapter you'll find some links to online and print resources that I've found useful in creating Group Policy solutions for networks of all sizes.

Controlling the Registry and File System

One of the largest headaches for most network admins is the need to secure large numbers of client workstations in a quick and efficient manner. We've already seen how you can import security templates into Group Policy to deploy network-based security settings like minimum password lengths and account lockout policies, but you can also use a GPO to enforce security standards on your users' local hard drives. By browsing to **Computer Configuration ➤ Windows Settings ➤ Security Settings** within the GPMC, you can add entries to the following Group Policy nodes:

- System Services
- Registry
- File System

In the case of System Services, you can define how local services will behave on system startup, and which users and groups have permission to start, stop, or modify those services. If you remember the Code Red and Nimda worms, they attacked many workstations that had the IIS services installed. In many cases, the owners of these workstations didn't even know that their machines were running an instance of the IIS web server, and so were taken completely by surprise when these network attacks hit. You can use the System Services node to universally disable a service like World Wide Web Publishing, Telnet, or any other service that really shouldn't be running on a workstation. That way, even if a virus or spyware program attempts to start the service, the malicious software will be unable to do so.

The Registry and File System nodes allow you to set NTFS permissions on specific registry keys or file/folder paths. Simply add the full name of the Registry key or the folder path that you want to secure, and you'll see a familiar **Properties** sheet that will allow you to specify permissions just as though you were sitting at the console of the workstation itself. You'll also have the option to propagate the permissions to any subfolders or subkeys of the folder or key you specify.

■**Caution** Note that none of these settings will *create* a service, Registry key, or file system path. These GPO settings are simply used to configure security on existing workstation configurations.

Using Restricted Groups

When you're protecting your domain and local user accounts, restricting membership to sensitive groups like Domain Admins, Enterprise Admins, and the like is absolutely critical. If malicious users, either external or internal, can somehow create an account for themselves that is a member of one of these groups, then the security of your entire Active Directory infrastructure can become irrevocably compromised. The solution to this is the use of restricted groups within Group Policy. By right-clicking the Computer Configuration\Windows Settings\Security Settings\Restricted Groups node and selecting **Add Group**, you can specify the following information:

- Which users or groups should belong to the restricted group, and
- Which users or groups should not belong to the group

Let's say you've restricted the Domain Admins group so that it can only contain the user accounts for yourself and two of your staff members. If you accidentally add (or delete) an account from Domain Admins membership, the Restricted Groups policy will re-create the membership list the next time that the policy is applied: every 90 minutes by default. You can also use this setting to restrict local group memberships on member servers and workstations.

Summary

In this chapter, we looked at the wide, wonderful world of Group Policies, and how they can make your life as an Active Directory administrator so much simpler by allowing you to specify security and usability settings for an entire site, OU, or domain from a single location. We started by looking at the Group Policy Management Console, which is a new Group Policy management tool that greatly simplifies the process of creating and managing Group Policy Objects. We then talked about the different configuration settings that you can control through Group Policy, including security settings like password policies and account lockout policies. You can also use a GPO to customize and control your users' desktops, removing access to potentially harmful items like the Control Panel and the command prompt. To further control security in your environment, you can use security templates that will allow you to configure numerous machines with the same security settings without risking data entry errors from entering the same information multiple times. You can also use Group Policy to centrally deploy software applications to your users and computers, as well as controlling the software that's allowed to run by using Software Restriction Policies. We closed out the chapter with a look at some more advanced Group Policy tricks, such as configuring permissions on Registry keys and NTFS files and folders, and controlling the startup behavior of Windows services.

Additional Resources

Windows Server 2003 Active Directory: http://www.microsoft.com/ windowsserver2003/technologies/directory/activedirectory/default.mspx.

Moskowitz, Inc., Group Policy Resource Center: http://www.gpanswers.com —Check out the forums and newsletter!

Group Policy, Profiles, and Intellimirror for Windows 2003, Windows 2000, and Windows XP by Jeremy Moskowitz. Sybex Publishing. ISBN 0-7821- 4298-2—Order it from http://www.gpanswers.com and the author will even sign it for you.

Microsoft Technet Script Center: http://www.microsoft.com/technet/ scriptcenter/default.mspx—Great for the scripting or WMI beginner, including a repository of ready-made scripts and filters that you can use right away.

Active Directory Discussions Mailing List: http://www.activedir.org— Moderate traffic (50 messages in a day is pretty busy). Required reading for anyone who is serious about managing their Active Directory network well.

CHAPTER 5

■ ■ ■

Active Directory Security

In an era where "always-on" Internet access is becoming the norm rather than the exception, securing the Active Directory infrastructure is a critical element of any administrator's or consultant's job. The information stored in the Active Directory database makes up the "keys to the kingdom" for any network: allow even one domain controller to be compromised, and you can never be sure of your network's security again. So I'll spend the rest of this chapter showing you some of the ways that you can secure an Active Directory network using Windows operating system built-in tools. This includes securing network transmissions between your network workstations and servers, and using auditing to ensure that no unauthorized changes are being made on your Active Directory network.

In this chapter, you'll learn how to do the following:

- Recognize vulnerabilities on a TCP/IP network.

- Create an IPSec policy using GUI tools.

- Use **netsh** to control IPSec from the command line.

- Harden the TCP/IP stack in Windows 2000 Server and Windows Server 2003.

- Increase security on Active Directory domain controllers.

- Eliminate weak authentication protocols on your network.

- Control anonymous access to Active Directory.

- Configure an audit policy to monitor for malicious activity.

Using IP Security

While IPSec (short for IP Security) isn't specifically designed to secure Active Directory per se, it's certainly a technology that you can put to good use on a Windows 2000/2003 network. IPSec's mission in life is to secure IP traffic of all kinds, which makes it quite useful for securing an Active Directory network. Specifically, IPSec is designed to protect the contents of IP packets traversing a network, and to help you protect yourself against network attacks using packet filtering, signing, authentication, and enforcing trusted communications.

IPSec can secure traffic in one of two ways. The first is *transport mode*, which establishes secure, end-to-end transmissions from a source IP address all the way to its destination IP, so that all Transport Layer packets that move between them are encrypted. This is different from *tunneling*, because the sender and receiver are the only ones who are aware that any encryption and security is taking place; IPSec packets traverse a network just like unsecured packets, and the two machines can send both encrypted and unencrypted traffic in the same way. You can see how this is different from using a Virtual Private Network (VPN), where a full-time secure tunnel gets created between a sender and a receiver. The other IPSec mode is much closer to this VPN-like configuration, and is called *tunnel* mode. You'll use tunnel mode primarily when you need to create secure communications between two devices where one of the devices is not the originator. Tunnel mode is used in cases when security is provided by a device that did not originate packets—as in the case of VPNs—or when the packet needs to be secured to a destination that is different from the actual destination. In this case, IPSec will only secure traffic between two static IP addresses, usually between the router on each side of the connection.

Understanding IP Security Vulnerabilities

Before we get into configuring IP Security for your network, let's take a quick look at the different kinds of security risks that you need to protect yourself against. If your network traffic is unsecured and unencrypted, then it's going across the wire in plaintext. This means that any attacker with a packet sniffer can eavesdrop on your network traffic, and capture and analyze any plaintext information he can find. Packet sniffers are pretty easy for an attacker to install and configure, and even the Network Monitor that is included with the Windows Server operating systems can allow a malicious user to intercept unencrypted traffic. Using these sniffers, a malicious user can intercept any kind of data as it moves across the network, including usernames and passwords if they're being transmitted in plaintext. (We'll talk more about user authentication at the end of the chapter.) This is particularly dangerous because, once an outsider obtains a legitimate username and password on your network, most of your security controls become meaningless: the attacker now has all the rights and privileges of the user whose account she's compromised. IPSec helps to guard against these eaves-dropping attacks by encrypting the *payload*, or IP packet contents, so that even if an attacker intercepts it, she'll only see a bunch of unintelligible gib-berish rather than any useful information.

Beyond this kind of passive eavesdropping, we move into more active attacks where hackers will try to modify or corrupt your information. This is probably the best argument in favor of securing and encrypting your data; even if you don't think your network information is sensitive enough to war-rant encryption as it's being transmitted, you probably don't want it being modified in route to the sender. A common example of this is the "man in the middle" or "session hijacking" attack, where an attacker intercepts and changes data as it's being transmitted between two parties. Typically, the people who are transmitting won't even realize that their information has been altered; they simply see a successful transaction and take the informa-tion at face value, even though it's been intercepted and compromised. In this case, IPSec will guard against data modification by placing a *checksum* on any packet that gets transmitted. This checksum is basically a seal on the packet in the form of a mathematical equation that was run on the packet just before it got transmitted. If the packet gets modified in any way, then that checksum won't be accurate anymore, and the receiving computer will know that the packet was altered somewhere in transit.

Another security vulnerability that IPSec can protect against is *spoofing*, which is when an intruder falsely uses an IP address to compromise packet filter security. IPSec uses Kerberos, public key certificates, or preshared key authentication to verify the identity of computer systems before the applica-tion-level communication can take place, which will work to prevent a malicious user from spoofing IP addresses on your internal network.

Moving away from attacks involving a single user or piece of data, IPSec can also help you to prevent Denial of Service (DoS) attacks, in which your network bandwidth gets flooded by a worm or virus, or just an attacker transmitting bad data across your network. The point of a DoS attack is to overwhelm your network bandwidth with false or useless queries and data so that the servers can't respond to legitimate requests from your actual users. This is especially dangerous if someone mounts a DoS attack against your DNS servers or other critical points in your network infrastructure, since it can render Active Directory dog-slow at best, unusable at worst. In many cases, these DoS attacks actually begin as an Application Layer attack against the operating system of the server, since an attacker can use an unpatched security vulnerability to take control of an application or even an entire server. And if attackers can take over your server to the extent that they can load, install, or execute programs or run their own commands, then it's quite simply not your server anymore. IPSec can help you guard against these kinds of attacks by permitting only authenticated traffic to your critical servers, and effectively not giving any "strangers" access to the box.

Creating an IPSec Policy

An IPSec policy consists of a few different elements that work together to secure communications on your network. When you create or modify an IPSec policy, you'll be working with the following configuration items:

- *IPSec policy*: This is the overall framework that manages the security configuration, especially the different rules that you've configured to respond to traffic going to and from machines on your network. The IPsec Policy also controls the name and description of the policy, and how frequently Group Policy will look for new changes to the policy. This defaults to 90 minutes for workstations and member servers, and 2 minutes for domain controllers.

- *Filter list*: This is a list of filters you've defined that IPSec will use to look for a particular subset of inbound or outbound network traffic that should be secured. Once the policy finds a packet that matches a specific filter you've created, it will take a particular filter action in response to the packet. A filter list can contain one or multiple individual filters, but each filter list can only be associated with one filter action.

- *Filter action*: Like it sounds, this dictates what IPSec will actually do with a packet that matches the criteria of a particular filter list. The possible filter actions available are **Block**, **Permit**, or **Negotiate Security**. **Negotiate Security** is the default, and you can specify one or more authentication methods that should be used to secure traffic.

- *Authentication methods*: You can specify one or more authentication methods to secure traffic, and place them in an order of preference if you've listed more than one. You can use Kerberos version 5 protocol for authentication, certificates from a Certification Authority (CA), or a preshared IPSec key if you have clients that require it. (Though I don't recommend this last one because it's a relatively weak security approach compared to the other two, since the preshared key gets stored in plaintext.)

- *IPSec rule*: A rule defines a combination of policy, filter list, and filter action that will determine how IPSec responds to traffic encountered by a machine on your network.

- *Tunnel endpoint*: Specifies whether you're using transport or tunnel mode, and the IP address of the tunnel endpoint if it's the latter.

- *Connection type*: Specifies whether this rule will apply to LAN-based communications, remote access connections, or both.

You'll create an IPSec policy within a Group Policy Object to assign it to every machine in a site, domain, or Organizational Unit (OU). Within the Group Policy Editor, simply navigate to **Computer Configuration ➤ Windows Settings ➤ Security Settings ➤ IP Security Policies**. Three IPSec policies are created within Active Directory by default:

- *Client (Respond Only)*: Machines configured with this policy will only use IPSec to encrypt packets if they're communicating with a machine that specifically requests it. In all other cases, communications will remain unencrypted.

- *Server (Request Security)*: Machines configured with this policy will request secure communications from any machine that contacts them. But if the remote machine refuses, this policy will still allow unsecured communications to take place.

- *Secure Server (Require Security)*: This is for a high-security environment. A machine configured this way will request secure communications from any machine contacting it. It's important to note that both the Server and Secure Server policies will allow unsecured *incoming* traffic in order to support clients configured with the Client (Respond Only) policy. The difference between this policy and Server (Request Security) is that this will secure *all* outgoing traffic, not just traffic that's sent to clients that support it.

You can assign one of these policies to your domain computers, or you can create a new policy by following the steps listed here. Keep in mind that you can have only one IPSec policy configured for a domain at any one time. To create a new IPSec policy for your domain, follow these steps:

1. Right-click IP Security Policies and select **Create IP Security Policy**. Click **Next** to bypass the initial **Welcome** screen.

2. Give your policy a name and a description, and then click **Next**.

3. The next screen gives you the option to activate the Default Response rule. The Default Response rule will try to enable secure communications with any machine requesting a connection, even if that machine doesn't fall under the parameters of the rule you're creating manually. It's usually a good idea to leave this enabled unless you're supporting a lot of downlevel clients that don't speak IPSec. Unlike other IPSec rules, you can only modify the security and authentication methods used by the Default Response rule, not the action that the rule will take: because it's the default rule, it will only use the Negotiate filter action. Click **Next** to continue.

4. Assuming that you activate the Default Response rule, the next screen will ask you to specify the authentication method that the Default Response rule should use. As I mentioned previously, you can use the Kerberos version 5 authentication protocol, certificates from a Windows Certificate Authority, or a preshared IPSec key. If you use certificates for authentication, you can specify the CA, as well some optional settings. Click **Next** to continue. There are also some optional settings that you can specify for certificate authentication, which include the following:

- **Exclude the CA Name from the Certificate Request**: You should enable this if your Public Key Infrastructure (PKI) certificates will be transmitted over the Internet, to protect your internal network structure from being revealed to malicious outsiders.

- **Enable Certificate to Account Mapping**: Use this if you have a PKI set up to distribute certificates to your Active Directory user and computer accounts.

At this point, you've successfully created a basic IPSec policy. You're probably going to want to configure more settings than this, though, so the **You're done!** screen has the **Edit Properties** option enabled by default when you click **Finish**. You'll see the screen shown in Figure 5-1.

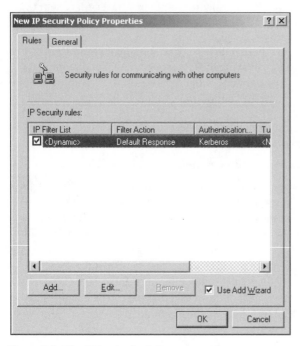

Figure 5-1. *The IPSec Default Response rule*

Notice that the only IPSec rule that's listed is the Default Response rule. To create a new rule, click **Add**, and use the following steps:

1. Click **Next** to bypass the initial **Welcome** screen. Your first question involves IP tunneling: if you need to configure IPSec in tunneling mode, this is where you'll specify the endpoint of the tunnel on the opposite end of the connection. If you're using IPSec in transport mode, just hit **Next** to continue.

2. Next you'll configure whether you want the IPSec encryption to apply to all networks, the Local Area Network (LAN) only, or to remote access connections only. In most cases, you'll want to apply your IPSec policy to all network connections unless you've got a performance or backwards-compatibility issue that's preventing you from doing so. Click **Next** to continue.

3. Select the IP filter list that this policy should apply to. The default filter lists are All ICMP Traffic and All IP Traffic. If you've created any additional filter lists, they'll be shown here as well. Let's create a new filter list to look for traffic on TCP port 6667, since that's one of the default ports for the Internet Relay Chat (IRC) protocol and a well-known transport mechanism for worms and other malicious code. Click **Add** to create a new IP filter list.

4. Now we need to create a new IP filter. First give it a name and a description, and then get rid of the check mark next to **Use Add Wizard**. (I think we're wizard-ed out by now, and would rather just get down to actually configuring IPSec.) Click **Add** again to configure a specific IP filter. You'll see the screen shown in Figure 5-2.

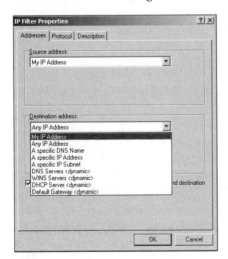

Figure 5-2. *IP filter properties*

5. When you're configuring an IP filter, you have available three tabs in the IP Filter Properties dialog box: **Addresses**, **Protocol**, and **Description**. As you can see in Figure 5-2, you have a number of possibilities to configure the source and destination IP addresses. You can also decide whether the filter should be mirrored, that is, applied to both incoming and outgoing traffic. So if you have a policy that's applying to traffic going from **Any** IP address to **My** IP address, the **Mirrored** setting would create a second policy that would apply to traffic going from **My** IP address to **Any** IP address. Your options for configuring an IP filter list are as follows:

- **My IP Address** (the IP address of the computer applying the policy)
- **Any IP Address**
- **A specific DNS Name**
- **A specific IP Address**
- **A specific IP subnet**
- **DNS Servers <dynamic>**
- **WINS Servers <dynamic>**
- **DHCP Servers <dynamic>**
- **Default Gateway <dynamic>**

■**Caution** The last four choices are configured dynamically based on the configuration of the local machine. They're new to Windows Server 2003, and can only be applied to computers running the Windows Server 2003 operating system.

---

6. The **Protocol** tab will let you choose the specific IP protocol that this filter should apply to. You can specify a particular source and destination port, or leave it at the default of **Any IP Address**.

7. Once you've finished configuring the IP filter, click **OK** until you're back at the screen from step 3.

8. Your next step will be to configure a filter action. Select the IP filter list you just created, and click **Next**.

9. Here you'll configure the filter action. By default, you can choose **Permit**, **Request Security**, and **Require Security**. You can create a new filter action to *block* traffic, or you can click **Edit** to modify one of the default actions. When customizing any Negotiate filter action, you can specify which security method your clients should use as follows:

- **Authentication Header (AH)**: For authentication only
- **Encapsulating Security Payload (ESP)**: For both authentication and encryption
- **Custom**: To create a customized security method

10. Your final step will be to select the authentication method that this policy should use. Your choices here are identical to the choices for the Default Response rule: Kerberos, certificates, and a preshared key.

At this point you've configured a fully functional IPSec policy. Click **OK** until you get back to the list of IP Security Policies in the Group Policy Editor. One final step that some people forget is that you still need to *assign* the policy within the GPO in order for it to take effect. (Windows isn't going to be a mind reader here, unlike the joy I'm having trying to convince Word that I don't need its help configuring my numbered lists right now!) Simply right-click the IPSec policy you just created, and click **Assign**. The policy will take effect the next time that Group Policy gets refreshed, or you can run **gpupdate** from the command line to enforce the changes right away.

Managing IPSec from the Command Line

A new feature in Windows Server 2003 is the ability to manipulate your IPSec settings from the command line using the **netsh** utility. You can use this to automate IPSec configuration for your network, to access some advanced IPSec functionality that you can't get to using the GUI, and to use in a disaster recovery setting so that you can re-create your security configuration quickly. You can either work with **netsh** interactively, so that you're entering one command or submenu at a time, or by entering an entire command at once.

To start working with **netsh** commands that are specific to IPSec, just type **netsh -c ipsec** at a command prompt. This will give you access to a number of other menus and options to configure IPSec on your network, using **netsh** interactive mode. To execute an entire command at once and eliminate the need to navigate the different menus within interactive mode, just eliminate the -c and enter the entire command string at once. I'll list some of the more useful **netsh** options for you here, and you should check out the URL in the "Additional Resources" section of this chapter for a link to the full **netsh** syntax. These examples will assume that we're working in interactive mode, since it makes things easier to read on the page.

■**Note** **netsh** is one of those really powerful tools that you should definitely become familiar with if you're interested in securing your network with IPSec. The number of available options can be a bit intimidating, but just start with the list here and look up additional commands as you need them. Just like with VBScript, even a little bit of **netsh** knowledge will make you a much better administrator.

Start by typing **netsh -c ipsec** at a command prompt. You'll be taken to the top-level IPSec interactive menu, and you'll see the following prompt:

```
netsh ipsec>
```

From here, you can enter one of the following subcontexts:

- **static**: This will take you to static mode, which you'll use to create, modify, and assign IPSec policies, without immediately affecting the configuration of the active policy.

- **dynamic**: Commands issued from the dynamic mode will immediately affect the active IPSec policy, except for some commands that will require you to restart the IPSec Service for the changes to take effect.

Let's move to the static context to create an IPSec policy from the command line. Just like when you're using the GUI, you need to create a policy, add a filter list to the policy, and then add individual filters and filter actions to the policy. We'll do each of these in order. From the netsh -c ipsec static command prompt, type **static** and press Enter:

```
netsh ipsec static>
```

From here, you use the add policy command, which uses the add policy name syntax shown next. This command needs a number of parameters at the command line that you'll see listed after the actual code:

```
add policy name = Policy name  [description =
    Policy Description (this is optional)]
```

Now that you've created your IPSec policy, you need to create a filter list. The add filterlist command just creates a blank filter list using the following syntax:

```
add filterlist name=Filter List Name [description=
    Description (this is optional)]
```

Next you need to add one or more filters to the filter list you just created. As you can probably guess, you'll use the add filter command, which takes the following syntax:

```
add filter filterlist= srcaddr= dstaddr= [description=][protocol=]
[mirrored=] [srcmask=][dstmask=][srcport=] [dstport=]
```

To add a filter from the command line, you'll need the following required information:

- *Source address for the filter*: This can be an IP address, DNS name, or server type (WINS, DNS, DHCP, or gateway). You can also use Me for the **My IP Address** option, and Any for the **Any IP Address** option.

- *Destination address of the filter*: This has with the same options as the source address.

- *Filter list*: This is the name of the filter list that you're adding this filter to.

You'll probably also want to specify at least some of the following optional information:

- *Description*: This refers to a description of the filter list.

- *Protocol*: Use this if you're specifying a particular protocol to be filtered. You can use ANY, ICMP, TCP, UDP, RAW, or a numeric port number.

- *Mirrored*: Use yes to create two identical filters for inbound and out-bound traffic, no if the filter should only work in one direction.

- *Source subnet mask, or* srcmask: Use this to specify the subnet mask of the source addresses being used. You can use the subnet mask syntax, like 255.255.255.0, or a CIDR prefix like 24 to specify the default Class C subnet mask.

- *Destination subnet mask, or* dstmask: This uses the same syntax as srcmask.

- *Source port and destination port*: Use srcport=*Some number* and dstport=*Some number* if you're filtering specific ports in either the source or destination.

Now that you have a filter list created, you need to specify the action that will take place when IPSec encounters any packets that meet the filter requirements. The add filteraction command takes the following common parameters:

```
add filteraction name = Filter Action Name [description =
    Descripton Name (optional) ][inpass=] [soft=][action=]
```

- inpass =: Do you want to allow incoming packets to be unsecured, but require security when replying? This parameter, which is optional, takes either yes or no and defaults to no if it's not specified.

- soft =: Specifies whether to use unsecured communications if you're working with a downlevel client that doesn't speak IPSec, or if IPSec fails for any reason. This optional parameter, which takes either yes or no, defaults to no.

- action =: This parameter takes the values permit, block, and negotiate. It defaults to negotiate to secure IP traffic that matches the filter list.

Now you're in the homestretch. All that's left is to create a rule that ties the policy, filter list, and filter action together. The add rule command takes the following required parameters:

```
add rule name = Rule Name  policy = Policy Name
     filterlist = Filter List name  filteraction = Filter Action Name
```

■**Note** I intentionally glossed over a number of optional parameters in each of these steps so that you could get the overall idea of how to configure an IPSec policy using **netsh**. You can customize these command strings to a pretty granular level, including specifying authentication methods, and whether to use Perfect Forward Secrecy (PFS) to generate the master key used by IPSec.

To review, here are the basic command sequences to create an IPSec policy using IPSec interactive mode:

```
C:\>netsh -c ipsec
netsh ipsec>static
netsh ipsec static>add policy name = Netsh Policy assign = yes
netsh ipsec static>add filterlist name = Netsh Filterlist
netsh ipsec static>add filter filterlist = Netsh Filterlist
     srcaddr = ANY dstaddr = ME mirrored = NO
netsh ipsec static>add filteraction name = SecureAll action =
     Negotiate
netsh ipsec static>add rule name = SecureTraffic policy = Netsh
     Filterlist = Netsh Filteraction = SecureAll
```

Some other useful **netsh** command-line tricks include show all, which will display the configuration information for all of your IPSec policies, rules, filter lists, and filter actions. You should also make frequent use of exportpolicy and importpolicy, which will let you save and restore IPSec policy information. This is particularly useful in a disaster recovery situation, and you should export your IPSec policy information before you make any production changes in case something really heinous happens and you need to roll things back to keep people from screaming at you.

IPSEC: NEW AND IMPROVED FOR 2003

Windows Server 2003 has enabled a number of useful IPSec features that weren't available in Windows 2000 Server. This is great if you're running a pure 2003 environment, of course. But if you're still supporting a mix of 2000, 2003, and XP clients, you should test out these features in a test lab before you deploy them on your production network. (And, of course, you can use the `exportpolicy` and `importpolicy` options in **netsh** to back up and restore policy settings quite easily.)

The most noticeable change is the ability to use **netsh** to manage your IPSec policies so well, but you also now have the IPSec Security Monitor available as an MMC snap-in. The snap-in allows you to monitor IPSec information for local and remote computers, and view details about the active IPSec policies.

IPSec also improves the way a machine behaves on startup, so that IPSec is up and running before the network connection becomes active: no more getting hit by an Internet worm in the time it takes you to boot the machine and get to Windows Update! (You're actually better off using Software Update Services, a free download from the Microsoft web site that allows you to centralize the patch management process for your internal clients and servers.) And this won't infringe on your clients' startup, either, since you can configure exemptions so that they can still get to DNS and DHCP servers to obtain IP addressing information. You can also configure a *persistent* IPSec policy that will stay in place even if the Active Directory policy isn't reachable, due to a network outage or some other issue.

Another big security improvement is that IPSec has removed most of the default traffic exemptions that existed in 2000. In 2000, there were a number of IP packets that IPSec wouldn't process, including broadcast, multicast, and Kerberos traffic. In 2003, the only type of traffic that doesn't get IPSec applied to it is Internet Key Exchange (IKE) traffic, since this is what's used to set up IPSec communications in the first place.

Strengthening TCP/IP Stack Security

Let's look at some other ways that you can strengthen TCP/IP stack security for your domain controllers. Now, a number of these changes involve editing the Windows Registry, and I'm sure you know that I can't talk about modifying the Registry without issuing the following warning.

■**Caution** Improperly editing the Windows Registry can lead to system instability, or the inability to start your operating system. Be sure you have a known-good backup of your operating system and system state, and attempt these changes in a test environment before rolling them out to your production servers. Be especially mindful of Registry changes between Windows 2000 and Windows Server 2003.

Now that I have that out of the way, let's get started. One of the first changes you can make is to protect your server against what's called a *SYN Flood attack*. SYN Flood attacks try to take advantage of the way that the TCP protocol sets up a network connection, which is by using a three-step "handshake." Basically, you have two machines that want to set up a TCP connection, to transfer files using FTP. Machine 1 sends a SYN (for synchronize) packet to Machine 2, effectively saying, "Are you there?" Machine 2 sends an SYN/ACK (for synchronization acknowledgement) packet back to Machine 1, basically saying, "Yes, I'm here. Are you ready to start?" Finally, Machine 1 sends an ACK back to Machine 2, saying, "Okay, we're both ready. Let's start."

But what happens if some part of this three-way handshake doesn't occur? If Machine 2 receives a SYN packet, sends a SYN/ACK packet, and then doesn't receive the final ACK packet, the connection is in a *half-open* state. Machine 2 will leave this half-open connection active for a time, in case Machine 1 just got delayed and will be sending the final ACK packet along soon. So a SYN Flood attack works by an attacker sending thousands of SYN packets to a target machine, but never sending the final ACK. As a result, the target machine is left maintaining thousands of these half-open connections, and each connection requires a certain amount of memory to keep open. This will eventually lead to Denial of Service when the target machine's memory gets completely taken up by maintaining these half-open connections that are simply never going to be completed.

Hardening the TCP/IP Stack in Windows 2000

Windows 2000 includes SYN Flooding protection to help you avoid this kind of attack. In Windows 2000, you specify certain thresholds for the maximum number of half-open connections that a server can have at any time. If these thresholds are exceeded, the server will consider itself "under attack," and will start closing these half-open connections much more quickly. You can modify any of the following Registry keys, all of which are DWORD values in the HKEY_LOCAL_MACHINE\SYSTEM\CurrentControlSet\Services\Tcpip\Parameters node:

- *SynAttackProtect*: This is the key that causes Windows 2000 to trigger an attack response if certain thresholds are exceeded. The recommended value here is **2**.

- *TcpMaxHalfOpen*: Establishes the threshold for the maximum number of half-open connections a server can maintain without considering itself under attack. The recommended value is **500**, but you can set it anywhere from 100 to 0xFFFF.

- *TcpMaxHalfOpenRetried*: Specifies the maximum number of half-open connections where a server has tried to resend the SYN/ACK packet at least once. You can set this anywhere from 80 to 65535; a good starting point is **400**.

■Note Windows Server 2003 handles these changes a bit differently, so we'll look at hardening the TCP/IP stack for 2003 in the next section.

Another type of attack is an *ICMP Redirect* attack. ICMP is the protocol that a host uses to respond to **ping** and **tracert**, and is how Windows 2000 and Windows Server 2003 detect slow links when processing Group Policies. Occasionally, routers will need to redirect ICMP packets if they have multiple routes between hosts and one of the routes is unavailable. But malicious users can exploit this by forging redirection packets, thereby attempting to redirect your legitimate network traffic away from where it's supposed to go, and possibly even routing it to a malicious host. You can protect against this by verifying that the following DWORD value exists under the HKLM\System\CurrentControlSet\Services\Tcpip\ Parameters key:

- *EnableICMPRedirect*: A setting of **0** will disable ICMP Redirection from a Windows 2000 server. **1** will enable it.

In most cases, you'll also want to disable *IP Source Routing*. This is a feature that allows the machine that's sending a packet to see the path that it took to get to its destination. Now, this is a normal part of the TCP/IP protocol, but once again malicious users have found a way to exploit it to bad ends. Attackers will use this feature to attempt to "spoof" IP packets; that is, to attempt to insert packets into your network by fooling your routers and switches into thinking that they actually originated from within your network. You can disable this feature by adding the DisableIPSourceRouting DWORD value to the HKLM\System\CurrentControlSet\Services\Tcpip\ Parameters key, and setting it to **2** to disable IP Source Routing on your network.

Hardening the TCP/IP Stack in Windows Server 2003

Windows Server 2003 makes this a lot less scary by adding many of the settings from the last section to the Group Policy and Security Templates MMC snap-ins, so that you can modify these changes using a GUI interface rather than futzing around inside the Registry. However, because these are still advanced settings, you'll need to edit an .INF file on the 2003 machine in order to enable the settings in the MMC.

In order to access these settings via Group Policy, you'll need to edit the SCEREGVL.INF file that is stored in the %SYSTEMROOT%\INF directory on a Windows Server 2003 server. There are two sections that you'll need to add information to: the [Register Registry Values] section, and the [Strings] section. Once you've made these changes, you'll need to reregister the Security Configuration Editor DLL by typing **regsvr32 scecli.dll** at the command line.

■Note You'll find a link to the actual text that you'll add to the SCEREGVL.INF file in the "Additional Resources" section at the end of the chapter; the text is freely available to cut and paste into Notepad from the Microsoft website.

Once you've edited the .INF file, you'll have a number of new entries available in the Computer Configuration\Windows Settings\Security Settings\ Security Options node of the Group Policy Editor. To enable protection against SYN attacks, ICMP Redirection, and IP Source Routing on a 2003 server, simply enable the following settings in a GPO linked to a site, domain, or OU:

- **MSS: Allow ICMP redirects to override OSPF generated routes**: Set to **Disabled**.

- **MSS: Syn attack protection level (protects against DoS)**: Set to **Connections time out sooner if a SYN attack is detected**.

- **MSS: IP source routing protection level (protects against packet spoofing)**: Set to **Highest protection, source routing is completely disabled**.

Securing Domain Controllers

In addition to setting up IPSec to secure IP traffic in your Active Directory domain, you can take a number of steps to specifically increase the security of your domain controllers. Since every DC in Active Directory contains a fully editable copy of the AD database, maintaining the security of these machines is absolutely paramount. If an attacker gains any type of administrative access to a domain controller, you're pretty much faced with starting everything over from scratch, because you can never really be sure that your directory information hasn't been irrevocably compromised. Since this isn't the type of scenario that *anyone* wants to deal with, the best way to avoid it is to prevent it from happening in the first place. In this section, we'll look at specific ways that you can improve the security of your Active Directory database, as well as the domain controllers that are hosting it.

I'm going to dispense with a detailed discussion of the most obvious tips right off the bat, since I'm sure you're using them already anyway, but I'd be remiss if I didn't mention them briefly. When you're configuring and administering a domain controller, make sure that you've taken care of these basic security essentials:

- *Physical security*: There isn't a firewall or Registry fix in the world that can protect your Active Directory installation if the only thing a hacker needs to do to compromise a domain controller is to walk up to it and reboot it with a boot disk. If an attacker can physically get his hands on a machine, he can wreak all kinds of havoc: deleting files, copying sensitive information, changing configuration settings, or even just shutting it down to prevent your users from accessing it. Because of this, your domain controllers need to be kept in a secure and controlled location that only network administrators have access to. Now, this can get tricky if you're working with branch offices that have a DC deployed locally without onsite support. But even in these cases, you need to make sure that that remote server is physically secured in a controlled area. If this sounds more like a policy measure than a technical one, that's because it is: you need to impress on all levels of management that your domain controllers are invaluable physical assets that need to be protected accordingly.

- *Use the NTFS file system*: This one should be a no-brainer, but I'll mention it anyway. The NTFS file system provides infinitely better security than the FAT or FAT32 alternatives, since the latter will restrict you to relying on share-level security. If someone gains access to the local machine or otherwise manages to bypass security on a file share, FAT and FAT32 provide no local file system security. NTFS provides this, as well as letting you use more advanced features like EFS file encryption. You should format or convert all of the hard drives on your domain controllers to the NTFS file system in order to provide the best security possible.

- *Use strong passwords for administrative accounts*: Since these accounts are literally the keys to your Active Directory kingdom, be sure that any of your Domain Admin and Enterprise Admin accounts use strong passwords. If anything, I'd recommend using a pass *phrase* for even better security—instead of trying to come up with a 7-character password with a bunch of nonalpha or special characters, use a 15-character or higher pass phrase that will create even better security. Mathematically speaking, a 15-character pass phrase is almost unbreakable by even the most powerful of modern computing hardware, and your admins will have a much easier time remembering something like "MyFavoriteMortalKombatCharacterIsJohnnyCage". Another advantage to a longer pass phrase is that it disables the LM hash, which is a legacy Windows function that makes it so easy for those hacker tools like L0PHTCrack to break your passwords. We'll talk more about disabling the LM hash for the other users on your network in the next section.

- *Install and update antivirus software and security patches regularly:* Most antivirus software vendors release new virus definitions daily, or at least several times a week. You should have antivirus software running on your domain controllers, and check for new AV definitions on a regular basis. As for installing security patches and updates? I know that some admins are skittish about installing patches as soon as they're released, since we've all been bitten by the occasional "fix" that ends up breaking some critical application or even the operating system itself. (Anyone remember the first release of Windows NT 4.0 Service Pack 6, which broke Lotus Notes installations because it affected the TCP/IP stack? I was working in a team of Windows and Notes administrators when that happened, and the hue and cry when we realized what was going on is certainly not something I'd want to repeat.) But network attacks based on security flaws are being released on the Internet at a rapid pace, so we really don't have the luxury of just waiting around for a few days or weeks to see if a new patch is really working. In the time that you wait around to install a new patch, your server could have already been compromised by the vulnerability the patch was meant to fix. Ideally, you should have some sort of test server set up that mirrors your production hardware and software, so that you can test software updates when they get released. But for those of us who don't have the budget to set up such an elaborate test environment, I will admit that even I have become an advocate of "patch first, ask questions later"— just be sure to take a backup of your operating system and system state data so that you've got something to roll back to.

Note If you don't have the budget for a full-fledged test lab, you can create a decent approximation with "virtual machines" configured using Microsoft Virtual PC or VMWare.

- *Disable the Administrator account:* Since this account can't be deleted on a Windows server, it creates a common attack point for attackers trying to break into a Windows machine. While you can't delete the Administrator account outright, you are able to disable and rename it. Once you've renamed the original account, you can then create a "dummy" account with the name Administrator, but with no access to your Active Directory network. Granted, this recommendation will only foil the least sophisticated of network attacks, but it's still a good place to start.

- *Move the Active Directory system files to an alternate location*: Just like renaming the Administrator account, this is only a small step for security since it will only thwart the most casual of attackers. But even if it stops one potential security breach on your network, I'd say it's worth the few minutes of effort. By moving the NTDS.DIT file and its associated log files out of the C:\WINDOWS\NTDS directory, you'll be outsmarting an attacker who is specifically targeting that default location. If you move them to a separate disk controller from the rest of the operating system, you'll also get a performance boost for your troubles. To move the Active Directory files, you'll need to do the following:

  1. Reboot the server in Directory Services Restore Mode, using the [F8] menu on startup.

  2. Go to a command prompt and type **ntdsutil**.

  3. From **ntdsutil**, type **files**.

  4. From the files menu, type **move db to** *driveletter:\path*, and **move logs to** *driveletter:\path*. Reboot the server normally, and you're done.

- *Disable unnecessary services and components*: This is pretty simple—if you're not going to be using a particular service, set its startup mode to Disabled. If you're not going to use a Windows component like SMTP on a particular server, either don't install it to begin with or else uninstall the application that is using the service through Add/Remove programs. Windows Server 2003 makes this a lot easier by not installing much of anything during the initial setup, but the pre–Service Pack 4 Windows 2000 installation CDs will still install IIS by default. This is a big part of how worms like Code Red and Nimda happened: you had server admins finding their machines compromised when some of them didn't even realize that they were running IIS. Use Table 5-1 as a starting point to determine which services you can and can't live without on a domain controller.

Table 5-1. *Recommended Services for Domain Controllers (Partial)*

Service Name	Recommended Startup Mode	Comments
Alerter	Disabled	Disabled by default on Windows Server 2003, Automatic on Windows 2000. Used to send administrative alerts to users and computers on a LAN. In most cases, you'll find that you can live without this one.
Computer Browser	Automatic or Manual	Set to Manual if your clients don't need to use the Master Browser functionality to locate network resources.
DHCP Client	Manual	Your DCs should be using static IPs anyway. If you're using DHCP for domain controllers, obviously leave this set to Automatic startup.
DNS Client	Automatic	Leave this service enabled so that DNS resolution will function.
DNS Server	Automatic or Disabled	Automatic if your DC is running the DNS server service, Disabled if you're relying on third-party DNS, or if DNS is installed on a member server.
Fax	Disabled	Disable this service if your DC is not being used as a fax server.
IIS Admin Service	Disabled	Disabling IIS and IIS-related services on a DC will help reduce its exposure to network attacks.
Indexing Service	Disabled	Disable this service to prevent users from searching for sensitive files on your domain controller.
NetMeeting Remote Desktop Sharing	Disabled	Do you really want someone taking over your DC using NetMeeting? Terminal Services and Remote Desktop are much better alternatives for remote management, especially in Windows Server 2003 where you can connect directly to the console session.
Print Spooler	Disabled	Disable this service if you don't need to do any printing from your domain controller.
Secondary Logon	Automatic	Always enable this service to allow the **RUNAS** option, so that you can log on to a workstation using an ordinary user account and only use administrative privileges for specific tasks.

Service Name	Recommended Startup Mode	Comments
Simple Mail Transfer Protocol (SMTP)	Disabled	Only enable this service if you need to use SMTP-based replication between Active Directory sites. It should be disabled in all other cases.
Telnet	Disabled	Disable this service to prevent anyone from attaching to the Telnet server on your domain controller.

Configuring User Rights

User rights control what different users and groups of users can do, both on and *to* your domain controllers. You can configure user rights centrally using Group Policy, from the Computer Configuration\Windows Settings\ Security Settings\User Rights Assignment node. To maintain a secure environment, configure a GPO in the Default Domain Controllers Policy (or another GPO linked to the Domain Controllers OU) as follows:

- **Access this computer from the network**: Should only be permitted for Administrators, Authenticated Users, and Enterprise Domain Controllers in Windows Server 2003. This will prevent nondomain users from gaining access to your domain controllers. There are a few exceptions to this that I'll cover in a few minutes, but this configuration is appropriate for most Active Directory environments.

- **Log on locally**: Should only be granted for the Administrators group. By default, this right is given to Administrators, Account Operators, Backup Operators, Print Operators, and Server Operators. Now, if you make extensive use of the Account Operators or Server Operators groups, you may want to include them as well. But there's almost no earthly reason why Backup Operators or Print Operators should be allowed to log on locally to the domain controllers in your environment.

- **Enable computer and user accounts to be trusted for delegation**: This setting allows an Administrator or another user to change the **Trusted for Delegation** setting on a user or computer object in Active Directory, particularly to configure a service account. By default, this right is undefined in Windows 2000 and Windows Server 2003. For best security, restrict this to Administrators only.

- **Load and unload device drivers**: By default, this right is configured for Administrators and Print Operators. But unless you're configuring printer shares on your domain controllers (and I really hope you're separating them out to a file server instead), you can safely remove Print Operators from the list so that only Administrators have this right.

- **Shut down the system**: Nearly identical to **Log on Locally**, this defaults to Administrators, Server Operators, Backup Operators, and Print Operators. And, once again, I can't think of a good reason why a Backup Operator or a Print Operator would need to shut down a domain controller in most environments. Leave this to the Administrators, and to the Server Operators if you use that group a lot.

■**Note** Unlike password policies, account lockout policies, and Kerberos policies, you can configure multiple user rights assignments within a domain. This means it's simple to configure a stricter set of user rights for domain controllers than for member servers or workstations on your network. The trick is in ensuring that your domain controllers aren't being used for other functions that can compromise their security. I once found myself stuck supporting an application that had been installed on a domain controller that required all users accessing it to have the **Log on locally** right. And since the app was running on a domain controller, I therefore had to grant that permission to the Domain Users group. You can probably imagine how unhappy that made me, and it should serve as a reminder to plan your server usage carefully so that you can avoid finding yourself in a similar situation.

PROTECTING PHYSICAL SECURITY WITH SYSKEY

You can improve the physical security of your 2000 and 2003 domain controllers by using the **Syskey** utility, which sets an extra level of encryption on the Active Directory database. Once you've enabled **Syskey**, you'll need to provide either a password or a floppy disk containing the encryption information in order to boot or reboot a domain controller. This can be great for increasing the security of domain controllers that aren't under your direct physical control, like DCs housed in remote branch offices. By requiring this **Syskey** information whenever a machine reboots, you can be much more confident that a malicious user hasn't compromised your machine. But this is one of those security measures that you really need to weigh the pros and cons of before you implement it. By using **Syskey**, you're effectively requiring user intervention whenever you reboot a domain controller, either to insert the **Syskey** floppy disk or to enter the password.

This is great from a security perspective since you know that all reboots are happening in a controlled manner. But it can be a real nuisance if you find that you need to reboot a remote DC at 2 a.m. on a Saturday and can't find anyone from the branch office to go to the office and enter the password. (Or even if you *do* find someone to take care of it, I can't imagine that the conversation would be all that pleasant.) You're also running the risk of having the personnel in the remote office simply leaving the **Syskey** password written on a clipboard next to the server, which will render the security of **Syskey** pretty much useless. Another potential drawback of **Syskey** is that if you lose the **Syskey** floppy or forget the password, you won't be able to reboot that domain controller again—your only option will be to restore the system state to a point before **Syskey** was enabled, or rebuild the machine entirely.

Now, it may seem like I've spent this whole time telling you what's wrong with **Syskey**. But the utility is incredibly helpful in creating a high-security environment for your domain controllers by encrypting the Active Directory database, as long as you're aware of the caveats that go along with its use. If the trade-off between security and convenience is one that you're willing to live with, **Syskey** can be a valuable tool in your security arsenal.

Enabling Restricted Groups

While your Active Directory installation as a whole is in need of protecting in and of itself, you need to be especially careful in ensuring that only authorized users have administrative access to your network. Any hacker's ultimate goal will be to create her own administrative account on a network, thereby allowing her unlimited access to a compromised network. Windows 2000 and Windows Server 2003 allow you to configure certain restricted groups on your network, so that you can control membership to sensitive groups like Domain Admins, Enterprise Admins, or the local Administrators group on a workstation. The Restricted Groups setting works by checking the membership of the Restricted Group whenever Group Policy refreshes: every 90 minutes for a workstation, every 2 minutes for a domain controller. When the GPO refreshes, any authorized members of the restricted group that have been removed will be re-added. Any *unauthorized* members of the restricted group will be removed. So if a junior administrator accidentally adds an ordinary user account to a sensitive group like Schema Admins or removes an existing administrator from the Domain Admins group, the Restricted Groups setting in Group Policy would restore sensitive group memberships to the appropriate state.

To configure Restricted Groups, navigate to the Computer Configuration\ Windows Settings\Security Settings\Restricted Groups node of a GPO linked to your domain. By default, there aren't any Restricted Groups configured in a 2000 or 2003 domain. When you click **Add Group**, you can configure the settings shown in Figure 5-3.

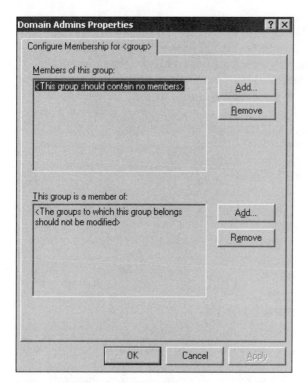

Figure 5-3. *Configuring a Restricted Group*

As you can see, you have two settings you can configure for each Restricted Group: **Members of this group** and **This group is a member of**. You'll enable the users and groups that should belong to the Restricted group from the "Members . . ." pane. Likewise, you'll configure the groups that the Restricted Group should be a member *of* in the ". . . member of" pane.

■**Note** You can also create a Restricted Groups policy within a Security Template that can be applied to multiple computers. From the Security Templates MMC snap-in: 1) Open the Security Templates console; 2) In the console tree, click **Restricted Groups** (**Security Templates ➤ Template path folder ➤ Security template ➤ Restricted Groups**).

Configuring Authentication Protocols

In addition to securing your domain controllers themselves, you should also take some time to configure how your network clients are accessing your DCs, and what authentication protocol they're using to do so. If you're running a pure Windows 2000/2003/XP environment and you'll never ever have a single downlevel client attempt to access any Active Directory resources, then you're set: these three operating systems will use Kerberos version 5 all the way. But if even one single downlevel client attempts to connect to your domain controllers (and I'm including machines belonging to potential intruders, mind you), then you need to be concerned with how LM and NTLM is configured on your network.

The LAN Manager, or LM, authentication protocol is a legacy (read: really, *really* old) protocol that was used by Windows 95 and Windows 98 machines to connect to LAN Manager networks in the very earliest days of Windows networking. Network operating systems have certainly improved since then, and newer server OSs allow for much more secure authentication like NTLM, NTLM version 2, and Kerberos. But the Microsoft stance for the longest time has been that it's always allowed for "lowest common denominator" authentication. That is, most Windows server operating systems have been configured to be backwards-compatible to LM authentication even if your environment doesn't require it, because of the continued prevalence of Windows 95 and 98 machines.

The problem here is that, at this point, LM authentication is just plain *broken*. It uses really weak encryption, only allows for 14-character passwords, and your users' passwords get stored in Active Directory as an *LM hash* that can be easily cracked by any number of freeware utilities available on the Internet. But despite this, Windows 2000 servers will still allow a remote computer to provide an authentication request using LM, which exposes your entire Active Directory database to attack.

So now we have two questions:

1. "Do I need to allow LM authentication on my network?"

   In almost every case, that answer is a definitive "No." Even if you're still supporting Windows 95 and/or 98 workstations, you can install the Active Directory Client Extensions to allow these older operating systems to use the newer and much more secure NTLM version 2 authentication protocol. And any NT 4.0 clients and servers will speak NTLM version 2 as well, as long as they're running Service Pack 4 or later.

■**Caution** In what might be the best decision to come out of Redmond in quite some time, Windows Server 2003 finally disables this default acceptance of LM authentication. So if you've just upgraded to 2003 and your 9x clients aren't able to connect to a domain controller, the Active Directory Client Extensions will probably fix them right up.

---

2. "If I don't need it, how can I turn it off?"

Disabling LM authentication is a three-step process. First you need to configure your network clients so that they'll only use NTLM version 2. And it's unfortunately not as simple as just installing the Directory Services Client Extensions (DSClient) or Service Pack 4 on NT. On your Windows 95 and 98 machines, you'll need to create the following Registry key and DWORD value after you've installed the Directory Services Client Extensions:

- HKEY_LOCAL_MACHINE\System\CurrentControlSet\Control\LSA

- HKLM\System\CurrentControlSet\Control\LSA\LMCompatibility, set to **3**

For your NT 4.0 machines, the LSA key is already in place, and you'll just need to create the LMCompatibilityLevel DWORD value. Set the DWORD value to **4** to reject LM and use NTLM and NTLM52, or set the value to **5** to reject both LM and NTLM and use only NTLM version 2.

Luckily, the process is much simpler for your Windows 2000, XP, and 2003 machines. Just edit a Group Policy Object that's linked to your domain, and enable the Computer Configuration\Windows Settings\Local Policies\ Security Options\Network Security: LAN Manager Authentication Level policy. Set this to one of the following values, though I recommend the second whenever possible:

- Send NTLMv2 response only\Refuse LM

- Send NTLMv2 response only\Refuse LM & NTLM

Once you've configured your clients to only use NTLM version 2, you need to disable the creation of LM hashes on your domain controllers. On Windows 2000, create the following key (not DWORD value): HKLM\System\ CurrentControlSet\Control\LSA\NoLMHash. In Windows 2003 and XP, enable the Computer Configuration\Windows Settings\Local Policies\ Security Options\Do not store LAN Manager hash value on next password change setting in Group Policy. And finally, you'll need to set all of your user accounts to change their passwords in order to clear out any LM hashes that are already stored within Active Directory.

Controlling Anonymous Access to Active Directory

Another cause for concern in securing Active Directory is in dealing with anonymous users accessing your AD database to retrieve usernames and other information. In some cases, you need to allow anonymous access to provide downlevel support for older operating systems or particular configurations. For example, if you are supporting any NT 4.0 RAS servers, these machines will need anonymous access to AD in order to determine whether users have permissions to establish a remote connection. Also, users logging in from clients running pre-Windows 2000 operating systems will need anonymous access enabled in order to set and change their user account passwords. To address this, you have the Pre-Windows 2000 Compatible Access security group, which is a Domain Local group on Windows 2000 and 2003 domain controllers. The Pre-Windows 2000 Compatible Access group has read access to the entire Active Directory database, and by default, the Everyone group is a member of this group on servers that are running at the Windows 2000 mixed functional level.

■**Note** The Windows Server 2003 Active Directory installation defaults to **Permissions compatible only with Windows 2000 or Windows Server 2003 servers**, which will restrict anonymous access on a 2003 domain.

If you're managing an existing domain that already has Pre-Windows 2000 Compatible Access enabled, you need to figure out whether you actually need to allow this level of anonymous access or if it can be safely eliminated. If all of your domain controllers are running Windows 2000 or higher, and if you aren't supporting NT 4.0 RAS servers, you can remove the Everyone group from the Pre-Windows 2000 Compatible Access group without suffering any adverse effects. In Windows Server 2003, you'll also want to configure the following two settings in Group Policy:

- Set Computer Configuration\Windows Settings\Security Settings\ Local Policies\Security Options\Network access: Do not allow anonymous enumeration of Security Accounts Manager (SAM) accounts and shares to **Enabled**. This will prevent anonymous users from obtaining a list of your Active Directory user accounts and using it to orchestrate password attacks against your domain.

- Set Computer Configuration\Windows Settings\Security Settings\ Local Policies\Security Options\Network access: Let Everyone permissions apply to anonymous users to be **Disabled**. This will avert any security headaches if you inadvertently configure the Everyone group with inappropriate permissions to any of your Active Directory resources. If this setting is **Enabled**, anonymous users will have the same permissions as those applied to the Everyone group.

To restrict anonymous access to a Windows 2000 domain, navigate to the Computer **Configuration ➤ Security Settings ➤ Local Policies ➤ Security Options** node. Double-click **Additional restrictions for anonymous connections**, and then select **No access without explicit anonymous permissions**.

Caution Be careful when combining these two settings in a mixed Windows 2000/2003 environment! Windows 2000 Server and Windows Server 2003 use different (and somewhat incompatible) Registry settings to effect the changes listed here. If you have a mix of Windows 2000 and Windows Server 2003 domain controllers, create separate OUs for them, and create a GPO for each one, using the appropriate operating system.

Creating an Audit Policy

Even after you've configured your domain controllers to be as secure as possible, you'll still want to configure auditing of your domain resources to be sure that no internal users or external attackers are attempting to access or alter information inappropriately. You can configure an audit policy within a Group Policy Object for any container in Active Directory; for now we'll concentrate on creating a policy to monitor your domain controllers and Active Directory in particular. When you enable auditing in Active Directory, you'll get an entry in the Security Log of the affected domain controller recording *what* action was performed, *who* performed the action, and *when* the action took place. (If you audit for both successful and failed actions, you'll also get entries when someone *tried* to perform an action but couldn't.) Using auditing, you can monitor the following types of events on your Active Directory network:

- Account Logon Events
- Logon Events
- Account Management
- Directory Service Access
- Policy Change
- System Events
- Process Tracking
- Object Access
- Privilege Use

All of these are basically useful, but some will create a substantially larger number of entries in your security logs than others. So it's useful to look at what auditing features will give you the most "bang" for your administrative "buck." "Account Logon Events" and "Logon Events" sound nearly identical, but there's a subtle difference between them that's important to understand so that you know what you're looking at. *Account Logon Events* will record an event every time a particular computer needs to validate a user's logon. *Logon Events* record a user simply logging on to or off of a computer. Sounds like gibberish? To me, too. Try this on for size:

You have an Active Directory domain that has auditing enabled for Account Logon Events as well as Logon Events, with a single domain controller called DC1. User *JaneD* needs to log on to her workstation, called \\WKS1. She does the Ctrl+Alt+Del shuffle, enters her password, and reaches her desktop. But what happened in the audit logs during that process?

1. \\WKS1 had to validate JaneD's user account against the Active Directory database on \\DC1, since she was logging on using a domain account. So a successful Account Logon Event gets recorded to the Security Log on \\DC1.

2. Since JaneD is logging on to \\WKS1, as well as the domain, a successful Logon Event gets recorded to the Security Log on \\SRV1.

If Jane logged on to \\WKS1 using a local user account (stored in the local SAM on \\WKS1), then both an Account Logon Event and a Logon Event would get recorded to the Security Log of \\WKS1, and nothing would get recorded to \\DC1. But in this case, to get the complete picture of logon activity for JaneD's user account, you would need to examine the Security Logs for both the workstation and the domain controller.

Another pair of useful items to audit is Account Management and Audit Policy Change events. The events that get audited through these policies are fairly self-explanatory: Account Management will track when a user gets created or deleted, group memberships change, someone changes his password, etc. Audit Policy Change will keep track of changes to user rights assignments, as well as changes to the audit policy itself. This last bit is especially useful since the first thing an attacker will often try to do is turn off auditing so that there's no record of her actions.

A third pair to watch is Directory Service Access and Object Access. These will both audit access to different objects on your network, the difference being that Object Access will audit attempts to open files, folders, and Registry keys. Directory Service Access will capture events associated with accessing objects within the Active Directory database: someone views the properties of a user object or Group Policy Object, for example.

■**Caution** Enabling Object Access auditing is actually a two-part procedure. First, you enable Object Access auditing within an audit policy, and then you specify individual objects that should be audited. We'll go through this step-by-step later in this section.

A Privilege Use event gets generated whenever a user does something associated with a user right—logging on locally, accessing a computer from the network, and so on. Process Tracking audits events like launching a program or exiting a process. These items can be really useful to you if you run into a troubleshooting situation, but they generate a *whole lot* of event entries. You'll have to decide if the signal-to-noise ratio is worth leaving these enabled all the time, or if you only want to enable them when you're trying to solve a particular problem. Finally, there's the Audit System Events category, which creates an audit log event whenever a computer system starts up or shuts down or when an event occurs that affects either the system security or the security log. Your best bet for a consistent security configuration will be to set an audit policy for your entire Active Directory domain. You can do this through Security Templates like we talked about in Chapter 4, or you can edit audit settings directly through a Group Policy Object that's linked to the domain. Just open the Group Policy Editor, and then browse to Computer Configuration\Windows Settings\Security Settings\Audit Policy. For each audit category, you can enable auditing of Success entries, Failure entries, or both. You may think that you only need to enable Failure entries, but imagine this scenario: you check your audit logs and see hundreds of failed account logon attempts for a Domain Admin account coming from a workstation that's not on your network. These failed logon attempts took place from 1 a.m. to 2 a.m. of the previous night . . . and then stopped. Now, can you tell from that information whether the hacker just stopped trying to log on? Or does the end of the Failure entries mean that the attacker succeeded in guessing the password of the Domain Admin account that he was hammering away at? You'll only know for sure if you've enabled Success auditing in addition to Failure.

WHY I LOVE WINDOWS SERVER 2003
by Laura E. Hunter

It used to be that those failed Account Logon Events would only record the date and time of the event, and the NetBIOS name of the offending machine. This was frustrating to no end, since there was no good way of matching the NetBIOS name to the IP address for any machines that weren't a part of your local network. In 2003, the Account Logon Event entries now include the IP address of the offending machine. As sort of a "Band-Aid" measure, you can use this information to create a Router Ban IP filter list within IPSec when you notice a machine that's hammering away at your accounts. Or you can get creative with scripting technologies to pull the IP address information directly from the Security Log, and then use **netsh** to update your IPSec policies automatically.

As a general guideline, try enabling the audit settings for your domain that you see in Table 5-2.

Table 5-2. *Recommended Audit Settings for Active Directory*

Event Category	Success	Failure
Audit Account Logon Events	X	X
Audit Account Management	X	X
Audit Directory Service Access	X	X
Audit Logon Events	X	X
Audit Object Access	X	X
Audit Policy Change	X	
Audit Privilege Use		X
Audit System Events	X	

Monitoring User Activity

As I mentioned in the previous section, auditing Object Access on your AD network is a two-step process. First, you need to enable Object Access auditing for your domain, site, or OU using Group Policy or a Security Template. But that by itself won't do it: you'll pop open your Security Logs and find page upon page of . . . absolutely no information gathered. Since auditing resources takes up a certain amount of processor time and memory usage, you need to enable it manually for the files and folders that you want to monitor. The good new is that, just like NTFS permissions, audit settings can be inherited down through the directory tree; so you can enable auditing for a single parent directory and have those same audit settings propagated to any new files or folders created within that directory. To enable auditing for a particular folder, follow these steps:

1. Right-click the folder in Windows Explorer, and then select **Properties**.

2. From the **Security** tab, click **Advanced**, and then **Auditing**. As you can see, there are no auditing entries enabled on any folder by default. To add an auditing entry, click **Add**. Enter the name of the user or group that you want to audit, and then click **OK**. You can choose the Everyone group to audit all access to a file or folder, or narrow the scope of your auditing to a particular user or group of users.

3. At this point, you'll see the screen shown in Figure 5-4. Select the types of activity that you want to audit: auditing **Full Control** will create an audit entry for all activity performed on the object. Auditing only **Write** will only audit attempts to write to a file; auditing **Delete** will monitor attempts to delete a file or folder. To audit more than one user or group, simply repeat steps 2 and 3 as many times as you need to.

By default, any auditing entries that you create will become part of the inheritance structure for the directory tree: any new files or folders created underneath the folder you enabled auditing for will receive the same auditing settings. You can restrict this by modifying the **Apply Onto** drop-down list on the **Auditing** tab. Using this drop-down list, you can restrict auditing entries to apply to the following:

- This folder only
- This folder and subfolders
- This folder, subfolders, and files
- This folder and files
- Subfolders and files only
- Subfolders only
- Files only

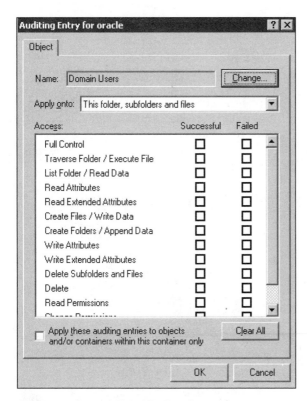

Figure 5-4. *Creating individual audit entries*

Collecting Auditing Information

So now you have all of these audit entries configured on your domain controllers, file server, and workstations. And you're a dutiful network administrator who spends the first hour of every morning poring over the previous day's logs to see if anything untoward went on, right? And you check on your logs at several points throughout the day to make sure that there are no ongoing security risks that you need to react to, right?

I'll take it by the sounds of silence just now that you, like most of us, need a better way to manage your security auditing information than just opening up Event Viewer whenever you have a spare moment. (Since, let's be realistic, when does that actually happen, anyway?) Unfortunately, I can't offer you the perfect solution that's free, easy to use, and perfectly effective all at the same time. But I'll give you a few options here that will hopefully hit at least two out of the three.

One solution that's been available from Microsoft since nearly the beginning of time is the **EventCombMT** utility, available for download at http://go.microsoft.com/fwlink/?LinkId=4544. This is a freeware utility that

will read through the Event Logs on specified servers in your domain, and produce output on all or selected Event Log events. You can output these events to
a text file, Excel spreadsheet, or even to a Microsoft SQL database. Once you
install and launch **EventCombMT**, you'll see the screen shown in Figure 5-5. At
this point it's fairly intuitive to run: just select the server or servers you want to
monitor, including any time or date restrictions and any specific information
that you want to search for. **EventCombMT** will return the events that meet
any criteria that you specified. It even includes some canned preconfigured
searches to look for File Replication System (FRS) errors and account lockouts
for your domain accounts.

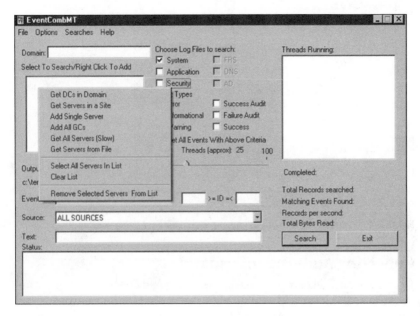

Figure 5-5. *Using EventCombMT to browse Event Log details*

You can also run **EventCombMT** from the command line to automate
the collection process as well, using the following command-line switches:

- /load:*<previously saved search>*: Runs **EventcombMT** with a previously configured search.

- /dc: Adds all domain controllers in your domain to the list of servers
  EventCombMT will search.

- /dc:*domain name*: Adds domain controllers from a different domain.

- /file:*path*: Adds servers to the search list from a text file, one IP or DNS name per line.

- /s:*servername*: Adds a single server name to the search list.

- /evt: *Event IDs*: Specifies the numeric event IDs that you want to search for. So you could use /evt: "644 529 538" to limit your search to these specific Event IDs.

- /et: *event type*: Restricts your search to specific event types. w is for warning, e is for error, i is for informational, sa is for success audit, fa is for failure audit, and su is for success. So you can specify /et:wei for only warning, error, and informational errors, or /et:all for all event types.

■Note Using /et:weisafasu will have the same effect as specifying /et:all.

- /log: *log type*: Specifies a particular log to search. sys is for system, app is for application, sec is for security, ds is for directory services, frs is for file replication service, and dns is for the DNS log. So you can restrict your search to only the System and Security Logs by specifying /log:syssec at the command line.

- /outdir: *path*: Specifies the output directory, not including the file name.

- /text: *text string*: Specifies a particular text string in the Event Log that **EventCombMT** should search for.

- /after: *and* /before:: Specify the starting and ending points for the events you're searching for. Both parameters require input in the form of MMDDYYYYHHMMSS, or Month-Date-Year-Hour-Minute-Second.

Another tool that you can use to collect log information is the Microsoft Log Parser, available for download at the time of this writing at http://www.microsoft.com/windows2000/downloads/tools/logparser. This is one of those freeware tools that got bundled into a Resource Kit, but because it was only released as an afterthought, the documentation for it is sparse at best. It's much more powerful than **EventCombMT**, but doesn't come with the same friendly GUI. Basically, if you know how to put together SQL command-line queries, you'll love Log Parser. The most recent version, available for download from the Microsoft website, will also create graphical bar, pie, and other chart types on the fly.

Summary

Since your Active Directory database contains all of the security principals needed to access and administer your network resources, it should go without saying that securing this information should be a top priority for any AD administrator or consultant. But before you can secure your network, you need to recognize the kinds of threats that it is vulnerable to. This chapter began with a look at the most common security vulnerabilities that affect Active Directory domain controllers, including threats to physical security and vulnerabilities in the TCP/IP protocol stack. We then talked about one of the most powerful tools available to safeguard your Active Directory information: the IPSec protocol that is included with Windows 2000 and Windows Server 2003, which is used to encrypt network traffic as it passes between two hosts. You can create and manage IPSec *policies* using a graphical interface, or from the command line using **netsh**. We then looked at ways to increase the security of the Windows operating system on an Active Directory domain controller, and how to configure audit policies to alert you to different types of malicious activities on your network.

In our next chapter, we'll look at tools and techniques to manage Active Directory on a larger scale, in an environment that contains multiple physical locations, domains, or forests.

Additional Resources

Microsoft Security Guidance: http://www.microsoft.com/technet/security/default.mspx—Step-by-step walk-throughs and recommendations to secure various operating systems and server roles, including domain controllers. At last count, the article containing the text you needed to add to the SCEREGVL.INF file is available from http://www.microsoft.com/technet/security/topics/threatsandcountermeasures/secmod57.mspx.

Mark Minasi's Homepage: http://www.minasi.com—Mark's monthly newsletters take a detailed look at a new Windows topic every month, many of which focus on security. The April 2003 newsletter delivers an exhaustive breakdown of the LM hash menace and why it's so important to disable it on your Active Directory network.

The *Hacking Exposed* series from the good people of Foundstone: http://www.hackingexposed.com—This is a good series of books on "hacks" like the ones we went over in this chapter, focusing on what specific Windows vulnerabilities hackers might try to exploit, and how to prevent them from doing so.

Microsoft Log Parser Toolkit, by Gabriele Guiseppini and Mark Burnett. Syngress. ISBN 1-932266-52-6—This book features a detailed description of this powerful, yet not-well-documented, tool.

"Using Netsh": http://www.microsoft.com/resources/documentation/windows/xp/all/proddocs/en-us/netsh.mspx—A full description of the various options available with **netsh**.

■ ■ ■

CHAPTER 6

Managing Large-Scale Deployments

Because Active Directory domains can scale to contain millions of objects, many Active Directory deployments will consist of a single domain within a single forest. Even more than that, the proliferation of high-speed connectivity will also often allow a network to be contained within a single site for easy replication. In some situations, though, you'll find it necessary to create a more complex logical or physical design. This can be because of lower-speed links between different locations that require more precise control over your replication scheme, or from a need to create trust relationships with external networks. In this chapter, you'll learn how to:

- Delegate administrative authority in a large environment.
- Configure domain and forest functional levels.
- Set up trust relationships with outside networks.
- Manage an Active Directory network spread across multiple sites.
- Configure replication within a single site.
- Configure replication between sites.
- Troubleshoot replication issues.

Managing Multiple Domains and Forests

In a larger Active Directory environment, you'll probably have a large IT support and administrative staff—or at least it'll hopefully be more than just you. To meet the challenges of managing a more complex domain and forest environment, you'll need to be able to delegate administrative authority effectively so that local administrators can tend to their own resources, as well as allowing junior staffers to handle everyday tasks without granting them too much authority. You'll also need to have an understanding of Active Directory trusts so that you can grant access to resources across multiple domains and forests.

Delegating Authority

In situations where you have a large and/or decentralized environment to manage, it may not be feasible for a single small group of people to perform every possible task relating to Active Directory administration. In Windows NT 4.0, your options for delegating administrative authority to junior administrators were fairly limited, but this is very much not the case with Active Directory. Using *delegation of authority*, you can assign authority over a portion of the Active Directory database to an onsite administrator, or grant a less experienced administrator the ability to perform only specific tasks. You can delegate authority at the site, domain, or Organizational Unit level.

For example, let's say that you have an OU that contains user and computer objects for your Customer Service department. The employees in this department are constantly forgetting their passwords, creating numerous help desk calls to unlock user accounts and reset passwords. The department head for the Customer Service area is someone you've worked with for a few years, and you are sufficiently confident in her technical abilities that you would like to give her the ability to reset passwords and unlock accounts for her own department members. However, you still don't want to grant this manager the ability to access user accounts in other departments, or to have more administrative authority than she needs to do these two things. You can delegate the authority to reset passwords quite easily, using the Delegation of Control Wizard as follows:

1. Right-click the Customer Service OU, and select **Delegate Control**. Click **Next** to skip the initial screen.

2. Click **Add** to select the user or group objects that should have authority over this OU. In most cases, you'll want to delegate authority to a group so that you can add and remove individual users as needed. Click **Next** when you've selected the accounts you want.

On the screen shown in Figure 6-1, you can see that the Delegation of Control Wizard has a number of preconfigured tasks that you can delegate permissions for, in addition to delegating a custom set of permissions. The preconfigured tasks you can delegate include the following:

- **Create, delete, and manage user accounts**
- **Reset user passwords and force password change at next logon**
- **Read all user information**
- **Create, delete, and manage groups**
- **Modify the membership of a group**
- **Manage Group Policy links**

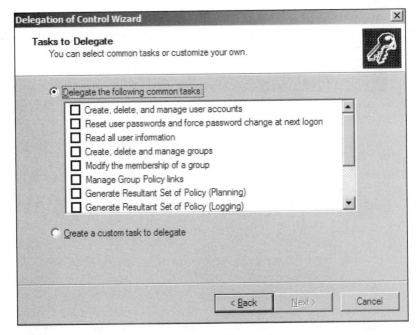

Figure 6-1. *Using the Delegation of Control Wizard*

3. Place a check mark next to **Reset user passwords and force password change at next logon**.

4. Click **Next** and then **Finish** to delegate this task.

You probably noticed that the Delegation of Control Wizard didn't allow you to delegate the ability to unlock user accounts using one of the precon-figured tasks—I keep hoping that Microsoft will include this in a future service pack, since it's a pretty common delegation. To allow your depart-ment manager to reset account passwords *and* to unlock user accounts, you'll need to delegate a custom task:

1. Right-click the OU and select **Delegate Control**. Click **Next**, and then **Add** to add the user or group objects that you're delegating authority to.

2. When you reach the screen from Figure 6-1, switch the radio button to **Create a custom task to delegate** and then click **Next**.

3. Your first step here is to indicate what *type* of objects you're delegating authority over. You can delegate authority over every single object within an OU, or restrict it to only specific object types. Since the Customer Service manager only needs to perform administration on user accounts,

we'll select the radio button for **Only the following objects in the folder** as shown in Figure 6-2, and then place a check mark next to **User Objects.** Click **Next** to continue.

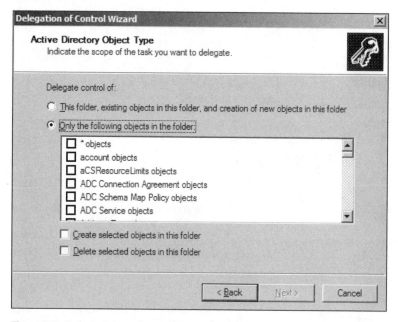

Figure 6-2. *Delegating authority over specific objects*

4. On the next screen, you'll indicate what permissions you want to delegate. You can delegate general permissions such as **Full Control**, **Read**, **Write**, etc., that apply to all Active Directory objects, as well as property-specific permissions. In this case, we'll need to delegate both of these permissions. Place a check mark next to **General** and **Property-specific**, and then select the permissions in the scroll list shown in Figure 6-3.

   - **Reset Password**
   - **Write lockoutTime**: Allows you to unlock an account
   - **Write pwdLastSet**: Lets you set the **User must change password at next logon** option
   - **Read and Write AccountRestrictions**: Lets you read the necessary account options

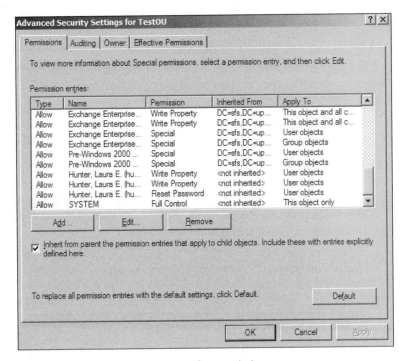

Figure 6-3. *Assigning property-specific permissions*

5. Click **Next** and **Finish** to create this delegation.

■**Caution** If you're working in Windows 2000 Active Directory, you may not see the **Write lockoutTime** permission here. If that's the case, use Notepad to open the dssec.dat file in the *%Windows%*\system32 directory and look for a line that reads `lockoutTime=7`. Change that seven to a zero and restart the Delegation of Control Wizard.

Another common scenario would be if you had a number of different departments organized into OUs, each of which have a dedicated IT support staff. In this case, you would want to delegate permissions to the entire Organizational Unit, not just specific objects within the OU. This type of delegation is often useful for defusing political landmines, so that decentralized departments can have full control over their own resources without interfering with your ability to administer your domain or forest as a single entity. To delegate control over all of the objects within an OU, follow these steps:

1. Right-click the OU, select **Delegate Control**, and click **Next** on the initial **Welcome** screen. Add the users or groups you want to delegate control to, and click **Next**.

2. Select **Create a Custom Task to Delegate** and click **Next**.

3. This brings you back to the screen in Figure 6-2 to select the objects that you're delegating control over. Leave the radio button on the default of **This folder, existing objects in this folder, and creation of new objects in this folder**. Click **Next** to continue.

4. On the **Permissions** screen, shown in Figure 6-4, place a check mark next to **Full Control**. You'll notice that every other permission gets selected automatically when you do this.

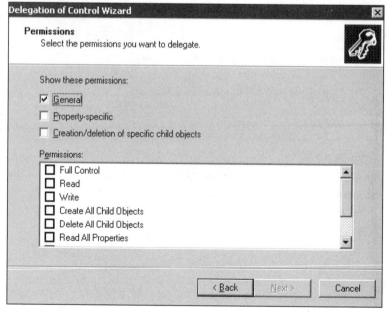

Figure 6-4. *Delegating custom permissions*

5. Click **Next** and **Finish** to create this delegation.

WHERE'S THE "UNDO" BUTTON?

One thing you may have noticed when creating these different delegations is that there's no obvious way to remove, delete, or otherwise undo what the Delegation of Control Wizard has done. In order to remove permissions that you've delegated, you'll need to go directly to the object's Access Control List (ACL) within Active Directory Users & Computers. You'll access this from the **Security** tab of the object's **Properties** sheet. From the **Security** tab, you can edit or remove any entries that were created by the wizard just like you would for an NTFS file or folder. You can also create new entries directly from this screen; the Delegation of Control Wizard is really just a way to simplify the process.

You can also use the **dsacls.exe** utility from the Windows 2000 and Windows Server 2003 Support Tools. This will let you modify ACLs on Active Directory objects from a command line or a script. **dsacls.exe** has a pretty obtuse syntax, but it's useful for automating permission assignments if you're taking over an AD infrastructure and need to reset permissions on a larger scale than one or two objects.

Another question is, what if you need to reclaim authority over an "orphaned" object? Say you granted **Full Control** over an OU to a local administrator who then decided to remove all other administrative access to the group. In this case, you can use the **Owner** tab in the object's **Properties** sheet to reclaim ownership of the object and reset its permissions, much like a file or folder in the NTFS file system.

Managing Trust Relationships

If you've configured multiple forests or domains, at some point you'll probably need to configure resources in one domain to be accessed by users in another domain. To allow for this, Active Directory uses *trust relationships* just like in previous versions of Windows. Unlike Windows NT, though, Active Directory establishes a number of trust relationships automatically so that you might not even need to manage the process at all. Within an Active Directory forest, the following trust relationships are created by default:

- A two-way transitive trust relationship gets created between a parent and a child domain. So if you have the mycompany.com domain and then create the sales.mycompany.com domain, users in the child domain will be able to access resources in the parent domain and vice versa.

- A two-way transitive trust relationship is created between the root domain of each domain tree within a forest. So if you have the mycompany.com, airplanes.com, and example.com domain trees within the mycompany.com forest, users in each domain tree will be able to access resources in any other domain tree.

These default trust relationships are both *two-way* and *transitive*. A two-way trust relationship means that if Domain A trusts Domain B, then Domain B automatically trusts Domain A without requiring additional configuration. A transitive trust means that if Domain A trusts Domain B and Domain B trusts Domain C, then Domain A trusts Domain C. You can see how these default trust relationships combine to allow access to resources throughout your Active Directory forest. Because the default trust relationships are transitive, a user in the sales.mycompany.com domain would be able to access resources in mycompany.com, airplanes.com, example.com, and any other child domains of these root domains. And because the trust relationships are two-way, any user in the forest can also access resources in the sales.mycompany.com child domain.

Creating External Trusts

In addition to these default trust relationships, you may need to configure access between your Windows 2000 or Windows Server 2003 forest and one of the following:

- A Windows NT domain
- A Windows 2000 or Windows Server 2003 domain in another forest

In this case, you'll configure an *external trust*. External trusts in Windows Server 2003 can be one-way or two-way in nature, but are nontransitive. External trusts in Windows 2000 can only be one-way and nontransitive—to create a two-way external trust relationship in Windows 2000, you'll need to create two separate trust relationships just like in Windows NT 4.0. This means that if you configure an external trust between your AD forest and an external NT domain, and the NT domain has a trust relationship with yet *another* NT domain, your AD forest does not automatically have a trust relationship with this third NT domain. Because external trusts are nontransitive, you would need to manually configure another external trust relationship with this third NT domain in order to allow access to it. This also means that users in the external domain will not be able to access any other Active Directory domains that you have a default trust relationship with; the trust relationship exists with your domain and your domain only.

You can configure an external trust using the Active Directory Domains & Trusts MMC, as well as the **Netdom** command-line utility. To use Active Directory Domains & Trusts, follow these steps:

1. Open the Active Directory Domains & Trusts MMC. Go to the **Properties** sheet of your domain.

2. Go to the **Trusts** tab and select **New Trust**. Click **Next** to skip past the initial screen.

3. Enter the name of the domain that you want to establish the trust relationship with. This can be either a NetBIOS domain name for an NT 4.0 domain or a DNS domain name for an external forest. Click **Next**.

4. On the **Trust Type** screen, select **External trust** and click **Next**.

5. On the **Direction of Trust** screen, select one of the following options:

   - **Two-way**: Users in both domains can access resources in both domains.

   - **One-way: incoming**: Users in your Active Directory forest will be able to access resources in the external domain. Users in the external domain will *not* be able to access resources in your domain.

   - **One way: outgoing**: Users in the external domain will be able to access resources in your domain. Your users will *not* have access to resources in the external domain.

6. Click **Next** to continue. On the next screen you'll have the option to create both sides of the trust relationship if you have administrative credentials for both domains. Select the option to create both the local and the external domain, and then click **Next**.

7. Enter administrative credentials for the external domain, and then click **Next**. If you're creating a trust in Windows Server 2003, you'll then be asked to specify the **Scope of Authentication**. Here you have two options:

   - **Forest-wide authentication**: Users in the trusted domain will be automatically authenticated whenever they try to access resources in the trusting domain. This is a more open authentication strategy than the second option, and is useful if you're joining two forests within the same organization.

   - **Selective authentication:** Users in the trusted domain will only be able to access resources that they've been specifically granted access to, rather than having **Authenticated User** access to all resources by default. This is more appropriate for an extranet or business partnership between two forests that belong to different companies or organizations.

8. Click **Next** and then **OK** to create the new trust.

■**Caution** Selective authentication isn't available in Windows 2000. Windows 2000 external trusts will use forest-wide authentication by default.

Creating a Realm Trust

You'll use a realm trust in a larger environment where you need to coexist and interact with UNIX machines, usually running MIT Kerberos for centralized authentication. Like an external trust, a realm trust can be one-way or two-way. Unlike external trusts, you have the choice to configure a realm trust as either transitive *or* nontransitive. The steps to create a realm trust are pretty similar to creating an external trust:

1. From the **Properties** sheet of your domain in the Domains & Trusts snap-in, go to the **Trusts** tab and select **New Trust**. Click **Next** to skip past the initial screen. Enter the DNS name of the UNIX realm that you want to establish the trust relationship with and click **Next**.

2. On the **Trust Type** screen, select **Realm trust** and click **Next**.

3. On the **Transitivity of Trust** screen, choose whether you want this trust to be

   - **Nontransitive**: This trust relationship will only apply to the two domains that it's been configured for.

   - **Transitive**: The trust will allow access to these two domains, as well as any other trusted domains or realms.

4. On the **Direction of Trust** screen, select **Two-way**, **One-way incoming**, or **One-way outgoing**.

5. Click **Next** and then **Finish** to create the new trust.

Creating Shortcut Trusts

Shortcut trusts are a bit of an oddity, since they don't actually create a new trust relationship between two untrusting domains or forests. All a shortcut trust will do is to improve the efficiency of the default Active Directory trusts, to make the authentication process run faster and improve performance for your users. By default, when a user tries to access a resource in a trusting domain, he is authenticated along the *trust path* to that domain. Say you have three domain trees within a single forest: mycompany.com, airplanes.com, and example.com. A user in sales.mycompany.com needs to access a file share located in sales.example.com. When this person tries to access this resource, his authentication information is passed along the following path:

1. From the sales.mycompany.com child domain to the mycompany.com parent domain

2. From the mycompany.com domain root to the example.com domain root

3. From the example.com parent domain to the sales.example.com child domain

This is a fairly simple example, but you can see how the default trust path could become pretty long in a large environment. Because of this, accessing resources in trusting domains can create a performance drain if the trust path is lengthy or traverses over any low-speed links. If you have users who access resources in trusted domains on a frequent basis, you can create a shortcut trust to speed the process. In this example, creating a shortcut trust between sales.mycompany.com and sales.example.com would allow the user's authentication information to pass directly to the trusting domain without going through any of the intermediary steps. A shortcut trust can be one-way or two-way: in a one-way trust, the user in sales.mycompany.com will be able to use the shortcut path to access resources in sales.example.com, but a user in sales.example.com would need to follow the default trust path to get to sales.mycompany.com. In a two-way shortcut trust, the shortcut path is available for authentication requests in both directions. To create a shortcut trust, do the following:

1. From the **Properties** sheet of your domain in the Domains & Trusts snap-in, go to the **Trusts** tab and select **New Trust**. Click **Next** to skip past the initial screen. Enter the DNS name of the UNIX realm that you want to establish the trust relationship with and click **Next**.

2. On the **Trust Name** screen enter the DNS or NetBIOS name of the domain you want to configure a shortcut path to, and then click **Next**.

3. On the **Direction of Trust** page, select one of the following:

   - **Two-way**: The shortcut trust is available for authentication requests in both directions.

   - **One-way incoming**: Users in your domain will be able to use the shortcut path to access their destination.

   - **One-way outgoing**: Users in the destination domain will be able to use the shortcut path to access your domain.

4. Click **Next** and **Finish** to create the shortcut trust.

Using Forest Trusts

Prior to Windows Server 2003, your only option for creating trusts between two forests was to use an external trust. In 2003, you can now use a *forest trust*, which will create a transitive trust relationship between a forest root domain and a forest root domain in another Windows Server 2003 forest. So unlike the external trust that only extended to a single domain in your forest, the forest trust will allow any user in your forest to access resources in the trusted forest, and vice versa. Forest trusts also allow users to log on to different domains using a single UPN suffix: with a forest trust, a user could log on to the mycompany.com, example.com, and airplanes.com forest, all using a single **jsmith@mycompany.com** logon.

■**Caution** While a forest trust creates a transitive trust with every domain within the containing forests, it is not transitive *between* forests. So if you create a forest trust between Forest 1 and Forest 2, and a second forest trust between Forest 2 and Forest 3, Forest 1 will *not* have a trust relationship with Forest 3 unless you create one manually.

Because this is an advanced feature, both forests need to be operating at the Windows Server 2003 forest functional level before you'll be able to create a forest trust. This means that every single domain controller (DC) in both forests must be running Windows Server 2003; any 2000 or NT DCs need to be upgraded or retired. To raise the forest functional level, right-click the topmost node in Active Directory Domains & Trusts and select **Raise Forest Functional Level**. Select **Windows Server 2003** from the list of available functional levels, and then click **Raise**. Active Directory will check the DCs in your forest to determine that they are all running Windows Server 2003 before raising the forest functional level. You'll need to do this for both forests in order to create a forest trust.

■**Caution** Remember that raising a domain or forest functional level is a one-way operation: once you change it, you won't be able to go back.

Once you've determined that both forests are running at the Windows Server 2003 forest functional level, use these steps to create a forest trust:

1. In Active Directory Domains and Trusts, go to the **Properties** sheet of the forest root domain. Go to the **Trusts** tab and select **New Trust**. Click **Next** to continue.

2. Enter the DNS name of the external forest and click **Next**. On the **Trust Type** page, select **Forest trust** and click **Next**.

3. On the **Direction of Trust** page, configure the forest trust as two-way, one-way incoming to allow your users to access resources in the external forest, or one-way outgoing to allow external users to access your resources.

4. Click **Next** to continue. On the next screen you'll have the option to create both sides of the trust relationship if you have administrative credentials for both domains. Select the option to create both the local and the external domain, and then click **Next**.

5. Enter administrative credentials for the external domain, and then click **Next**. Then select forest-wide or selective authentication for both the outgoing and incoming trusts, and then click **Next**.

6. Click **Next** and then **OK** to create the new trust.

DOMAIN AND FOREST FUNCTIONAL LEVELS

Active Directory obviously makes a number of advanced features available to manage your users and network resources. To allow for backwards compatibility with earlier operating systems, AD creates certain *functional levels* that will keep the more advanced features disabled until you manually enable them. In order to change to a higher functionality level, all domain controllers in your domain need to be running the necessary level of the Windows operating system. If you are working in a multidomain forest, you can have different domains operating at different functionality levels to allow for rolling migrations. At the domain level, you can enable the following functionality levels:

- *Windows 2000 mixed mode*: This is the default domain functional level, and supports domain controllers running Windows NT 4.0, Windows 2000, and Windows Server 2003. Because this mode provides the most backwards compatibility, it only enables the minimum features of Active Directory like support for the Global Catalog server.

- *Windows 2000 native mode*: This domain functional level supports Windows 2000 and 2003 only; any NT 4.0 Backup Domain Controllers (BDCs) will need to be upgraded or demoted before you switch to this functional level. Because AD no longer needs to communicate with NT 4.0 domain controllers, native mode allows for more advanced functions like universal security groups and the SIDHistory function.

- *Windows Server 2003 interim mode*: This functional level is only available if you're upgrading directly from Windows NT 4.0 to Windows Server 2003.

- *Windows Server 2003*: This level will support only Windows Server 2003 DCs, supporting the domain rename function and the InetOrgPerson class to allow for coexistence with third-party LDAP directory services.

Windows Server 2003 also enables *forest functional levels*, which enable advanced features for an entire Active Directory forest. Unlike domain functional levels, forest functional levels require every DC in an entire forest to be running the appropriate operating system. Windows Server 2003 provides three forest functionality levels:

- *Windows 2000*: This is the default forest functional level, and supports DCs of all three operating systems. It enables only the minimum features of a Windows Server 2003 Active Directory forest, including Universal group caching, application partitions, and the Install from Media functionality.

- *Windows Server 2003 interim*: Like interim mode at the domain level, this is only available when upgrading directly from NT 4.0 to Windows Server 2003.

- *Windows Server 2003*: This is the highest forest functional level and requires a pure Windows Server 2003 environment. It allows for forest trusts and domain renaming.

Creating Trusts from the Command Line

You'll use the **Netdom** utility from the Windows Support tools to create and manage trust relationships from the command line. To use **Netdom**, you'll need to understand the distinction between the *trusting* domain and the *trusted* domain—this was terminology that was more important in NT when you could only create one-way trust relationships. The trusted domain is the domain that contains *user* accounts—the accounts that are being "trusted" with access to external resources. The trusting domain is the domain that contains *resources* being accessed—as the administrator of the trusting domain, you are "trusting" the other domain's users with access to your stuff. The beginning syntax of **Netdom** looks like this:

```
netdom trust TrustingDomainName /d:TrustedDomainName
/ud:Domain\User /pd: password | * /uo:User /po:password | *
```

In this case, /ud and /pd refer to the username and password of a user with administrative credentials in the trusted domain; /uo and /po refer to the credentials of an administrative user in the trusting domain. You can either specify the passwords at the command line or use a * to be prompted for a password when you run the command.

Once you have this basic information, you can use **Netdom** to add, verify, and remove trust relationships. Here's an example of how you would add an external trust relationship between your AD domain called mycompany.com, and an NT 4.0 domain called NT. In this case, you want users in the NT domain to be able to access resources in the mycompany.com domain, so NT is the *trusted* domain and mycompany.com is the *trusting* domain:

```
netdom trust /d:NT mycompany.com /add /ud:NT\administrator /pd:*
/uo:mycompany.com\administrator /po:*
```

If you've created a two-way trust between the mycompany.com and example.com Active Directory forests, you can verify that the trust was created by using the following syntax:

```
netdom trust /d:mycompany.com example.com /verify /twoway
```

Granting Access to Resources

Once you've established your trust relationships, you'll want to allow access to network resources in an efficient manner so that it becomes simpler to manage and troubleshoot. In order to do this effectively, you need to understand how to use the different group types available in Active Directory, and how you can nest different groups together to grant access to network resources. In Windows 2000 and 2003 Active Directory, you can configure either *security groups* or *distribution groups*. Distribution groups are used exclusively to send e-mail using Microsoft Exchange or another e-mail server; you can't use them to assign permissions to resources. Both distribution and security groups can have one of three different *scopes*, which will dictate how they can be used within Active Directory. Because we're concerned with controlling security, we'll focus our discussion on security groups here. The possible scopes you can use are

- *Domain Local*: A Domain Local group can be used to assign permissions to resources within the same domain. Domain Local groups can have members from anywhere in the forest, from trusted domains in other forests and from trusted downlevel domains, as well as other Domain Local groups from the same domain.

- *Global*: A Global group can be used to assign permissions to resources in *any* domain in the forest, but it can only contain user accounts and other Global groups from within the same domain. Because Global groups can only contain resources within the same domain, Global group memberships don't get replicated to other domains within Active Directory.

- *Universal*: A Universal group can be assigned permissions to resources in any domain in the forest, and can contain user accounts and Global groups from any domain. Universal group membership information gets replicated to the Global Catalog servers, and so they should not be overused since they have an impact on network bandwidth.

These three group scopes can be combined to simplify how you assign permissions to resources across domains. In all cases, you should create a Domain Local group in the same domain as the resource you're securing, and assign permissions only to that Domain Local group. This gives you a single point of contact when assigning permissions to the resource, rather than trying to remember to update four or five different groups any time you need to make a change. Once you've assigned permissions to the Domain Local group, you have several options. If you're assigning permissions across multiple domains within a *single forest*:

1. Create a Global group in each domain, containing the users within that domain that need access to the resource. Because Global group information doesn't get replicated outside of the domain, this will cut down on replication traffic when you need to update membership in the Global group.

2. Add each Global group to the Domain Local group in the domain containing the resource. Because the group names themselves will tend to be static, this means that you won't be updating the membership of the Domain Local group very often. So the bulk of the administration for this resource will consist of changing the permissions that are assigned to the Domain Local group and having each domain administrator update the membership of each domain's Global group.

If you're assigning permissions to domains in multiple forests, this will change slightly:

1. Create the Domain Local group in the domain containing the resource and assign permissions just like before.

2. Create a Global group in each domain of each forest, just like before.

3. Create a Universal group in the domain containing the resource. Add the Global groups from the different domains and forests into the Universal group. Because changes to Universal group memberships are replicated to the Global Catalog server, you should add group objects to Universal groups instead of individual accounts. This will cut down on replication traffic since you'll primarily be making changes to the membership of the Global groups, not the Universal groups.

4. Add the Universal group to the Domain Local group in the domain containing the resource. This once again simplifies administration of resources across forests so that the bulk of the changes will fall on the domain administrator responsible for each domain's Global group.

Managing Active Directory Sites

Like we talked about in Chapter 1, Active Directory *sites* allow you to separate your physical network topology from your logical Active Directory design. This lets you configure domains and forests according to your administrative and security requirements, without being restricted by geography or bandwidth limitations. You can deploy a single domain in a single site, multiple domains in a single site, or a single domain that spans multiple physical locations.

Once you've created your logical Active Directory structure, you'll then configure sites to control how replication takes place on your network. Active Directory uses sites and *site links* to figure out the most efficient path to replicate data to all of the domain controllers and Global Catalog servers that need to receive updates, so it's critical to the performance of your network that you design your site topology correctly.

You'll also use sites to control how your clients log on to your network: AD will use site information to pick the closest domain controller to any client that's logging on to the domain. This will allow your clients to authenticate against a domain controller in the same subnet, rather than going across a slow or expensive WAN link in order to log onto Active Directory. There are also other Active Directory–aware applications that will use site information to direct clients to servers that are located physically close to the client requesting the resource.

You'll configure sites and subnets using the Active Directory Sites & Services MMC snap-in. When a client logs on to your domain, Active Directory will automatically figure out which site it needs to belong to based on its IP address and subnet mask. Site information for your domain controllers gets determined by the machine's location within Active Directory. When you first install Active Directory, your new domain controller gets placed into a new site called (imaginatively enough) Default-First-Site. (You can rename this just by right-clicking the site and selecting **Rename**.) Until you create additional sites, every domain controller you install will be placed into this default site, regardless of its location.

Within each site, you'll configure one or more subnets to correspond with the physical addressing scheme of your network. It's important to configure subnet objects correctly so that your clients will contact the appropriate domain controllers, since clients will first attempt to contact a DC within the same subnet for authentication. To add a subnet for an Active Directory site, do the following:

1. In Active Directory Sites & Services, browse to the Subnets node. Right-click Subnets, and select **New Subnets**.

2. Fill in the network address and subnet mask and select the site that this subnet should be associated with, as shown in Figure 6-5. Click **OK** when you're done.

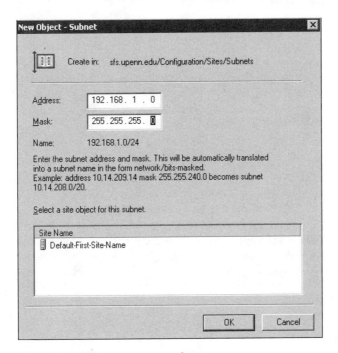

Figure 6-5. *Configuring a new subnet*

■**Note** You can change the site that a particular subnet is associated with, but you cannot associate a single subnet with more than one site at a time.

DEFINING IP SUBNETS

This is the part of the chapter where I think I'm legally obligated to give you a quick review of TCP/IP network addressing, and how that's used to define a subnet. If you know this stuff like the back of your hand already, go ahead and skip past this. (I won't be offended, honest.)

Each TCP/IP address is made up of four sections or *octets*, so called because IP addresses are actually 32-bit binary numbers that get converted to four decimal numbers to make it easier for humans to read. This is called *dotted decimal notation*, and creates the familiar 192.168.1.101 IP addresses that you're probably quite familiar with.

Every IP address is broken up into two parts: the *network* address and the *host* address. You can think of the network address as the street address of an office building, while the host address corresponds to a particular suite number. Any office located at the same street address is located in the same building; similarly, any IP addresses with the same network address are in the same subnet.

Each IP address also has a corresponding *subnet mask* that indicates where the network address ends and the host address begins. But when a network device like a computer or router looks at an IP address, it looks at the binary equivalent of the IP that we're familiar with. Binary numbers consist of nothing but 1s and 0s, and computers are designed to process binary information very quickly. So 192.168.1.101 would look like this in binary:

11000000 10101000 00000001 1100101

A subnet mask uses all 1s in binary to indicate the network address of a particular IP address. So if you're looking at the preceding IP address, and its subnet mask looks like this (255.255.255.0 in decimal):

11111111 11111111 11111111 00000000

then the first three octets of the IP address make up its network address. So you have 192.168.1.101 with a subnet mask of 255.255.255.0, and its network address is 192.168.1.0. The following IP addresses, therefore, would all be in the same subnet, since they all have the same network mask and subnet mask:

- 192.168.1.101
- 192.168.1.115
- 192.168.1.25
- 192.168.1.4

An Active Directory site represents the physical layout of your network, and consists of machines that are *well connected* with each other. What does "well connected" mean? Like many things in the world of Microsoft, this is a great big "it depends." The textbook answer is that well-connected sites should be connected by at least a 128Kbps dedicated link, usually located in the same building or office complex. But if you're interested in actually running a network and not just passing a Microsoft certification test, that 128Kbps mark may or may not be enough for you. As we'll discuss next, intra-site replication (replication that takes place between domain controllers in a single site) can be fairly bandwidth-intensive compared to replication that occurs between two different sites. So you'll want to do some functional testing to determine if 128Kbps is really going to be sufficient bandwidth, or if you need to mandate higher bandwidth requirements for sites on your network. In reality, you'll probably want to stick with areas where your domain controllers are connecting at LAN speed (10Mbps) or higher.

So how do you determine how many sites to deploy on your network? If your entire network is connected by high-speed, reliable links, you'll probably want to opt for a single site. Using a single site simplifies how you manage Active Directory replication, since all replication takes place within the same site. We'll talk about the differences between *intrasite* and *intersite* replication in the next section, but briefly: this simplifies replication because you don't need to configure it manually. When all of your domain controllers exist in a single site, they will replicate information to each other automatically whenever a change gets made to Active Directory.

If you're dealing with multiple geographic locations that use low-speed connections, you can create multiple sites to make more effective use of your Wide Area Network (WAN) connectivity. Replication between sites takes place less frequently than within a single site, so you can exert more granular control over how your WAN connections get used.

Configuring Replication

If you need to configure multiple sites within your organization, you'll need to configure *replication* to control how the different sites will communicate with each other. This is especially important in Active Directory because it uses *multimaster replication*. Unlike Windows NT, each Active Directory domain controller contains a writable *replica* of the AD database. This means that an administrator can make changes from any domain controller on your network, so these changes need to be synchronized between the various domain controllers.

Active Directory uses sites to configure how replication takes place, and uses the *Knowledge Consistency Checker (KCC)* to generate replication connections between your DCs. The KCC runs on each domain controller to automatically generate a replication topology for your network by adjusting for any DCs that are added or removed from Active Directory or moved between sites.

Configuring Intrasite Replication

Since the information that's replicated within a site is generally more critical to local clients than information that's going between sites, intrasite replication is more concerned with speed than efficiency. This means that any time you make a change to the Active Directory database (either by creating, deleting, or modifying an object), the KCC on the domain controller where you made the change will send an *update notification* to each of its replication partners. This notification gets sent to the closest replication partner 15 seconds after the change is made, and then to any other replication partners at 3-second intervals. Once each partner receives this update notification, each partner will then send a *directory update request* to the DC that sent the notification to grab any changes that have been made.

■**Note** Some changes to Active Directory are considered important enough to bypass this 15-second waiting period. For changes like account lockouts and password changes, changes are replicated immediately using *urgent replication*.

Within a single site, the KCC will automatically create connections between DCs within the site. When you have multiple sites, a single DC in each site is designated as the *intersite topology generator* to create connections between sites. You can see each of these connection objects within the Active Directory Sites & Services snap-in by browsing to *SiteName* ➤ **Servers** ➤ *ServerName* ➤ **NTDS Settings**. Any connection objects generated by the KCC will have *<automatically generated>* listed as the name of the connection. By default, the KCC on each domain controller will automatically generate a connection with two other DCs for fault tolerance. You can also create a manual connection by right-clicking NTDS Settings, selecting **Create new Active Directory connection**, and browsing to the other server. However, any manually created connection objects won't be controlled by the KCC. This means that manual connection objects won't be automatically updated if you add or remove domain controllers from Active Directory.

■**Note** The KCC on each DC will also periodically check the status of its existing connection objects. If one of the DCs it connects to is unavailable, the KCC will create a temporary connection to another DC in the same site to ensure that replication continues to function correctly.

Controlling Replication Between Sites

Unlike with intrasite replication, Active Directory will transfer information between sites in a way that will maximize the efficiency of the network connection between two sites, even when this efficiency means that changes aren't replicated as quickly from site to site. Just like with intrasite replication, the KCC can also build your intersite replication topology automatically, using information that you've entered in the AD Sites & Services console. But to correctly configure replication between sites, you need to configure more information than simply the subnets that make up each site. You'll also need to create and configure *sites*, *site links*, and *site link bridges*.

To create a new site, do the following:

1. Right-click Sites and select **New Site**.

2. Enter a name for the site, and select a site link to connect the new site to the rest of your network. (We'll configure site links next.)

A site link is an Active Directory object that represents a physical connection between two sites—typically this will correspond to a T1 link or some other type of WAN link that's connecting two physical sites on your network. The main purpose of a site link is to assign a *cost* to a physical connection to help the KCC figure out the most efficient route to replicate Active Directory information. The cost of a site link is simply a number that you assign when you create or modify the link, where a higher number indicates a lower-priority or "more expensive" link. Let's say you configure two site links between two Active Directory sites. You then assign a site link cost of 100 to Site Link A, and a cost of 200 to Site Link B. When Active Directory replication takes place, the KCC will transmit information using Site Link A whenever possible, and Site Link B will only be used if the first link is unavailable. This is actually a pretty common scenario if you have a high-speed WAN link between two sites, but still maintain a dial-up link to communicate if the WAN link fails. In this case, you'd configure the higher-speed link with the lower site link cost; when the WAN link goes down, Active Directory replication will revert to the backup dial-up link. Site links also have two other configurable items that you can use to control how replication occurs between sites:

- *Replication interval*: Dictates how frequently replication will occur on this link. Unlike intrasite replication, which takes place whenever a change is made, intersite replication only occurs on a scheduled basis. By default the replication interval for a site link is every 3 hours.

- *Replication schedule*: Dictates the times and days that a link is available. By default, a site link will be available 24 hours a day, 7 days a week. You can exclude certain dates and times if you want to restrict traffic on a heavily used T1 connection, for example. By clicking **Change Schedule** you can modify the dates and times that a site link is available, as you can see in Figure 6-6.

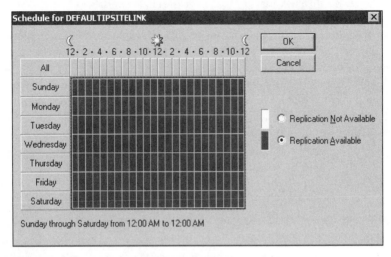

Figure 6-6. *Modifying the default replication schedule*

Whenever you create a new site, you need to connect the new site to an existing site by way of a site link. Windows 2000 and Windows Server 2003 create two default site links when Active Directory is installed:

- *DefaultIPSiteLink*: This default site link has a cost of 100 and a replication interval of 15 minutes.

- *DefaultSMTPLink*: You can use SMTP in cases where you don't have a reliable connection between sites. However, using SMTP for replication is limited in functionality, since it doesn't use schedules, and requires a Certificate Authority (CA) to be in place on your network.

To create a new site link, follow these steps:

1. Browse to **Sites ➤ Inter-site Transports ➤ IP**.
2. Right-click IP and select **New Site Link**.
3. Enter a name for the new site, and configure at least two sites to be connected by this link.

4. Click **OK**, and then double-click the newly created link to configure the site link properties.

5. Change the cost of the link to 150 and the schedule to every 30 minutes, and then click **OK** to save your changes.

When you connect two sites, the KCC will designate a domain controller in each site as a *bridgehead server* to control replication between the two sites. This further cuts down on bandwidth utilization on a WAN link by ensuring that only one server from each site will be replicating information over a low-speed link. In Windows 2000, this created a potential single point of failure if the bridgehead server in a site went offline. This was corrected in Windows Server 2003 by allowing more than one DC in a site to be designated as a *candidate* bridgehead server, so that another server could take over replication functions if the bridgehead server was no longer available.

■**Note** You can also use the **ADLB.EXE** Resource Kit utility to disperse replication traffic across multiple Windows 2003 servers.

By default, all site links in Active Directory are transitive, which means that the KCC will automatically replicate information between sites even when they're not directly connected. This is a lot like trust transitivity with Active Directory domains, where if Domain A trusts Domain B, and Domain B trusts Domain C, then Domain A automatically has a trust relationship with Domain C. With site links, if you configure a site link between Site 1 and Site 2, and another site link between Site 2 and Site 3, the KCC will automatically replicate information from Site 1 to Site 3. In this way, you can configure links to a large number of sites by using a relatively small number of site links. This is referred to as *site link bridging*. This default behavior means that all site links belong to the same site link bridge, so that you don't need to configure a site link "mesh" between each site and every other site.

If you disable this default behavior, you would need to manually configure site link bridges to set up site link transitivity. This will have the effect of preventing replication traffic from entering certain portions of your network, which can be useful in isolating a high-security portion of your network. You'll also use manual site link bridging if your network isn't fully routed—in other words, if you don't have a direct physical connection between each site in your network. You may also want to manually configure site link bridging if your network consists of a large number of sites, to prevent replication traffic from taking up too much bandwidth.

To create a manual site link bridge, do the following:

1. Browse to **Sites ➤ Intersite Transports ➤ IP**. Right-click the IP node and select **Properties**. You'll see the screen shown in Figure 6-7.

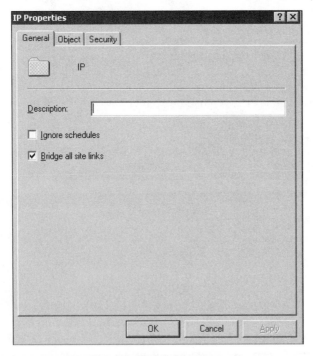

Figure 6-7. *Disabling site link bridging*

2. Remove the check mark next to **Bridge all site links**, and click **OK**.

3. Right-click IP and select **New Site Link Bridge**.

4. Enter a name, and select at least two site links that should be included in this site link bridge.

5. Click **OK** to create the new site link bridge.

■**Note** If you are using manual site link bridging and you've created two potential paths for replication traffic, the KCC will take the *sum* of the site link costs for each "leg" of the bridge. It will then compare the sums of each bridge to determine the lowest-cost path to use for transmitting replication traffic.

CONFIGURING REPLICATION OVER FIREWALLS

When you're dealing with intersite replication, you'll often find that you're trying to pass replication information over firewalls. This presents some unique challenges in terms of being able to transmit the information you need without compromising the security of your firewall. There are a few different ways that you can configure this. Your first option is to open up the necessary ports on your firewall to allow Active Directory replication. This is the simplest approach from the standpoint of a Windows administrator, since you don't need to configure anything on the server side. The bad news? You're opening up a whole bunch of ports on your firewall, many of which are well-known attack vectors that any firewall worth its salt should be blocking. You'd need to enable the following ports to allow normal replication to take place:

- TCP/UDP port 135
- TCP/UDP port 137
- TCP port 138
- TCP port 139
- TCP ports 1024–65535 (for dynamic RPC)
- TCP/UDP port 445
- TCP port 389

- TCP port 636
- TCP port 3268, 3269
- TCP/UDP port 88
- TCP/UDP port 53
- TCP/UDP port 1512
- TCP/UDP port 42
- TCP/UDP port 123

Once you've opened up all of these ports, that $30,000 firewall sitting at your network perimeter has essentially become a five-figure paperweight, so I'd recommend steering clear of this option. You can decrease the number of ports you're leaving open by configuring your domain controllers to use limited RPC instead of dynamic RPC. You can do this by choosing one port in the 1024–65535 range, and configuring each domain controller to use only that port by going to the HKLM\SYSTEM\CurrentControlList\ Services\NTDS\Parameters Registry key on each server and adding a new DWORD value for **TCP/IP Port**, configured to match the limited RPC port number. This is more secure than using dynamic RPC, but you're still opening up a number of high-risk ports on your firewall.

A better option would be to configure a Virtual Private Network (VPN) connection between sites, using either IPSec or a third-party VPN solution. This will provide strong encryption of your Active Directory information, especially if it's being transmitted over the Internet.

Configuring Global Catalog Servers

One consideration that affects both the physical and logical Active Directory layout in a large network is how you place Global Catalog servers. Like we talked about in Chapter 1, Global Catalogs are necessary for your users to log on to Active Directory, since they store Universal group membership for multidomain environments. In most cases, you'll want to configure a Global Catalog server in every site that supports more than 100 users, especially if the site is one that's connected to the rest of your network by a low-bandwidth connection. This will ensure that your users will still be able to log on to Active Directory in the event of a WAN failure.

In some cases, though, it's not practical to place a Global Catalog server in every site. With Windows Server 2003, you have the option to enable *Universal group membership caching*, so that you can minimize the replication traffic that needs to go across your WAN links. To enable this feature for a particular site, do the following:

1. Navigate to the site that you want to enable caching for.

2. Right-click NTDS Settings and select **Properties**. Place a check mark next to **Enable Universal Group Membership Caching**. In the **Refresh Cache from** drop-down list, you can specify a site that should be used to refresh the cache information, or leave it at **<Default>** to contact the nearest site that has a Global Catalog.

3. Click **OK** when you're done.

Using Application Directory Partitions

In a large environment, you can further control the behavior of replication on your network by using *application directory partitions*. These partitions contain data belonging to Active Directory or another application that only gets replicated to a subset of the domain controllers in your domain or forest. Application directory partitions can contain any type of object *except security principals*, and are not replicated to the Global Catalog, so no user or group objects are allowed. For example, if you're using Active Directory–integrated DNS in Windows Server 2003, you can use application partitions to only replicate DNS data to those DCs that are actually running the DNS service, either within a single domain or throughout your forest. This way, domain controllers that don't need to maintain a copy of DNS data won't need to participate in replicating it. You can also use application partitions to prevent information that's only needed by a few domain controllers from needing to replicate throughout your enterprise—like an application that integrates with Active Directory, but is only used by one division of a large corporation. Application partitions also allow easy integration with applications and services that use LDAP to access and store data.

Caution Application directory partitions can only be created on servers running Windows Server 2003.

Application directory partitions follow the same DNS naming scheme as the rest of Active Directory. So if you create an application partition called partition1 in the mycompany.com domain, its DNS name would be partition1.mycompany.com. And just like domain directory partitions (the "normal" partitions used to replicate Active Directory data), the KCC will automatically generate a replication topology for any application directory partitions in your domain or forest.

In most cases, the application that's creating the application directory partition will have its own management utility to tend to application directory partitions, like the DNS Management MMC for the ones created by DNS. But if it's necessary, you can manually create, manage, and delete application partitions using the **ntdsutil** or **ldp** command-line utilities, as well as the Active Directory Service Interfaces (ADSI) editor. To create a new application partition using **ntdsutil**, follow these steps:

1. From a command prompt, type **ntdsutil**.

2. Type **domain management**.

3. Type **connections**. From the connections menu, type:

   connect to *servername*

   where *servername* is the name of a domain controller for your domain.

4. Type **quit** to return to the domain management menu.

5. To create an application partition, type:

   create nc *ApplicationDirectoryPartition Servername*

   where *ApplicationDirectoryPartition* is the distinguished name of the partition, like dc=partition1, dc=sales, dc=mycompany, dc=com. *Servername* is the name of the domain controller that should host the application partition.

6. To delete an application partition, type:

   delete nc *ApplicationDirectoryPartition*

Tip You can create or delete a replica of an existing application partition by using the **add nc replica** or **delete nc replica** command from the same menu.

Troubleshooting Replication Issues

In most cases, you'll find that Active Directory replication works without a hitch. But every now and then you'll notice some issues where changes you've made to a particular Active Directory object don't appear, or you create a new object that doesn't get copied to other domain controllers in your environment. When this happens, you have a number of tools available to help you troubleshoot how replication is performing on your network.

Your first step should be to determine whether your replication issues are actually a matter of *object collision*. Because Active Directory uses multi-master replication, you can have multiple administrators making changes from different DCs. To address this, each object that you create in Active Directory possesses an *Update Sequence Number (USN)*, *timestamp*, and a *version number*. The Update Sequence Number gets replicated along with the object, and is updated every time a change gets made to the object. Each domain controller will use this USN to determine if it needs to retrieve an updated copy of the object. In a case where two DCs have the same USN for an object, Active Directory records a timestamp each time an object is updated. Active Directory uses the timestamp as a tie-breaker, where the most recent update will be the one that "wins."

Note To reduce the number of potential collisions, Active Directory uses *attribute-level replication*. So if you change a user object's display name from one DC, and change its group memberships from another one, this will not be considered a collision since the two updates involved different attributes of the object.

If you've determined that your replication issues are not a matter of object collision, there are a number of other potential causes for trouble. One of the most powerful troubleshooting tools available is **repadmin.exe**, which is included with the Windows Server 2003 Support Tools. **repadmin** is a command-line utility with a number of switches to show you detailed information about how replication is functioning, as you can see in Listing 6-1.

Listing 6-1. *Syntax of the repadmin Tool*

```
Usage: repadmin <cmd> <args> [/u:{domain\\user}] [/pw:{password|*}]
                            [/rpc] [/ldap]
                            [/csv] - see /csvhelp
Command-line arguments:
    /bind [DC_LIST]
    /bridgeheads [DC_LIST] [/verbose]
    /checkprop [DC_LIST from which to enumerate host DCs]
```

```
        <Naming Context>
        <Originating DC Invocation ID> <Originating USN>
/dsaguid [DC_LIST] [GUID]
/failcache [DC_LIST]
/istg [DC_LIST] [/verbose]
/kcc [DC_LIST] [/async]
/latency [DC_LIST] [/verbose]
/notifyopt [DC_LIST] <Naming Context> [/first:<value>]
        [/subs:<value>]
/queue [DC_LIST]
/querysites <From-Site-RDN> <To-Site-RDN-1>
        [<To-Site-RDN-2> ...]
        (may not be called with alternate credentials)
/replicate <Dest_DC_LIST> <Naming Context> /allsources
        [/force] [/async]
        [/full] [/addref] [/readonly]
/replicate <Dest_DC_LIST> <Source DC_NAME>
        <Naming Context> [/force] [/async]
        [/full] [/addref] [/readonly]
/replsingleobj <DC_LIST> <dsa-source-guid> <obj dn>
/replsummary [DC_LIST] /bysrc /bydest /errorsonly
        [/sort:{ delta | partners | failures | error | percent |
            unresponsive }]
/showattr <DC_LIST> <OBJ_LIST> [OBJ_LIST OPTIONS]
        [/atts:<att1>,<att2>...] [/allvalues] [/long]
            [/dumpallblob]
/showcert [DC_LIST]
/showchanges . <SourceDC> <NamingContext> [/cookie:<file>]
        [/atts:<att1>,<att2>,...] [/long] [
/showchanges <Dest_DC_LIST> <SourceDCObjectGUID> <NamingContext>
        [/verbose] [/statistics] [/noincremental] [/objectsecurity]
        [/ancestors] [/atts:<att1>,<att2>,...] [/filter:
            <ldap filter>]
/showconn [DC_LIST] {serverRDN | Container DN | <DC GUID>}
        (default is local site)
        [/from:serverRDN] [/intersite]
/showctx [DC_LIST] [/nocache]
/showism [<Transport DN>] [/verbose] (must be executed locally)
/showmsg {<Win32 error> | <DS event ID> /NTDSMSG}
/showncsig [DC_LIST]
/showobjmeta [DC_LIST] <Object DN> [/nocache] [/linked]
/showoutcalls [DC_LIST]
/showproxy [DC_LIST] [Naming Context] [matchstring]
        (search xdommove proxies)
```

```
/showproxy [DC_LIST] [Object DN] [matchstring] /movedobject
    (dump xdommoved object)
/showreps [DC_LIST [Source DC object GUID]] [Naming Context]
    [/verbose]
    [/nocache] [/repsto] [/conn] [/all] [/errorsonly]
        [/intersite]
/showsig [DC_LIST]
/showtime <DS time value>
/showtrust [DC_LIST]
/showutdvec <DC_LIST> <Naming Context> [/nocache] [/latency]
/showvalue [DC_LIST] <Object DN> [Attribute Name]
    [Value DN] [/nocache]
/syncall <DC> [<Naming Context>] [<flags>]
/viewlist <DC_LIST> [OBJ_LIST]
```

You can start with the repadmin /showreps command. If replication is functioning normally, this will return a listing of each DC that is configured as a replication partner of the DC you're working from. If not, the /showreps option can produce several different error messages, including the following:

- No inbound neighbors: This means that there are no connection objects between this DC and any other DCs, or that the DCs referenced in the connection objects can't be contacted. Create any necessary connection objects, or determine if there's a connectivity issue.

- Target account name is incorrect: This is typically a DNS or connectivity issue.

- No more endpoint mappings are available: This is typically caused by a faulty DNS entry, where the DC's DNS name is registered with the wrong IP address.

■**Note** You can also use the **dcdiag /test:replications** utility to verify that replication is functioning on a particular domain controller.

Another useful tool to troubleshoot Active Directory replication is **replmon**. **replmon** is a graphical utility that you can use to view the replication history for a particular DC, display the current replication topology, force the KCC to rebuild the topology, and to force replication to take place. You can see an example of **replmon** in action in Figure 6-8.

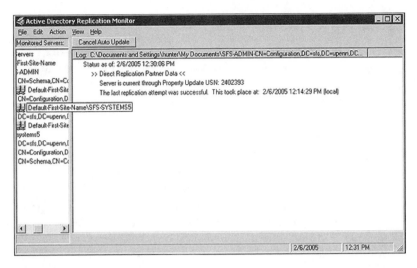

Figure 6-8. *Using the replmon utility*

Summary

In Chapter 6, we moved from the tasks needed to administer and secure a single Active Directory domain and looked at concepts that are specifically geared toward larger environments. In a decentralized environment, you'll often have multiple locations that each have its own IT staff. With Active Directory, you can delegate authority over portions of the Active Directory tree to onsite administrators, or else delegate the ability to perform only certain tasks to lower-level administrators or help desk employees. You can also set up many different types of trust relationships to allow easier authentication between different domains, forests, and UNIX Kerberos realms. Moving from the logical layout of Active Directory to the physical, you'll also often need to deploy multiple Active Directory sites, either within a single domain or supporting multiple domains. In order for a multisite environment to be successful, you need to configure replication correctly so that Active Directory information can be transmitted between different sites without impacting network performance for your users. This chapter closed with a look at different tools that are available for you to troubleshoot and replication issues in your environment.

Additional Resources

"How to Optimize Active Directory Replication in a Large Network": http://support.microsoft.com/kb/244368/EN-US/—Detailed charts on memory usage by the KCC, based on the number of sites and domains that you're supporting.

"Designing a Site Topology for Active Directory Replication": http://www.microsoft.com/windows2000/techinfo/reskit/ deploymentscenarios/scenarios/repl_design_sitetopology_active_ directory_repl.asp—This gives you a step-by-step walk-through of a case study in designing a site topology for an enterprise network.

"Active Directory Replication in Windows 2000": http://www.microsoft.com/ technet/security/prodtech/windows2000/w2kccadm/adsites/ w2kadm37.mspx—Describes the replication topology for Windows 2000 Server.

Active Directory Services for Microsoft Windows .NET Technical Reference, by Mike Mulcare and Stan Reimer. Microsoft Press. ISBN 0-7356-1577-2 —Detailed technical information straight from technical writers at Microsoft. Makes a wonderful reference, even if you might not be reading it from cover to cover on an airplane.

■ ■ ■

CHAPTER 7

Active Directory Migrations

In many situations, you probably won't be deploying a brand new Active Directory forest completely from scratch. Larger companies will already have some sort of network in place, and it becomes up to you to upgrade or migrate that network to Active Directory. The most common upgrade path to Active Directory is from Windows NT 4.0, so that's what we'll focus on in this chapter. We'll look at migration scenarios ranging from a simple in-place upgrade to a full restructuring of an enterprise NT 4.0 environment. Along the way, we'll look at some of the tools available to help you in the migration process, most notably the **Active Directory Migration Tool**. We'll also talk about planning steps to prepare for a migration, as well as some maintenance that you can perform once a migration has been finished. By the end of this chapter, you'll be able to

- Plan an Active Directory upgrade from NT 4.0.
- Create a rollback plan to recover from a failed upgrade.
- Perform an in-place upgrade of a single domain.
- Restructure a multidomain NT 4.0 environment.
- Migrate domains within the same Active Directory forest.
- Migrate domains between separate forests.

Upgrading from Windows NT 4.0

If you're still working with NT 4.0, an Active Directory upgrade can range in difficulty from simple to nightmarish, depending on the complexity of your existing infrastructure. This is because Active Directory has completely changed the way that your user accounts and network resources can be arranged with the introduction of a hierarchical organization structure, using DNS for name resolution, and allowing for a separation between the logical and physical design of your network. Many of the features of Active Directory are also not available in NT 4.0, including Group Policy Objects and delegation of authority.

Unlike Active Directory, Windows NT 4.0 uses the Security Accounts Manager (SAM) to store account information. SAM has a flat-file structure instead of the hierarchical structure of Active Directory, which presents a number of issues in terms of scalability and the size of domains that you could realistically deploy. For example, a single NT 4.0 domain could have a SAM database that is no larger than 40MB in size; beyond that you would need to create additional domains. This size limitation often requires NT 4.0 administrators to create two separate kinds of domains for their network:

- *Account domains* to hold user and group accounts, and
- *Resource domains* to hold files and applications that users needed to access

As an NT 4.0 admin, you then need to create one- or two-way trust relationships between the account and resource domains, which could add up to a large number of trusts to manage if you are dealing with more than a few domains. If you had a network with ten separate domains, and you want every domain to trust every other domain, you would need to create 90 separate trust relationships to make that happen. (This is because NT 4.0 only supports one-way nontransitive trusts.) And that's 90 different trust relationships that need to be administered, updated, and examined for errors in a troubleshooting situation. Pretty un-fun, huh?

■**Note** Because the SAM database is a flat file, each object in the SAM also needs to have a unique name within the network. This gets pretty interesting if you have more than two or three users named "smith" to contend with.

Let's look at a more common scenario where you have two account domains and four resource domains. You configure eight separate trust relationships, one between each account domain and each resource domain, and another two between the two account domains. When upgrading a network like this to Active Directory, you can potentially collapse these six domains into one, since AD doesn't set the 40,000-object size limitation. You can then create Organizational Units to house the servers that used to live in the resource domains, so that you can delegate administration of them as needed. This addresses another limitation of NT 4.0, which is that it has no real way to delegate control over a subset of domain resources without granting someone control over the entire domain, or else spinning the resources in question out to their own domain. You can't easily allow a departmental administrator to perform maintenance on a single Windows NT 4.0 domain controller without making them a member of the Domain Admins group, for example. We'll talk more about these kinds of considerations when we discuss domain restructuring later in the chapter.

Performing In-Place Upgrades

The simplest upgrade to perform is one where you're going from a single Windows NT 4.0 domain to a single Windows 2000/2003 domain. In this case, most of your system settings and applications will be retained during the upgrade, and your end users might not even notice the change. There are a number of reasons to consider using an in-place upgrade. Most notably, your user and group accounts will remain intact during the upgrade process, so you don't need to reconfigure security on any file shares or objects because of a change in user or group Security Identifiers (SIDs). Remember that Windows file and object permissions are keyed to the SID of a user or group, not to the name that you see displayed in any management utilities. By retaining your existing domain structure, all of your SIDs stay the same. Your users will also retain their existing user profiles, instead of having a new one created when they log on to a new domain for the first time.

The first question you need to ask when you're planning an in-place upgrade is whether your existing servers meet the hardware and software requirements for a Windows 2000 Server or Windows Server 2003 upgrade. There are certain supported *upgrade paths* for each operating system that you need to use when upgrading from a particular version of NT 4.0. Table 7-1 lists the supported upgrade paths for both Windows 2000 Server and Windows Server 2003. In addition, you should verify that all of the hardware components installed in your NT 4.0 Servers are listed in the *Windows Catalog* (formerly called the *Hardware Compatibility List*, or *HCL*) for Windows 2000 Server or Windows Server 2003, since some legacy hardware might not have a 2000 Server or 2003 driver available for it. You can view the Windows Catalog for Windows 2000 at http://go.microsoft.com/fwlink/?linkID=14201, and the Windows Catalog for Windows Server 2003 at http://www.microsoft.com/windows/catalog/server/.

Table 7-1. *Upgrade Paths for Windows 2000 Server and Windows Server 2003*

If You're Currently Running . . .	You Can Upgrade To . . .
Windows NT 3.51 Server	Windows 2000 Server, full version
	Windows 2000 Server, upgrade version
	Windows 2000 Advanced Server, full version
Windows NT 4.0 Server	Windows 2000 Server, full version
	Windows 2000 Server, upgrade version
	Windows 2000 Advanced Server, full version
	Windows Server 2003, Standard Edition
	Windows Server 2003, Enterprise Edition
Windows NT 4.0 Terminal Server	Windows 2000 Server, full version
	Windows 2000 Server, upgrade version
	Windows 2000 Advanced Server, upgrade version
	Windows Server 2003, Enterprise Edition
Windows NT 4.0 Enterprise Edition	Windows 2000 Advanced Server, full version
	Windows 2000 Server, upgrade version
	Windows Server 2003, Enterprise Edition
Windows 2000 Server	Windows Server 2003, Standard Edition
	Windows Server 2003, Enterprise Edition
	Windows Small Business Server 2003, Standard Edition
	Windows Small Business Server 2003, Premium Edition
Windows 2000 Advanced Server	Windows Server 2003, Enterprise Edition
Windows 2000 Datacenter Server	Windows Server 2003, Datacenter Edition

In addition, you should also determine whether your existing NT 4.0 domain controllers meet the hardware requirements to be upgraded to Windows 2000 or Windows Server 2003. Of course, there are the "minimum" hardware requirements listed on the Microsoft website, and then there's the kind of hardware that you'd actually want to run on a domain controller out in the real world. After all, according to Microsoft you can install Windows 2000 on a Pentium 133 on as little as 128MB of RAM, though 256MB is the recommended minimum. While I'm sure it's true that you might be able to get away with such a small amount of installed RAM, I'm equally certain that you wouldn't be all that happy with the results. Personally, I wouldn't recommend deploying Windows 2000 or Windows Server 2003 on a machine running much less than a 1GHz processor, with at least 512MB of RAM.

A final area of concern will be to ensure that your existing applications will make the transition well: does your current version of SQL, MS Exchange, and the like function on Windows 2000/2003? Or do you need to plan for an application upgrade before you perform the Active Directory upgrade?

Creating a Fallback Plan

Even the smallest upgrade calls for a rollback plan, a means of getting back to "the way things used to be" if something really horrible goes wrong. In the case of an NT 4.0–to–AD upgrade, you'll find that this usually stems from application incompatibility between Windows NT 4.0 and Windows 2000/2003, or it could be something as unforeseen as encountering a power outage in the middle of the upgrade process. The good news is that there's a (relatively) simple way to roll back from a failed Active Directory upgrade. By default, an NT 4.0 domain that's been upgraded to Active Directory will be running in the Windows 2000 mixed domain functional level. This means that any NT 4.0 Backup Domain Controllers (BDCs) will still be able to function on your network, since the PDC Emulator FSMO will translate the hierarchical Active Directory database into a flat SAM database that the BDCs can understand. And therein lies your safety valve to recover from an upgrade gone wrong. As long as your Windows 2000 domain controller is online, you've got yourself an Active Directory domain running in Windows 2000 mixed mode. But as far as your NT 4.0 BDCs are concerned, they're still happily sitting on an NT 4.0 network because of the PDC Emulator FSMO. If you take the 2000 DC offline, your NT 4.0 BDCs will *still* just think that they're members of an NT 4.0 domain.

So if you take an NT 4.0 BDC and promote it to NT 4.0 Primary Domain Controller, what you're effectively doing is reverting your domain to an NT 4.0 domain; any traces of Active Directory go away when you take the 2000 DC offline. Your remaining BDCs will still think that they're members of an NT 4.0 domain and will just point to the new NT 4.0 PDC for their replication updates rather than the 2000 DC that was holding the PDC Emulator role.

This failback plan will remain in place as long as

- You're running in Windows 2000 mixed mode (or Windows Server 2003 interim mode for 2003).
- You still have an NT 4.0 BDC in your domain.

So my best advice for the paranoid upgrader is this: keep an NT 4.0 BDC online until you're absolutely certain that you're happy with the Windows 2000/2003 upgrade, and only take it offline when you're ready to make the switch to a higher functionality level like Windows 2000 native mode. I also recommend installing a new machine to act as your PDC for the purposes of the upgrade—this will not only let you perform the upgrade on a clean machine, but also allow you to introduce a Primary Domain Controller with better hardware specifications than what you may have in your production environment. And the most important consideration for your failback plan, of course, is to have recent and *tested* backups in place. Before upgrading your domain to Active Directory, take a full backup of the Primary Domain Controller and at least one Backup Domain Controller as well.

Ensuring Client Connectivity

In addition to making sure that your network applications will function after the upgrade, you also need to be certain that your network clients will still be functional, since nothing says "migraine" like a thousand people who can't log on to the server first thing on a Monday morning. Any client machines running Windows 2000 or Windows XP will accept the upgrade without so much as a sneeze: as soon as they realize that they're hitting a Windows 2000/2003 domain controller, they'll stop using NT LAN Manager (NTLM) and start using Kerberos automatically. Clients running earlier operating systems will sometimes be a bit less cooperative, especially if you're upgrading directly to Windows Server 2003. Windows Server 2003 enables strong domain authentication by default, which means that it will disable LM and NTLM authentication requests from your clients. This feature will render Windows 95 clients unable to log on to the network unless you install the Active Directory Client Extensions, which is a free download from the Microsoft website at http://www.microsoft.com/windows2000/server/evaluation/news/bulletins/adextension.asp. The client extensions will run on Windows 95/98/ME, as well as on NT 4.0 running Service Pack 6a. And while your older clients won't be able to use some of the new features of AD, the client extensions will allow them to use at least a subset of them, including these:

- The Active Directory Services Interface (ADSI) scripting interface, which allows you to create administrative scripts

- Distributed File System (DFS) clients for fault-tolerant file shares published within Active Directory

- NTLM version 2 authentication

Even with the client extensions installed, though, your legacy clients won't be able to support certain features of Active Directory. This includes the following:

- *Kerberos support:* Your legacy clients will only be able to log on using some form of LM or NTLM authentication.

- *Group Policy:* Only Windows 2000, Windows XP, and Windows Server 2003 machines will be able to process Group Policy settings.

- *IPSec and L2TP for encrypting LAN traffic*

Another point to keep in mind about client connectivity during the upgrade process is where your clients will be pointing to for authentication when both Windows NT 4.0 and Windows 2000/2003 domain controllers exist on the network. Your NT 4.0/Windows 95/98/ME clients will use any available domain controller for authentication, but any Windows 2000 or Windows XP clients will home in on the Active Directory domain controller. This can create issues whereby your AD domain controllers get overloaded with requests, or your Windows 2000/XP clients find themselves unable to authenticate if the new DC goes offline. To provide for load balancing when authenticating newer clients, you should plan to bring a second Windows 2000/2003 DC online as soon as possible. This can either be a BDC that's been upgraded or a brand new Windows 2000/2003 server.

Configuring File Replication

If you made extensive use of the LANMAN Directory Replication (LMRepl) file replication service in NT 4.0, you'll need to do some jury-rigging during your upgrade to Active Directory, since Active Directory replaces the LMRepl file replication mechanism with the File Replication Service (FRS), and the two don't really play well together. So if your NT 4.0 PDC is configured as an LMRepl export server, you'll need to move that role to another server until you've migrated all of your NT 4.0 BDCs. Ideally, this should be the last NT 4.0 BDC that you take offline, so that the NT 4.0 replication process continues to function until you're fully prepared to make the switch to FRS.

Let's say that you have a machine called \\DC1 configured as your PDC and as an export server for LMRepl. Before you upgrade \\DC1, you want to configure another NT 4.0 controller, \\DC3, as the new export server. To do that, follow these steps:

1. Open the Windows NT 4.0 Server Manager utility. Select **\\DC1**, and then click **Computer ➤ Properties**.

2. Select **Replication** to view the current LMRepl configuration of DC1. Make a note of the directory that's being exported and the target domain that \\DC1 is replicating to.

3. Change the selected radio button from **Export Directories** to **Do Not Export**. Click **OK** to return to the Server Manager main window.

4. Select **\\DC3** from Server Manager and go back to **Computer ➤ Properties**.

5. From the Replication window, select the **Export Directories** radio button.

6. Click **Add**, and add the name of your NT 4.0 domain. Click **OK** to return to Server Manager.

7. Restart the directory replication service on all of your NT 4.0 domain controllers.

You can test the new replication configuration by placing a small test file in the export directory of \\DC3. After five minutes or so, the test file should have been copied to the import directories of your other NT 4.0 domain controllers. If the file replication succeeds, try deleting the file and waiting another five minutes to make sure that the deletion is propagated as well.

Of course, another way around this is to configure a brand new machine to act as your PDC during the upgrade process as I recommended earlier, and to demote your production PDC to BDC status. By doing this, you can leave your LMRepl file replication configured as-is. In our example here, \\DC1 would be able to continue functioning as the LMRepl export server since it's no longer the initial target of the Active Directory upgrade. This is another example of how creating a new PDC for the purpose of the Active Directory upgrade will help you to minimize the impact of the upgrade on your production servers.

Whether you move the export server role to another machine or bring a clean PDC into your network for the upgrade, you'll still need to configure manual file replication between your NT 4.0 and 2000 domain controllers. LMRepl and FRS are *not* backwards-compatible, and you'll need to have a mechanism in place to replicate any changes to your logon scripts between your NT 4.0 and 2000 DCs so that all of your clients are receiving the same information when they log on. To do this, you'll create a batch file that will copy the contents of the SYSVOL share on the Windows 2000/2003 DC to the export directory on the NT 4.0 BDC that's acting as the export server. The Windows 2000 Resource Kit includes a preconfigured LBridge.cmd file to help you set this up quickly, as well as to give you the ability to purge older files. The batch file needs to run using the credentials of a user account that has the **Read** permission to the NETLOGON share of the 2003 server and the **Full Control** permission to the export directory on the NT 4.0 export server. You should schedule this batch file to run at several points during the day if you are making numerous changes to your logon scripts, or just once a day if your scripts are relatively stable.

■**Caution** If you're running this script from the NT 4.0 Server, you need to configure the Scheduler service to run with user credentials that have the necessary permissions. If you leave the Scheduler service to run under the Local System account in NT 4.0, any copy operations across the network will fail.

Once you've configured this scheduled task, you can test it by doing the following:

1. Create a test file in the NETLOGON share of your Windows 2000/2003 domain controller.

2. Manually execute the synchronization script.

3. Check the export directory of the NT 4.0 export server to make sure that the script copied the new file correctly.

4. Wait approximately five minutes, and then check your other NT 4.0 BDCs to make sure that the export server propagated the new file.

Performing the Upgrade

When you upgrade an NT 4.0 domain to Windows 2000/2003, the first machine that you need to upgrade is the Primary Domain Controller (PDC) on your NT 4.0 domain. The operating system upgrade will detect that you're upgrading a domain controller, and will automatically launch the Active Directory Installation Wizard once the OS upgrade completes. The AD Installation Wizard will import the existing NT 4.0 Security Accounts Manager database into Active Directory, including user accounts, local and global groups, and computer objects. The upgraded NT 4.0 Server will become the first DC in a new Active Directory domain, holding all five of the FSMO roles.

Before you perform the Windows 2000/2003 upgrade on your PDC, you need to first configure TCP/IP so that it's pointing to a DNS server that supports the Active Directory requirements of SRV records and preferably dynamic updates as well. You can do this by installing the DNS Server service on the PDC itself and configuring a zone for the new Active Directory domain, or by pointing the PDC to a DNS server elsewhere in your Active Directory structure if you are moving into an existing forest or tree. You should also perform the following preparatory steps:

1. Check the hardware and software installed on the NT 4.0 PDC using the Application Compatibility Toolkit, available for download from http://www.microsoft.com/downloads/details.aspx?FamilyID=7fc46855-b8a4-46cd-a236-3159970fde94&DisplayLang=en.

2. Perform any necessary hardware or software updates, including patches or BIOS updates.

3. Back up all sensitive data on the PDC to a tape drive or another backup device.

4. Check for any viruses on the PDC using an antivirus scanner with the most recent definitions installed.

5. If you have compression enabled on any NTFS drives, disable compression for the duration of the upgrade.

6. Uninstall any power management software or third-party disk management utilities.

7. Disconnect any UPS devices connected to the PDC. The hardware detection process that takes place during the upgrade can interfere with a UPS that's plugged into a printer or serial port.

■**Note** Windows NT 4.0 DNS supports SRV records as long as Service Pack 4 or better is installed, but does not support dynamic updates at any Service Pack level. Once you've upgraded the server to Windows 2000/2003, you will be able to enable dynamic updates.

Once you're ready to upgrade your NT 4.0 PDC, follow these steps:

1. Run Windows Setup from the Windows 2000/2003 Server CD or from a network installation point. Click **Next** to bypass the initial screen.

2. Click **Yes** to upgrade your system. The next screen will prompt you to upgrade the existing operating system or install a fresh copy of Windows on a separate partition. Select the **Upgrade** option, and click **Next**.

3. Select **I accept the License Agreement** and click **Next**.

4. The next screen will ask you if you want to upgrade to the newer version of the NTFS file system, which will support newer features such as disk quotas and the Encrypted File System (EFS). Select **Upgrade the file system** and click **Next**.

From here, the rest of the operating system installation pretty much runs on autopilot. You'll need to specify a few items such as the Windows 2000/2003 license key, but information like the current time zone and keyboard layout settings will be picked up from the existing NT 4.0 install. After the OS installation finishes, it will automatically launch into the Active Directory Installation Wizard. You'll run through the **dcpromo** process just as you would for a new Active Directory installation, as covered in Chapter 1.

Once you've finished the upgrade process, you can verify the Active Directory installation by opening Active Directory Domains & Trusts and verifying that the new Windows 2000/2003 domain appears. You can then right-click your domain and select **Manage** to open up Active Directory Users & Computers. You should see your new domain controller in the Domain Controllers OU, and your NT 4.0 users should appear in the Users container. In addition, the 2000 domain controller will appear in the NT 4.0 Server manager as a Windows NT 5.0 Primary. You should also check the System logs of your NT 4.0 BDCs for event entries indicating that synchronization with the new PDC has taken place.

■**Note** This will be event ID 5715, and will read "The partial synchronization replication of the SAM database from the primary domain controller *New-Windows-2000-DC* completed successfully."

Once you've done all of this? Congratulations, you've upgraded your domain to Active Directory, albeit at the most basic level. Any remaining Backup Domain Controllers will continue to function, and will access the new Windows 2000/2003 server as if it were the NT 4.0 PDC. The Active Directory account database will appear to your NT 4.0 machines as a flat SAM file that they can understand, while appearing to any Active Directory–aware machines and applications as, well, Active Directory. This means that you can create and change objects in Active Directory, and your NT 4.0 machines will still be able to pick up those changes during normal replication. It also allows you to perform your upgrades on a rolling timetable, where you can upgrade your BDCs and member servers one at a time. This will allow you time to migrate any applications to new versions or even to new hardware, and to perform your upgrade in small chunks to maintain the overall stability of your domain.

When you run the AD Installation Wizard on the NT 4.0 PDC, you have the same installation options that you would when creating any new Active Directory domain. You can create the new DC as

- The first domain controller in a new forest
- The first DC in a new domain tree within an existing forest, or
- The first DC in a new child domain within an existing domain tree

If you insert the new NT 4.0 domain into an existing Active Directory forest, all the usual trust relationships will be created automatically: if this is a new child domain, a two-way transitive trust relationship will exist between the child and the parent domains. If this is the first DC in a new domain tree, a two-way transitive Kerberos trust will get set up with the root domain of any other domain trees in the forest. Any *preexisting* trust relationships that you'd configured in the NT 4.0 domain will be retained as one-way intransitive trust relationships using NTLM. This will stay in place until you switch to native mode, since your NT 4.0 BDCs don't understand Kerberos or transitive trusts. Any new domains that you create after the upgrade will have the default Kerberos trusts created. If you upgrade an NT 4.0 domain to 2000 and then create a new 2000 child domain under the upgraded domain, the usual two-way transitive trusts will be created between parent and child.

■Caution If you want to configure your upgraded domain to join an existing forest, remember that you must have DNS name resolution configured on the NT 4.0 PDC before you begin the upgrade process.

Setting the Functional Level

Another new aspect of Active Directory that you'll need to address when upgrading from NT 4.0 is the idea of a domain functional level. Since you can have any combination of NT 4.0, Windows 2000, and Windows Server 2003 domain controllers present in a domain, Microsoft needed a way to throttle back the feature set that was available so that the older DCs could still function. So you now have four different domain functional levels available, each one supporting a different set of operating systems for your domain controllers, as shown in Table 7-2.

Table 7-2. *Domain Functional Levels*

Functional Level	Supported Domain Controllers
Windows 2000 mixed	Windows NT 4.0
	Windows 2000
	Windows Server 2003
Windows 2000 native	Windows 2000
	Windows Server 2003
Windows Server 2003 interim	Windows NT 4.0
	Windows Server 2003
Windows Server 2003	Windows Server 2003

Higher functional levels like Windows 2000 native and Windows Server 2003 make additional features available for your network, since they no longer need to worry about backwards compatibility with older operating systems that don't understand the new features. This includes features like universal security groups, domain local groups, group nesting, forest trusts, and the ability to rename an Active Directory domain.

■**Caution** Domain functional levels are new to Windows Server 2003. If you are upgrading to Windows 2000, you will either be in mixed mode or native mode. Mixed mode supports both Windows 2000 domain controllers and NT 4.0 BDCs; native mode supports only Windows 2000 domain controllers.

When you first upgrade an NT 4.0 domain, you will be in mixed mode (if you upgraded to Windows 2000) or interim mode (if you upgraded to Windows Server 2003). These two modes give you the maximum backwards-compatibility with NT 4.0, but they also provide you the least flexibility in terms of using new features of Active Directory. You might also still be subject to some of the same limitations as NT 4.0. If you think you might need to roll back to NT 4.0, for example, you should still keep your AD database under 40,000 objects so that an NT 4.0 BDC can still replicate the entire account database correctly.

If you have NT 4.0 BDCs that don't meet the hardware requirements of the upgrade process, you can decommission them entirely by transferring any files and applications to another server and removing the BDC from the network. You also have the option of having a slower BDC move into the Windows 2000 domain as a member server instead of a domain controller. You can do this by reinstalling Windows NT 4.0 before the upgrade and designating the server as an NT 4.0 member server instead of a BDC—remember that NT 4.0 only allows you to make this distinction during setup. This option isn't really my favorite, since you're running the risk of causing problems with the BDC before you even get to the upgrade. Luckily, the Windows 2000/2003 upgrade process will recognize that you are upgrading a BDC, and will give you the option to do one of two things:

- Configure the server as a domain controller in the Active Directory domain.

- Allow the server to act as a member server after the upgrade.

Once you've upgraded or decommissioned any remaining NT 4.0 BDCs on your network, you can switch to a higher functional level to gain access to these newer features. Your domain will actually remain at the mixed or interim functional level until you manually switch to a higher one. This is because changing your domain functional level is a one-way trip: if you make a mistake, the only way to go back is to reinstall your domain controllers from backups or re-create your domain from scratch. Switching to a higher functional level will prevent your NT 4.0 BDCs from receiving Active Directory updates anymore, so that your existing NT 4.0 BDCs will stop replicating and you won't be able to add any new ones. (An obvious side effect of this is that you lose the ability to revert to NT 4.0 just by bringing an NT 4.0 BDC back online and removing the new DCs.)

When you're ready to upgrade to a higher functional level, do the following:

1. Open Active Directory Users & Computers.

2. Right-click the domain and select **Properties**.

3. On the **General** tab, click **Change Mode** and select the new functional level you want.

4. You'll see a warning that this is a one-way operation, and that there's no going back if you've made a mistake, so are you *really* sure you want to do this? Click **OK**.

5. Assuming that all DCs in your domain are running the correct levels of the operating system, the functional level will change. Click **OK** to finish.

■**Note** Domain functional levels only really apply to the domain controllers that are present in your domain. You can still have member servers and workstations running older versions of the operating system after you switch to native mode; you just can't have any NT 4.0 BDCs still hanging around.

Domain Migration in Eleven Easy(-ish) Steps

So to boil it all down to a simple checklist, here's how I like to approach the mechanics of an NT 4.0–to–2000 domain upgrade:

1. Install NT 4.0 Server on a spare machine, called \\NT1 for this example. It doesn't need to be anything special, just enough to run the operating system. Configure the machine as a Backup Domain Controller and synchronize it with the PDC.

2. Once \\NT1 has a synchronized copy of your domain information, sit it in a corner and don't touch it until you're certain that the domain upgrade has been a success. This little puppy is your safety net: if something unforeseen happens, this is how you get your users back up and running as quickly as possible.

3. Install NT 4.0 Server on a second machine, called \\NT2 for this example. This one needs slightly better hardware than \\NT1, since it needs to handle an upgrade to Windows 2000. Configure it as another Backup Domain Controller and synchronize it with the production PDC.

4. Once \\NT2 has synchronized all domain information, promote it to be the PDC on your network. This will let you do your first "production" upgrade on a clean machine, so that none of your applications or file shares will get broken if a herd of crazed wildebeests storms your server room and tramples \\NT2 in the middle of the upgrade process.

5. Take a full backup of both \\NT1 and \\NT2, since in the world of network administration you can never be too paranoid.

6. If you're using file replication on your NT 4.0 Servers, verify that replication is taking place between \\NT1 and \\NT2, as well as any other BDCs on your network.

7. Verify that DNS is set up and working properly on \\NT2. Either configure the service locally, or point \\NT2 to another DNS server that supports SRV records (mandatory) and dynamic updates (preferable).

8. Run the Windows 2000 upgrade process on \\NT2, and configure Active Directory as necessary.

9. Once the upgrade has completed on \\NT2, verify that Active Directory has been installed properly.

10. Create a script to copy information between \\NT2\Netlogon and \\NT1\Repl$ on a regular basis. Test the script by creating a test file in the ~\Netlogon share and making sure that it copies to the export directory on your export server.

11. Create a new user from the Windows 2000/2003 domain controller, and check the system log of the NT 4.0 BDCs to verify that the object was replicated. Then take the new DC offline and make sure that you can log on to a workstation using the user account that you created after the upgrade.

Restructuring an NT 4.0 Environment

If you're working in a more complex NT 4.0 domain environment, you have numerous options when it's time to perform an Active Directory upgrade. One solution, of course, is to allow each NT 4.0 domain to remain as a separate Active Directory domain using the steps we just discussed. However, this often doesn't make for the most efficient Active Directory design, since designing NT 4.0 domains involves a number of physical constraints that are no longer present in Active Directory. Because of this, you may want to consolidate numerous Windows NT 4.0 domains into one or two larger Active Directory forests when you decide to make the move to AD. This restructuring process can take place along with a straight upgrade, where you do an in-place upgrade of a single NT 4.0 domain and then migrate your other NT 4.0 users and resources into this single forest. Or you can migrate your entire NT 4.0 domain structure, creating a brand new Active Directory environment and migrating your NT 4.0 users into it over a period of time.

Restructuring a multidomain NT 4.0 network into a single Active Directory forest will create a number of benefits for you as an administrator. First, Active Directory allows for much better scalability as your network expands. While your NT 4.0 domains were restricted to that 40MB SAM size limitation, a single Active Directory forest can house an almost unlimited number of user and group accounts. This will simplify how you administer your network, since it reduces the number of trust relationships that you need to manage between domains. You can also consolidate resource domains into Organizational Units, which will allow you to delegate administration of resources without losing your overall administrative control of the forest or domain.

If you decide to restructure your NT 4.0 network, many of the same design considerations will apply as when you design an Active Directory forest from scratch. You need to look at your existing NT 4.0 domains and determine whether they can be consolidated into a single domain, or whether there are groups of users that need sufficient isolation from the rest of the network that they require a separate domain or forest. Because of the introduction of Organizational Units, Active Directory gives you the ability to delegate administration of resources within a single domain in a way that you were unable to do in Windows NT 4.0. For example, you may have a department in your company that insists on maintaining its own servers, printers, and user accounts. In the NT 4.0 world, the only way to accomplish this (without granting the departmental administrators too much authority) is to create a separate domain for this department. In Active Directory, you can consolidate this departmental domain with the rest of your users, and create an OU to allow them to continue to administer their own resources autonomously.

Migrating to a single Active Directory domain creates the easiest possible environment to administer, postupgrade, because it creates a single authentication database for all of your users. It also allows you to create security policies, password settings, and user environment configuration, and then easily apply those policies to every user in your environment. The largest drawback, of course, is that it takes away the ease of performing an in-place upgrade for most, if not all, of your users. So you'll need to plan the migration process carefully in order to minimize any downtime, as well as the impact that this will have on your user population.

When consolidating multiple domains, you have two options in configuring the destination domain. You can either choose one of your existing NT 4.0 domains to upgrade to Active Directory, and then move your other users into this domain. Or else you can create a brand new Active Directory domain using all new servers and hardware, and migrate *all* of your NT 4.0 users and resources into this new domain. When you upgrade an NT 4.0 domain to Active Directory, you won't be able to change the NetBIOS name of the domain. If you choose the upgrade route, you need to select your domain carefully, so that the NetBIOS domain name will be applicable and acceptable to all users in the new Active Directory domain. While this is often more of a political issue than a technical one, it can still make or break your migration process and so needs to be given a certain amount of attention.

If you are going to be investing in new hardware anyway, I like the idea of creating a pristine environment for Active Directory whenever possible. Especially if your NT 4.0 domains have been around for a while, using a brand new domain for AD allows you to start fresh. This way, you're not allowing any lingering security misconfigurations in your NT 4.0 domains to carry over into Active Directory; this allows you to do everything the way you want, right from the start.

When consolidating multiple domains, your first order of business is to determine the order in which they should be upgraded or migrated. Typically, you'll want to upgrade your account domain first, followed by any resource domains. Especially if you have multiple account domains, upgrading these first will create the most benefits for you since you can consolidate your users into a single container for easier and better administration. This will also allow you to take advantage of Active Directory's improved administration features, perhaps taking some of the pressure off of your administrative staff by delegating certain low-level tasks to a help desk. This kind of granular control was impossible in NT 4.0—to allow someone to reset passwords or unlock user accounts, you had to make them Account Operators or even Domain Admins, which presented risks that many administrators weren't willing to live with.

If you have multiple account domains to deal with, you'll typically want to choose the *smallest* domain to upgrade first—this is sort of a Murphy's Law approach, so that if it breaks you've inconvenienced the fewest number of people. But this choice needs to be mitigated by other factors as well. You should also base this decision on which domains contain the best hardware and bandwidth to support an upgrade, and which domains provide you the best physical access to the domain controllers during the upgrade process. This can also be a political decision: if you have a large domain of slightly-more-technical-than-most users who are chomping at the bit to move to Active Directory, this might be a good choice to start with even if you'll be upgrading a larger number of people than in a smaller domain.

Securing the Migration Process

Each Windows user and computer account in a domain has a Security Identifier, or SID, associated with it. This SID gets generated automatically for each object, and contains a number that identifies the domain that's issuing the SID, as well as a Relative Identifier (RID) that uniquely identifies the user or computer object within the domain. Because SIDs are based on the domain that issued them, you won't be able to move a user or computer object to another domain without having its SID change. This can create issues in terms of how your users access resources, since all Windows Access Control Lists (ACLs) are based on SIDs and not the display name that administrators work with. This is one of the reasons why an upgrade can be preferable to a migration: since no SIDs will change during the upgrade process, user access to resources won't be interrupted because of a change in SID.

This is further complicated because of the behavior of group memberships in both Windows NT 4.0 and Windows 2000/2003. Because *global groups* can only contain user accounts that reside in the same domain, moving a user object from one domain to another will affect their global group membership. For example, let's say that you have an AcctUsers global group in the USERS domain that is used to grant access to resources in the ACCTG domain. If you migrate a member of the AcctUsers group to the new Windows 2000 domain, that user will lose her membership to the AcctgUsers global group, since she is no longer a member of the USERS domain. You can address this in one of two ways:

- Move the entire group and all of its members in a single operation. Groups are assigned SIDs just like user accounts, so the SID of the group object will also change when you migrate it from one domain to another. After you move all the members of the group, you can reassign permissions to resources in the ACCTG domain using the global group in the new Active Directory domain.

- Create a parallel group in the new domain, and maintain the membership list and permission assignments for both groups until all members of the group have been consolidated into the new domain. You would use this option if you needed to migrate the users in the USERS domain over an extended period of time, and needed to allow users in both the old and the new domains to access resources during the migration.

If your old and new domains will be coexisting for some time, you'll need to create trust relationships between the new Active Directory domain and any NT 4.0 domains that still contain production resources. You'll create an *external trust* in Active Directory Domains & Trusts, which will be a one-way nontransitive trust similar to the default trust relationships in Windows NT 4.0. The **Active Directory Migration Tool**, which we'll be talking about in a moment, also provides options to migrate trust relationships automatically.

During a migration, one of your primary goals should clearly be ensuring that your users do not lose access to the resources that they use on a daily basis. A number of third-party utilities can assist you with the SID migration problem by automatically searching for references to a user's old SID, and replacing it with a reference to his new SID. Windows 2000 often makes these kinds of tools unnecessary, however, because of an Active

Directory attribute called *SIDHistory*. The SIDHistory attribute will retain a reference to any old SIDs that applied to a user or group, and use these to access any resources with ACLs that reference the old SID. Because this can represent a security risk if it's used improperly, SIDHistory is only available in certain situations. You can only use SIDHistory in the following situations:

- You are *moving* objects between Active Directory domains within the same forest. Because you are essentially creating a new object and destroying the old one, the object will retain a unique SID.

- You are *copying* (or *cloning*) objects between domains that are in different forests. This includes cloning objects between Windows 2000/2003 domains that are located in different forests, or copying objects between an NT 4.0 and a 2000/2003 domain. Because both the new and the old object will still exist after the cloning process is finished, this can only take place between separate forests. You cannot clone Active Directory objects between two domains within the same forest.

In order to use SIDHistory, your *target* domain—the domain that you're moving or cloning user accounts into—must be running in Windows 2000 native mode or higher. You must also have a trust relationship configured between the source and target domains.

Migrating User Profiles

One aspect of the migration process that often gets overlooked are user profiles. You're all pleased with yourself that you've made the switch to this great new domain, gotten all of your workstations hooked into the new domain over a weekend so that nobody has to deal with any downtime . . . and then you start getting the phone calls on Monday morning:

"All of my Internet bookmarks are gone!"

"Can you come fix my e-mail? It's not working anymore."

"Where's my wallpaper with the picture of my granddaughter?"

When a user logs on to an NT 4.0 workstation, the profile that gets loaded is based on her SID, which will change when you migrate users to a new domain. So when the user logs on to the new domain for the first time, the workstation creates a whole new profile as if she were a brand new user. (Since, after a fashion, she *is*.) Unless you take precautions against it, this "disappearing profiles" problem will happen anytime you clone a user from an NT 4.0 domain into an Active Directory domain.

■**Note** This doesn't happen if you're running Windows 2000 or Windows XP on the desktop and moving users between Windows 2000/2003 domains within the same forest, since the newer client will look for a *Globally Unique Identifier (GUID)* that will follow a user object throughout an Active Directory forest.

You have two options for dealing with user profiles when you're migrating users into an Active Directory domain:

- Create a network share to host your user profiles. Make these shared profiles for each user available to both his NT 4.0 account and his Active Directory account. This can get ugly when once you start rolling out Group Policy settings and other Active Directory–specific features, so I'd recommend against it.

- Create a copy of the user profile under a Registry key named after the user's new SID. This way when the "new" user logs on to his workstation for the first time, the workstation will point him to the profile stored under his new SID, which will have all of his old information ready and waiting for him. While this option is preferable to the first one, it can still create some unpredictable behavior with any applications that you've deployed via Group Policy in the destination domain, where an application may uninstall or reinstall itself unexpectedly.

Using the Active Directory Migration Tool

Microsoft provides a number of free utilities that can assist you with the process of upgrading or migrating domains to Active Directory. The most powerful of these is the **Active Directory Migration Tool** (**ADMT**), which we'll be revisiting in the next section. But you also have a number of command-line tools that can be equally effective, and sometimes more so since they can be scripted. Some of the tools available to help you with your domain migration are as follows:

- **ClonePrincipal**: This tool is available from the Windows 2000 or Windows Server 2003 Resource Kit, and is used to clone user and group accounts from a Windows NT 4.0, 2000, or 2003 source domain to a Windows 2000/2003 native mode domain, without removing the source account. At the same time, the utility adds the original account SID to the SIDHistory of the new account to maintain resource access. The Resource Kit includes a number of Visual Basic scripts that will help you customize the behavior of this tool.

■**Caution** **ClonePrincipal** does *not* migrate user passwords.

- **Netdom**: Used to migrate computer accounts and create or re-create trust relationships.

- **Movetree**: Used to move (not copy) users, groups, and Organizational Units between Windows 2000/2003 domains within the same forest. **Movetree** is able to migrate user password information.

- **Active Directory Migration Tool**: This is the big kahuna of Active Directory migration utilities. **ADMT** provides a GUI front-end to perform a number of tasks, including migrating trust relationships, updating the SIDHistory attribute, cloning local groups, and changing computer accounts to reflect any new domain or OU memberships. **ADMT** also allows you to test how you've configured the migration process so that you can do a "dry run" before actually creating any new accounts. In most situations, **ADMT** is going to be your migration tool of choice.

■**Caution** Although **ClonePrincipal** and **ADMT** sound like they're interchangeable, they shouldn't be used during the same migration operation. These two tools use different mechanisms to move objects and to figure out whether an object has already been moved, and so using them together can produce some unexpected (and probably unpleasant) results.

Migration Scenarios

In this section, we'll look at migrating existing NT 4.0 domains to Windows Server 2003. The source domains are laid out in Figure 7-1, with two account domains called USERS and USERS1, and four resource domains called ACCTG, HR, SALES, and DEV. The USERS domain contains 10,000 user objects, and USERS1 contains an additional 5,000. As you can see, there are two one-way trust relationships configured between the two account domains, and a one-way trust relationship configured between ACCTG, HR, SALES, and the two account domains. The ACCTG, HR, and SALES domains contain only computer accounts to host resources for each of those departments. The DEV domain, on the other hand, contains all of the computer resources for the Development department, as well as 200 user accounts, including three local administrators who are members of the Domain Admins group for the DEV domain. Because the users in the DEV domain also require access to resources in the other three resource domains, you've also had to configure trust relationships between the DEV domain and the ACCTG, HR, and SALES domains. This is exactly the kind of convoluted environment that Active Directory was made for; by consolidating these six domains into a single Active Directory domain, you'll be able to greatly streamline how your users access company resources.

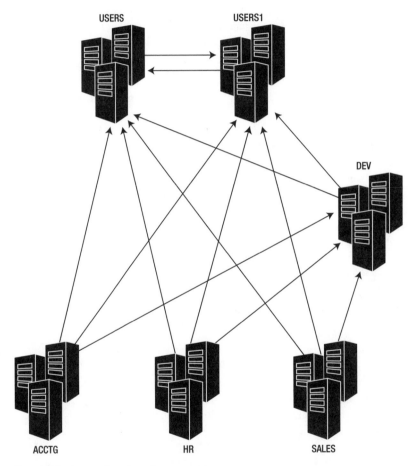

Figure 7-1. *A sample migration scenario*

Performing an Interforest Migration

So the first question is this: do you upgrade one of your existing domains, or migrate to a pristine environment? Say that none of your existing domain controllers are really beefy enough to run Windows Server 2003. In this case, you'll perform an interforest migration, consolidating the USERS and USERS1 domains into a single Active Directory domain. Each NT 4.0 resource domain will be consolidated into the one AD domain within its own Organizational Unit. This will allow you to maintain centralized control over the entire network, while still allowing the individual departments—especially the DEV department—to be able to maintain some control over their local resources. Performing an interforest migration involves several steps.

Creating the Destination Domain

The ability to create a pristine Windows Server 2003 forest to house your new Active Directory infrastructure is probably the most appealing part of the migration process. You can install and configure your Active Directory environment in precisely the way you want it to be, rather than trying to make it fit into the design constraints of your existing network. You'll create your destination domain using the concepts and steps we talked about in Chapter 1, since you're really just performing a fresh installation of Active Directory onto new hardware. As a part of this process, be sure to configure the necessary DNS servers for name resolution on an Active Directory network, especially if you weren't using DNS under Windows NT 4.0.

■**Caution** In order to use the **Active Directory Migration Tool** and the SIDHistory function, be sure that your new domain is running in Windows 2000 native mode or higher.

Once you have the destination domain in place, you'll have to decide what trust relationships you need to establish. When you're using **ADMT**, you should set up trust relationships between the source and the target domains so that **ADMT** can migrate objects successfully. At a minimum, you need to establish a one-way trust relationship, where the NT 4.0 domain is the *trusted* domain and the Active Directory domain is the *trusting* domain.

If you'll be consolidating all six domains in one long and sleepless weekend, then there won't be any need to set up other trust relationships because you're moving everything in one fell swoop. If, on the other hand, you'll be migrating your resource domains over a period of time, you'll need to set up an *external trust* between each resource domain and the Active Directory domain. This will ensure that your users will still be able to access network resources after you've migrated their user accounts but before you've consolidated the resource domains. In this case, you'll want to set up a one-way trust in which the Active Directory domain is the *trusted* domain and the NT 4.0 resource domains are the *trusting* domains. In the case of the DEV domain, you'll need to set up a two-way trust relationship with the Active Directory domain until the objects in the DEV domain have been migrated.

Preparing the Source and Target Domains

Now that your source and destination domains are ready, you can get down to the nuts and bolts of the migration process. You'll first install the **Active Directory Migration Tool** on a domain controller in the destination domain, using an account with Domain Admins credentials. If you'll be migrating password information, you'll need to take a few extra steps to prepare both the source and destination domains. The **Active Directory Migration Tool** uses a Password Encryption Server, or PES, to support interforest password migration. The PES can be any domain controller in the source domain that supports 128-bit encryption—which means that at least one of your NT 4.0 domain controllers needs to have Service Pack 6a installed.

You'll first need to prepare an encryption key in the target domain by logging on to the DC that has the **ADMT** software installed on it and running the following at the command prompt (this requires a blank floppy disk):

```
ADMT KEY SourceDomainNetBIOSName FloppyDrive Password
```

You can either enter a password at the end of this command, or type * to be prompted for one. Using a password will encrypt the key itself, and so it's highly advisable to use one. To prepare the target domain for password migration, you'll also need to add the Everyone and Anonymous Logon groups to the Pre-Windows 2000 Compatible Access group. If these groups need to be added, you'll have to restart the Server service on all the domain controllers in the target domain for the change to take effect.

To enable password migration on the source domain, you'll need the floppy disk containing the password encryption key, as well as the 2003 installation CD. Navigate to the \i386\admt\admigration.msi folder and run **pwdmig.exe**, and then enter the password that you set up on the floppy disk. After that, you'll make the following change to the Registry on the NT 4.0 controller:

1. Browse to the HKLM\System\CurrentControlSet\Control\LSA key.

2. Look for the AllowPasswordExport entry, and change its value from **0** to **1**.

As a final step to prepare the source domain, you'll need to create a local group called DomainName$$$. This group will be used to enable SIDHistory. Only create the group, don't add any members to it. You should also enable auditing of User and Group Management events (both successes and failures) on the target domain. This will allow you to verify that new user accounts are created, and will record error messages that you can use for troubleshooting if the migrations fail.

Migrating User and Group Accounts

Once **ADMT** has been installed, you'll find that it consists of a series of wizards that will help you migrate different parts of the source domain, including users, groups, computers, service accounts, and trust relationships. Your first step will be to migrate the *service accounts* for any applications that you'll be migrating over to the new domain. Since service accounts need to be granted the **Log on as a service** right, you should identify any services in your NT 4.0 domain that are running using an account other than the LocalSystem account, so that you can configure any services in the target domain correctly.

Identifying Service Accounts

To identify service accounts in your source domain, follow these steps:

1. Open the **Active Directory Migration Tool**. Right-click the top folder and select **Service Account Migration Wizard**. Click **Next** to bypass the initial screen.

2. Enter the source and the target domains, or use the drop-down boxes to browse for them. Click **Next** to continue.

3. On the **Update Information** screen, select **Yes, update the information**. This screen exists to let you use information that you collected previously on a "dry run" of the migration process.

4. On the **Service Account Selection** screen, click **Add** to include all machines in the source domain that use service accounts. This includes domain controllers, member servers, and workstations.

5. If you're prompted to, enter user credentials for the servers that you specified in step 4, and click **Next**.

   From here **ADMT** will send a software inventory agent out to each server that you specified. This agent will query all registered services to see what credentials they're running under, and return to you the names of any services that aren't using LocalSystem, and the name of the account that they're using.

6. If any of the accounts returned by the **ADMT** query shouldn't be marked as service accounts during the migration—you'll be reconfiguring the service, for example—click on the **Skip/Include** button to prevent a particular account from being marked as a service account. Click **Next**, and then **Finish**.

At this point, **ADMT** hasn't actually migrated any of the service accounts. It has merely marked the accounts in the **ADMT** database, so that when the accounts are migrated later they'll automatically be assigned the **Log on as a service** permission.

■**Note** You can also run this query from the command line by using the syntax ADMT SERVICE /N "*COMPUTERNAME1*" "*COMPUTERNAME2*" /SD:source domain, /TD:target domain. "*COMPUTERNAME1*" and "*COMPUTERNAME2*" are the NetBIOS names of machines in the source domain that use service accounts.

Migrating Group Accounts

In a process that's very similar to the Service Account Migration Wizard, you'll use the Group Migration Wizard in **ADMT**. When migrating from Windows NT 4.0 to Windows 2000/2003, any local groups in the source domain will be converted to Domain Local groups in Active Directory. Global groups will remain Global groups within the target domain. The group migration process goes like this:

1. Right-click the Active Directory Migration Wizard and select **Group Migration Wizard**. Click **Next** to get started.

2. On the **Test or Make Changes** screen, select **Make Changes** to begin migrating accounts and click **Next**.

3. Enter the source and destination domain names and click **Next**.

4. The next screen is for **Group Selection**. Click **Add** to select the groups that you want to migrate, and then click **Next**.

5. On the next screen, you can select the Active Directory OU that the group should be migrated into. Use the **Browse** button to select the correct OU and click **Next** to continue.

6. The next screen allows you to specify options for migrating groups. Your options here include the following:

- **Update user rights**: Takes the user rights assigned to these groups in the source domain and copies them to the target domain.

- **Copy Group Members**: Migrates the user objects that belong to the group. If you don't select this option, only the group object will get migrated, and you'll need to migrate the users separately.

- **Update Previously Migrated Objects**: If you migrate users over a long period of time, you may need to remigrate your global groups at the end of the migration so that the group membership in the target domain remains correct. By selecting this option, you can remigrate only the group members that have recently been migrated to the target domain without overwriting any users that had previously been migrated.

- **Fix membership of the group**: Adds migrated users to the new group in the target domain if they belonged to the group in the source domain

- **Migrate Group SIDS to target domain**: Migrates the Group SID in the SIDHistory attribute.

- **Naming Options**: Allows you to specify how migrated groups are named in the target domain. You can have migrated groups retain the same name, or specify a prefix or suffix to add to each group name.

7. Once you've specified the group options, click **Next**. If you're migrating the Group SID, you'll be prompted for administrative credentials on the next screen; once you've specified them, click **Next**.

8. Next is the **Naming Conflicts** screen, shown in Figure 7-2. Here you'll specify what **ADMT** should do if it encounters any name collisions during the migration process. You can choose not to migrate accounts with conflicting names, create a new object by renaming the conflicting account, or replace the conflicting account with the one being migrated.

9. Click **Next** and then **Finish** to perform the migration.

■**Caution** Because global groups can only contain user objects that reside in the same domain, you'll need to migrate your global groups before you migrate any user accounts.

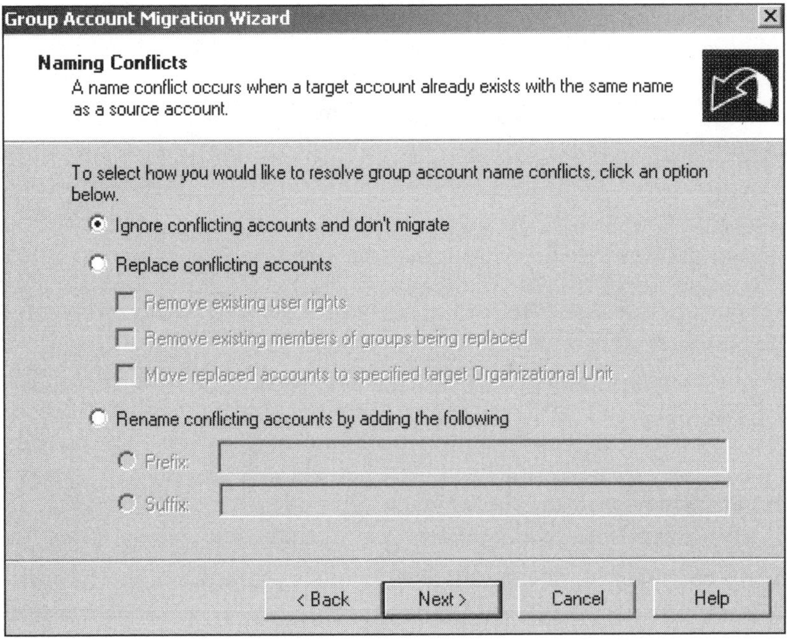

Figure 7-2. *Handling naming conflicts with ADMT*

Migrating User Accounts

To migrate user accounts, you'll use either the **ClonePrincipal** utility or the User Account Migration Wizard from the **ADMT**. The largest point of contention with user migration tends to be the question of passwords: what happens to them during the migration? **ADMT** will migrate passwords along with the associated user objects, unless the password in the source domain doesn't meet the password complexity requirements of the target domain. In other words, you have a Windows NT 4.0 user who's had the password "fluffy" for the last three years, and you're migrating to a Windows Server 2003 domain where you've enabled password complexity requirements and a minimum password length of eight characters. In this case, the password migration for that user will fail, and **ADMT** will generate a new complex password for the user account in the target domain. Any passwords that **ADMT** needs to create will be stored in a text file in the Program Files\ Active Directory Migration Tool\Logs\Password.txt file. At this point, you'll need to create a mechanism to communicate the new passwords to the users so that they'll be able to log on to the new domain.

■**Caution** Be sure to test the migration process with a few sample users before migrating any actual users. Some properties of user objects will not be migrated by **ADMT**, so you may need to massage the newly created accounts in the target domain once the migration is over.

To migrate user accounts using the **ADMT**, follow these steps:

1. Right-click the ADMT folder and select **User Account Migration Wizard**. Click **Next** to continue.

2. Select **Migrate Now?** to perform a migration instead of a test. Click **Next** to continue.

3. Specify the source and target domains and click **Next**.

4. Click **Add** to select the user accounts you want to migrate. Click **OK** when you've selected all the users to be migrated, and then click **Next**.

5. Select a target OU that the migrated users should be placed in, and click **Next**.

6. On the **Password Options** screen, select the option **Migrate Passwords**.

7. The **Account Transition Options** screen allows you to control how the source and domain target accounts. You have the option to disable the source account, the target account, or both. You can also set an expiration date on the user accounts in the source domain. This screen is also where you choose the option **Migrate User SIDs to target domain**. Click **Next** when you've got these options configured the way you want.

8. If you're using SIDHistory, you'll need to enter administrative credentials for the source domain and click **Next**.

9. Next is the **User Options** screen. This is similar to the options available for migrating user accounts, with the additional option of translating the UNC path for roaming profiles to reflect their location in the new domain. Click **Next** when you're ready to continue.

10. Your last step is to specify how the wizard should handle naming conflicts. Just like when migrating group accounts, you can choose not to migrate the conflicting account, replace the object in the target domain with the object that's being migrated, or rename the source domain by adding a prefix or suffix to the object name.

Migrating Computer Accounts

You'll want to migrate users' workstations at the time that you migrate their user accounts so that both objects are present in the target domain the next time a user tries to log on. Migrating workstation accounts is pretty simple, since the local SAM database doesn't need to be migrated and simply stays in place on the local workstation. You'll migrate these objects using the Computer Account Migration Wizard in the **ADMT**. By this point, the **ADMT** wizards have become pretty self-explanatory. The only real change is that you'll specify how long to wait after the migration to restart the target computer, since changing domain memberships is one of those operations that will require a reboot.

SID FILTERING AND SID HISTORY: SECURITY VERSUS CONVENIENCE

While the SIDHistory feature makes domain migration a much simpler task, there are certain instances where you won't be able to use it. To improve the security of your AD forest, you may decide to configure *SID filtering* for your AD forest. SID filtering prevents the SIDHistory attribute from working, in effect breaking the trust relationship between two domains in a separate forest. If you have configured SID filtering on your Windows 2000/2003 domain, the SIDHistory function will not work.

In order to ensure that your users can continue to access resources without SIDHistory in place, you'll need to *translate* security for resources in the target domain. This will go through any ACLs in the target domain (for file shares, printers, and the like) and replace any entries that include SIDs from the source domain with the updated SIDs from the target domain. You'll run the Security Translation Wizard on every member server that you migrate, as well as on at least one migrated domain controller. You can run the wizard in one of two modes:

- *Add*: Use this to add the object SIDs from the target domain to the ACLs on your migrated resources, while leaving references to the source domain in place.

- *Remove*: This will remove any references to SIDs from the source domain. Only use this option after all of your user accounts have been migrated to the new domain and the source domain is ready to be taken offline.

To run the Security Translation Wizard, you'll select the member server containing the ACLs that need translating, and then select the objects that should be updated—this includes files and folders, printers, the Windows Registry, and user profiles.

Summary

In this chapter, we looked at the task of planning for and performing a migration to Active Directory from an existing Windows NT 4.0 network. Windows 2000 Server and Windows Server 2003 allow you to perform a direct upgrade from an NT 4.0 domain, or you can use the **Active Directory Migration Tool** to migrate from an existing NT 4.0 domain to a pristine Active Directory environment. When you are performing an in-place upgrade from NT 4.0, the first domain controller that you upgrade must be the Primary Domain Controller of the existing NT 4.0 domain. Once the PDC has been upgraded, any Backup Domain Controllers can be upgraded to domain controller status, or else demoted to member server status during the upgrade to Windows 2000 Server or Windows Server 2003.

When you're performing a migration instead of an in-place upgrade, you have a great deal of flexibility in terms of how you will structure your new Active Directory environment. In many cases, you'll want to use the new scalability of Active Directory to collapse several account and resource domains into a single Active Directory domain, and use Organizational Units (OUs) to administer resources and delegate authority. The **Active Directory Migration Tool** will help you migrate user and computer accounts, as well as make special considerations for user profiles and Windows service accounts.

In the next chapter, we'll talk about disaster recovery and business continuity planning as it relates to your Active Directory network.

Additional Resources

"Windows 2000 Active Directory Migration Cookbook": http://www.microsoft.com/technet/prodtechnol/windows2000serv/deploy/cookbook/default.mspx—This was written specifically for an NT 4.0–to–2000 migration, so some of the specifics of the **ADMT** have changed, but it's still a good foundation on migration planning and other assorted topics.

"Using SID Filtering to Prevent Elevation of Privilege Attacks": http://www.microsoft.com/windows2000/techinfo/administration/security/sidfilter.asp—An older but still useful whitepaper, detailing everything you ever wanted to know about SIDHistory and SID Filtering.

Active Directory Migration Tool: http://www.microsoft.com/resources/documentation/windowsserv/2003/all/deployguide/en-us/dssbg_rent_gcrd.asp—Everything you can do with **ADMT** from the GUI, you can also use from the command line and with VBScript. This page lists the VBScript commands that you can use to script the **ADMT** process.

CHAPTER 8

Disaster Recovery

Or Not Only Was Murphy an Optimist, but I Think He Worked in IT

Even though this chapter falls almost last in our guide, it's important enough that I probably should have placed it first instead. Disaster recovery often winds up on the back burner of an administrator's life, since we're so busy dealing with the day-to-day administrative tasks on our networks that we might not think much about the things that could go wrong until they actually do. In this chapter, I'll show you ways to create a disaster recovery plan for Active Directory, so that you can protect your networks from failure and be able to restore mission-critical services quickly in the event of a failure. I'll start by talking about the importance of creating a test network to do "dry runs" of any major changes you're planning, so that you can minimize the impact of downtime and errors in your production environment Then I'll explain ways to troubleshoot a server that has had a software install go awry, or that just gets up on the wrong side of the bed one morning and decides not to boot properly just to ruin your day. You'll learn strategies for backing up and restoring your Active Directory database to ensure that your Active Directory database can be brought back online quickly when (not if) something untoward happens on your network.

In this chapter, you'll learn how to

- Create a test network to mirror your production environment.
- Back up the Active Directory database.
- Perform authoritative, nonauthoritative, and primary restores.
- Troubleshoot a failed server.
- Use the Recovery Console.
- Configure Automated System Recovery.
- Restore Active Directory in different disaster recovery scenarios.

Troubleshooting System Startup

So you perform some maintenance on one of your servers, and then reboot it just like you've done a hundred times before. Only instead of getting back to the Windows desktop in a normal fashion, something goes horribly awry. The server hangs up on "Applying computer settings . . ." or "Preparing network connections. . . ." Maybe it continuously reboots itself, or just leaves you hanging at the dreaded Blue Screen of Death. Being able to troubleshoot a misbehaving Windows machine is sometimes the difference between a good administrator and a great one, since it means the difference between a few minutes of downtime for your users versus a few hours or days. Luckily, Windows 2000 Server and Windows Server 2003 provide you with a number of options to revive a cranky server and get it back to a running state.

Using Alternate Startup Modes

Unlike Windows NT 4.0, Windows 2000 and 2003 allow you to boot into several alternate startup modes like Safe Mode and Safe Mode with Networking. (And unlike Windows 95 and Windows 98, using Safe Mode in Windows 2000 and 2003 actually does some good more often than not.) In Safe Mode, Windows uses certain default settings like a VGA monitor, Microsoft mouse driver, and no network connectivity. Basically, Safe Mode creates an environment that uses the minimum device drivers needed to start Windows. So if your Windows 2000/2003 server won't start after you install a new software package, you can try to restart the server using the minimal services in Safe Mode, and then change how the new software package is configured, or even remove it entirely to verify that it is actually the cause of the problem. You can even reinstall the latest Windows service pack or the entire operating system from Safe Mode, if necessary. If a server is misbehaving, and you restart the server in Safe Mode and the problem doesn't reappear, you can eliminate the Windows default settings and minimum drivers as the point of failure for the server. You can then set nonessential services to be disabled, and then reenable the services one at a time to see which one is the troublemaker.

The different startup modes available for you are as follows:

- *Safe Mode*: Starts the server using the basic system files and device drivers for the mouse, monitor, keyboard, and mass storage devices—usually a hard drive. It loads a base VGA video driver and default system services, and does not include any network support. If you can't even get a machine to start successfully using Safe Mode, you may need to go to the Recovery Console to repair your server. (We'll talk more about the Recovery Console in just a moment.)

- *Safe Mode with Networking*: Starts a Windows machine with the same features as Safe Mode, but enables networking support.

- *Safe Mode with Command Prompt:* Starts up a machine using only the basic system files and drivers, but boots the machine directly to a command prompt instead of to the Windows desktop. There is no networking support in this mode.

- *Enable Boot Logging:* Starts your system normally, and logs all the drivers and services that were loaded (or not loaded) to the *%systemroot%* ntbtlog.txt file. Safe Mode, Safe Mode with Networking, and Safe Mode with Command Prompt will all create this log file as well, in addition to starting up in a restrictive mode. You can use this boot log to determine exactly which services and drivers were able or unable to load, and isolate the cause of a system failure. You can see how a portion of this log file appears here:

```
Microsoft (R) Windows (R) Version 5.2 (Build 3790)
 7 29 2004 14:15:20.375
Loaded driver \WINDOWS\system32\ntoskrnl.exe
Loaded driver \WINDOWS\system32\hal.dll
Loaded driver \WINDOWS\system32\KDCOM.DLL
Loaded driver \WINDOWS\system32\BOOTVID.dll
Loaded driver ACPI.sys
Loaded driver \WINDOWS\system32\DRIVERS\WMILIB.SYS
Loaded driver pci.sys
Loaded driver isapnp.sys
Loaded driver pciide.sys
Loaded driver \WINDOWS\system32\DRIVERS\PCIIDEX.SYS
Loaded driver MountMgr.sys
Loaded driver ftdisk.sys
Loaded driver dmload.sys
Loaded driver dmio.sys
Loaded driver volsnap.sys
Loaded driver PartMgr.sys
Loaded driver atapi.sys
Loaded driver cercsr6.sys
Loaded driver \WINDOWS\system32\drivers\SCSIPORT.SYS
Loaded driver afamgt.sys
Loaded driver disk.sys
Loaded driver \WINDOWS\system32\DRIVERS\CLASSPNP.SYS
Loaded driver Dfs.sys
Loaded driver KSecDD.sys
Loaded driver Ntfs.sys
Loaded driver NDIS.sys
Loaded driver Mup.sys
Loaded driver crcdisk.sys
Did not load driver ACPI Multiprocessor PC
Did not load driver Audio Codecs
```

- *Enable VGA Mode*: Starts the computer using the base VGA video driver that gets loaded in Safe Mode. This is useful if you're specifically troubleshooting a new display driver you've installed that is preventing your system from booting properly.

- *Directory Services Restore Mode*: This mode is exactly what it sounds like—you'll use it on domain controllers to restore Active Directory and the SYSVOL share. We'll talk more about this mode in the section "Backing Up and Restoring Active Directory."

- *Debugging Mode*: A pretty advanced feature—it starts up the machine in kernel debugging mode while sending debug information to another computer through a serial cable, which allows you to use a kernel debugger to do really detailed troubleshooting and analysis. You'll almost never use this option unless you're instructed to do so by Microsoft Product Support Services.

- *Last Known Good Configuration*: A useful feature if your server stops responding immediately after you install a new piece of hardware or software. Last Known Good Configuration will start Windows using the Registry information and drivers that Windows saved at the last graceful shutdown. It can sometimes resolve configuration issues that have cropped up immediately after an install by loading the Registry settings and driver files that were present at the last shutdown, but it's also something of a weapon of last resort. Any driver settings or other system setting changes that you've made since the last successful logon will be lost, so using Last Known Good Configuration can actually be destructive to other configuration you've done on a server. It's because of Last Known Good Configuration that I always reboot my servers after performing any significant maintenance or installations, even if the OS doesn't prompt me to do so. While it's good that Windows 2000 Server and Windows Server 2003 don't prompt you to reboot nearly as often as NT 4.0 did, it becomes a double-edged sword if you ever try to use this particular troubleshooting mode. If you haven't rebooted a server since before you made some major changes to the IIS metabase, for example, using Last Known Good Configuration will wipe out all of those changes by reverting to the configuration that was set at the last graceful shutdown.

Caution Last Known Good Configuration in Windows 2000 Server and Windows NT 4.0 will save only the Registry settings that were present at the last shutdown. Driver files are only preserved in Windows Server 2003.

Using the Recovery Console

If you can't even start up a server in Safe Mode, you can try using the Recovery Console to bring the server back online before resorting to recovering from a backup. The Recovery Console allows you to access a Windows server without launching the GUI, enabling you to perform the following tasks at the command line:

- Obtain access to disk volumes on a server.

- Copy, rename, or replace files and folders within the operating system.

- Enable or disable services or device drivers.

- Repair the boot sector or the master boot record (MBR) of a physical hard disk.

- Create and format partitions on physical hard drives.

You can access the Recovery Console by booting from a Windows 2000 or Windows Server 2003 installation CD and selecting the option **Repair a Windows 2000/2003 installation** within the text portion of Windows setup. Type **C** when you reach the next screen to access the Recovery Console. You can also simplify this by installing the Recovery Console locally on the server hard drive. The Recovery Console installation takes up only about 8MB of space, and adds an entry for the Recovery Console to the boot.ini startup menu for your server. You can install the Recovery Console locally by running the `winnt32.exe /cmdcons` command from within Windows. When you launch the Recovery Console, you'll be prompted to enter the password for the local Administrator account. Be sure to remember that this is not the password for a domain account, but for the local Administrator—it's the one you were prompted to create when you ran **dcpromo** and needed to create a Directory Services Restore Mode password.

■**Caution** Because installing the Recovery Console locally can provide an alternative way for a malicious user to log on to a server, you should weigh the benefits of installing this feature locally with the potential security risk that it creates. If you are supporting a server in a remote location that does not have adequate physical security, for example, you shouldn't install the Recovery Console locally.

Because the Recovery Console can potentially provide an attacker (or a careless administrator) with the ability to wreak a certain amount of havoc on a server, it has certain limitations. Specifically, the Recovery Console can only access the root directory of the boot volume, the *%systemroot%* folder and any subfolders, the CMDCONS folder, and any removable media such as floppy drives and CD-ROMs. In addition, some Recovery Console commands will not work on dynamic disks or on an Itanium-based computer. You have the ability to copy files from a floppy or a CD to the local hard drive, although by default you're prevented from copying files from the local hard drive *to* removable media. When you're working in the Recovery Console, you can use the commands listed in Table 8-1.

Table 8-1. *Recovery Console Commands*

Command	Explanation
attrib	Changes the attributes of a file or folder.
batch	Executes multiple commands specified in a text file.
bootcfg	Makes changes to the boot configuration of a server. Bootcfg /add will add a Windows installation to the boot.ini file. Bootcfg /scan will scan all Windows installations on a machine so that you can choose which ones to add to boot.ini. Bootcfg /default will set the default boot entry. Bootcfg /list will list the Windows installations that are currently included in boot.ini.
cd	Displays the current working directory, or changes it to one that you specify.
chkdsk	Checks the hard disk for errors. Marks any bad sectors and repairs any errors it finds.
cls	Clears the console screen.
copy	Copies files.
del	Deletes files.
dir	Lists the contents of a directory.
disable	Disables a service. Uses the syntax disable servicename.
diskpart	Manages the partitions on your hard disks. Diskpart /add creates a new partition. Diskpart /delete deletes a partition.
enable	Enables a service or driver. Uses the syntax enable servicename start_type, where start_type can be SERVICE_BOOT_START, SERVICE_SYSTEM_START, SERVICE_AUTO_START, or SERVICE_DEMAND_START.
exit	Quits the Recovery Console and restarts the computer.
expand	Unzips a compressed file. Expand /y will overwrite existing files without prompting.
fixboot	Used with the syntax fixboot drivename to write a new boot sector on the system partition.

Command	Explanation
fixmbr	Used with the syntax fixmbr devicename to write a new master boot record to the boot partition.
format	Formats disk partitions.
listsvc	Lists all services and drivers that are available on a particular computer, as well as their startup types.
logon	Allows you to log on to a different Windows installation on the local machine. You'll be prompted for the local Administrator password for the other installation.
map	Lists drive letters, file system types, and partition sizes on physical disk drives.
md	Creates a directory.
more	Displays a text file to the screen, with the syntax more filename.
rd	Deletes a directory.
ren	Renames a file.
systemroot	Sets the current directory to the root of the *%systemroot%* directory.
type	Same use and syntax as more.

■Note If you install the Recovery Console to a hard drive configured with the .FAT file system, you should reinstall it in the event that you convert the file system to NTFS.

A final command available in the Recovery Console is the set command. You can use set to configure four different variables, using the syntax set VARIABLE = TRUE or set VARIABLE = FALSE. The four variables you can set are

- AllowWildCards: Allows you to use the * and ? wildcards with certain Recovery Console commands, such as del *.tmp.

- AllowAllPaths: Allows you to use the cd command to access any path on the server, not just the *%systemroot%* directory and its subdirectories.

- AllowRemovableMedia: Allows you to copy files from the hard drive to a floppy disk or other removable media types.

- NoCopyPrompt: Won't prompt you with an "Are you sure?" when you try to overwrite an existing file.

You won't be able to set any of these variables within the Recovery Console until you've first enabled it in the Local Security Policy or in a Group Policy Object. To be able to navigate the entire hard drive from the Recovery Console, you need to enable the **Recover Console: Allow floppy copy and access to all drives and all folders** policy setting under Local Policies\Security Options.

■**Caution** Another policy setting for the Recovery Console is **Allow automatic Administrative Logon,** which will automatically log someone on with the local Administrator password when he fires up the Recovery Console. Do I really need to explain the tremendous security hole you'd leave open on your domain controllers if you enabled this one?

Backing Up and Restoring Active Directory

Hopefully, I'm preaching to the choir when I talk about the importance of backing up the system state of your Windows servers. Protecting the information that's stored on your network servers, including the Active Directory database, is quite simply the most important thing you can do as a part of your disaster recovery planning. Provisioning for spare network hardware is useful as a time-saving mechanism and to prevent extended outages. Network and server hardware, though, is relatively simple to replace: in a worst-case scenario, you can simply take the CFO's credit card and go buy a new machine from your local electronics superstore to keep you up and running while your production hardware is repaired or replaced. Your network data cannot be replaced quite so easily, and your Active Directory data can be just as important as your data files. If you can't restore Active Directory from a backup, you'll be faced with the unpleasant task of re-creating user and group information from scratch. This is not only a long and laborious process, but it also creates a potential security risk, since you can't really be sure that you reconfigured everything correctly from memory. This can create lingering access and security problems that might not show themselves for weeks or even months after an outage. Because of this, your Active Directory database should be included in your nightly backups of critical network data.

■**Caution** Just like backups for your other critical network data, you should maintain copies of your Active Directory backups in an offsite location in case of a natural disaster or other mishap.

The built-in Windows **Backup** utility makes it quite simple to back up the Active Directory database, and almost any third-party server backup utility will do the same. (In fact, if you're using a backup utility that doesn't allow for easy Active Directory backups and restores, I'd personally recommend that you find yourself another one.) Unlike creating backups for your data files, where you need to decide between full, differential, and incremental backups, backing up the Active Directory is relatively straightforward. Backing up Active Directory involves creating a system state backup on each of your domain controllers. You can create a system state backup for any Windows machine, but the contents of the system state will vary depending on how each machine is configured. System state information needs to be backed up as a unit, and consists of the following:

- Registry
- COM+ class registration database
- System files
- Boot files
- Files protected by the Windows File Protection service
- Certificate Services database (for machines running Certificate Services)
- Active Directory database and SYSVOL directory (for domain controllers)
- Cluster database information (for machines running as part of a Windows cluster)
- IIS metabase (for web servers)

Using Windows Backup

To create a system state backup, you can use the built-in Windows **Backup** utility located at **Start ➤ All Programs ➤ Accessories ➤ System Tools ➤ Backup**. To create a system state backup, follow these steps:

1. Open the Windows **Backup** utility.

2. Select **Tools ➤ Backup Wizard**. Click **Next** to bypass the initial **Welcome** screen.

3. Click the radio button next to **Only back up the System State data** to perform a dedicated system state backup. Click **Next**.

4. Browse to the appropriate backup media, either backing up directly to a tape or backing up to a file. Give the backup a name and click **Next**.

5. Click **Advanced** to set additional options for your system state backup.

6. On the **Type of Backup** screen, leave the backup type as **Normal** and click **Next**. (System state backups cannot use incremental or differential backups.)

7. Place a check mark next to **Verify data after backup**.

8. Select whether you want to **append** this backup to any existing information, or **replace** any existing backups with the new information. Remember, if you choose to append to existing backups, you'll need to keep an eye on your disk space usage as the size of the backup file grows over time. Click **Next** to continue.

9. On the **When to back up** screen, click the radio button next to **Later**, and click **Set Schedule** to create a regular schedule for system state backups. Click **Next** to continue. You'll be prompted to enter a username and password to run the backup at a later time.

10. Click **Finish** once you've scheduled your system state backup.

It's important to remember that a system state backup isn't a backup of the entire system, just the key configuration components of a particular machine. System state backups don't include user data or the majority of the Windows operating system files; these need to be backed up separately. Because the entire system state needs to be backed up as a unit, you can only configure your backups as full backups; you can't use differential or incremental backups.

■**Note** You may have noticed that the Backup Wizard also offers you the option to **Back up everything on this computer**. If you select this option, the backup job you create will include the system state data along with all programs and data on the machine. This is a convenient way to create a backup plan to protect an entire server in one shot.

Using Automated System Recovery

Another necessary part of disaster recovery planning is to figure out what you're going to do in the event of a catastrophic hard drive failure on a particular machine, where you need to rebuild the operating system from scratch. (You'll hear this referred to as a *bare metal restore*.) In Windows 2000, the only way to do this is to manually reinstall the operating system and reconfigure it. Windows Server 2003 introduces Automated System Recovery, or ASR, which is a new tool that adds new functionality to Windows **Backup**, as well as third-party backup software. The purpose of ASR is really simple: it allows you to bring a server back online quickly after this type of major system failure. The files and settings restored by ASR create a really simplified configuration: ASR stores your boot and system drive configurations and works with Windows Setup to bring the failed server back to a point where it can boot successfully and has the same partitions and drives configured as before the drive failure. After this, you can then restore any data or application files. ASR replaces the Emergency Repair Disk feature in Windows 2000 and earlier versions of Windows. The major difference between ASR and

ERD is that ERD will replace any missing or corrupt system files without formatting any hard drives or reconfiguring any storage partitions. By comparison, ASR will reformat the boot and system partitions.

■Caution ASR only saves information that's stored on the system and boot partitions. Data stored on other volumes won't be included in an ASR backup and will not be restored as a part of the ASR process. You can either back up these other volumes separately or use the **Back up everything on this computer** option in the Windows Backup Wizard to create a full backup of all data on your server in addition to an ASR backup set.

Because ASR is a destructive process that reformats partitions before restoring them, and because it only restores a basic configuration, you should still think of ASR as a weapon of last resort to get a failed server back up and running. In addition, for some applications like SQL Server, Exchange, and IIS, ASR will not necessarily back up all of the files that you need to perform an automatic recovery. Before using Automated System Recovery, you should assess whether your hard disk has been physically damaged and have it replaced or repaired if necessary. If you need to install a new hard disk, it should have the same number of spindles (physical drives) as the old one, and each spindle must be as large as, or larger than, the corresponding spindle in the disk that failed. The ASR process will fail if the new hard disk contains fewer spindles, or if the spindles are smaller than the ones on the failed disk.

Using Automated System Recovery is a two-part process: creating an ASR backup and performing ASR restore. You'll create an ASR backup through the Windows **Backup** utility; like regular backups, the ASR creation process is extremely menu-driven and easy to follow. The ASR Wizard backs up the system state data, system services that are installed on your machine, and the configuration of the system and boot disks. It also creates a floppy disk that contains the disk configurations and provides information that Windows will use in an ASR restore.

To create an Automated System Recovery backup, follow these steps:

1. Click **Start ➤ All Programs ➤ Accessories ➤ System Tools ➤ Backup**.

2. If Windows **Backup** starts in Wizard Mode, click **Advanced Mode** to switch to the screen shown in Figure 8-1.

3. From the screen shown in Figure 8-1, click **Automated System Recovery Wizard**. Click **Next** to bypass the initial **Welcome** screen.

4. Select a destination for the backup file, which uses a .BFK extension. This can be stored on the local hard drive, or preferably on a network file share on another server. Click **Next** to continue.

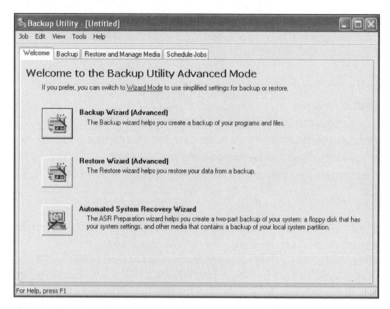

Figure 8-1. *Creating an ASR backup*

During the ASR creation process, you'll be prompted to insert a floppy disk to store the following two files:

- *asr.sif*: Contains information about the disk signatures on your server and how your disk volumes are configured

- *asrpnp.sif*: Contains information about the plug-and-play hardware devices installed on your system

If you don't have a floppy drive installed on your server, you can simply hit **Cancel** when you're prompted for the floppy. These two files also get copied to the *%systemroot%*\Repair folder on the boot volume of the server, so you can manually copy them from this location to manually create an ASR floppy disk. Even though you can perform an ASR backup without a floppy drive, it will still be necessary to perform an ASR restore. Because of this, you'll still need a floppy drive to perform an ASR restore, so I'd recommend that you drop a few bucks on an external USB floppy drive. This is especially true if you have a number of servers that you're creating ASR backup sets for. The files asr.sif and asrpnp.sif need to be copied into the root of the floppy disk in order to be used by the ASR restore process. If you misplace your ASR floppy disk, just create a new one by manually restoring the asr.sif and asrpnp.sif files from the *%systemroot%*\Repair directory of the backup set that you're restoring from.

■**Note** As an alternative, you can also use Remote Installation Services to automate the restore process for a server that does not have a floppy drive. This requires your server to have a PXE-enabled network adapter to allow for booting and installing remotely over a TCP/IP connection.

Performing a system restore using Automated System Recovery is relatively straightforward. (Otherwise, they'd be hard-pressed to keep calling it "Automated," wouldn't you say?) You'll need to have the following media available to do an ASR restore:

- The ASR floppy disk
- The ASR backup set, either stored on tape or otherwise accessible to the system being restored
- The Windows Server 2003 installation media and installation key
- Any third-party mass storage drivers for your server's hard disk controller, copied to a floppy drive

Once you have this information available, boot the server to the CD media, and press F2 when prompted during the text portion of Windows Setup. You'll be prompted for the ASR floppy disk, after which ASR will launch a setup routine that will format and re-create the hard disk partitions on your server and copy your data from the ASR backup set.

As you can probably figure out from reading a description of Automated System Recovery, it's really designed to re-create a Windows installation on the same hardware configuration that the ASR backup was created from. An ASR backup will function most effectively when the hardware you're restoring onto is identical to the original hardware, or as close as possible if an identical configuration isn't possible. We'll talk about restoring Windows and Active Directory to different hardware configurations in the "Restoring to Dissimilar Hardware" section.

Performing Active Directory Restores

You can use Windows **Backup** or a third-party utility to restore individual objects within Active Directory, or entire Organizational Units and even the entire AD database. This is extremely useful because there's no "Undo" button in any of the Active Directory utilities: once you make a change (complete with the confirmation button that accompanies any deletion), then the change is made and there's no going back from it without resorting to a data restore. Unlike the Windows file system, there's no Recycle Bin within Active

Directory for Windows 2000 to allow you to undelete objects. (Active Directory in Windows Server 2003 allows for this on a limited basis, but it's still pretty hairy.)

Active Directory restores are heavily dependent on Update Sequence Numbers, or USNs. In multimaster replication, each domain controller maintains its own copy of the AD database, and each object has an associated Update Sequence Number. When you modify an object from a particular domain controller, that DC updates the USN on its copy of that object. This way, when the various domain controllers replicate their information to each other, they will compare the USN of each object to see which DC has the most up-to-date copy of that object. Then the most current copy of the object, including the value of its USN, will be replicated to each domain controller in the topology. This becomes a concern for Active Directory restores when the USN of a restored object is lower than the USN that currently exists in the AD database, which will happen if an object gets modified after a backup is performed.

Another replication issue that's critical to the restore process is that, when you delete an object within Active Directory, the object is actually *tombstoned* rather than deleted outright. Active Directory is configured this way to allow for any delays in replication between domain controllers, so that your Active Directory data remains consistent. If you delete a user object from Domain Controller A, and Domain Controller B misses the replication update that includes the deletion, the object might get re-created during the next replication cycle, since Domain Controller B doesn't know that the user should have been deleted, and still has it listed as a valid object in its copy of the Active Directory database. Using the tombstone process eliminates this potential for messy replication: when you delete an object within Active Directory, the object is tombstoned for 60 days, and that tombstone record is replicated to the other domain controllers within Active Directory. Only after the tombstone interval has passed does the object actually get deleted.

■**Caution** Because of this tombstone interval, you should be careful about returning domain controllers to production that have been offline for longer than 60 days. Bringing old domain controllers back online in this way can create replication errors if the DC has missed the tombstone interval for objects that it still has a record for. In this case, it's better to demote the old domain controller to member server status before returning it to production, then run **dcpromo** again so that it can receive the most current replication information.

TAKING OUT THE ACTIVE DIRECTORY GARBAGE

The default tombstone interval in Active Directory also means that your backups have an effective useful lifespan of 60 days. This is because of the situation that occurs if you have an Active Directory object that was deleted after a backup was made, and you perform a restore after the tombstone interval for the deleted object has expired and the object has been permanently removed. When this happens, the restored domain controller will have a copy of the object the way it existed before it was deleted, but the other DCs in your environment would have no record that the object exists, or ever existed to begin with. Now you're in a situation where your restored domain controller will have a number of these "orphaned" objects that won't be replicated to the other domain controllers, which you'll need to manually delete on the restored DC once they've stopped confusing the heck out of you by trying to figure out where they came from.

If you need your backups to be valid for longer than 60 days, there are two Active Directory Configuration settings that you can modify, under the cn=Directory Service,cn=Windows NT,cn=Service,cn=Configuration,dc=*ForestRootDomain* node of the Active Directory schema:

- The **garbage collection interval** determines how frequently Active Directory will check for tombstoned objects that have been hanging around long enough that they can be deleted. The default is 12 hours, and it can run as frequently as every hour. The garbage collection process also performs an online defragmentation of the Active Directory database.

- The **tombstone lifetime** setting determines how long an object will remain tombstoned before the garbage collection process will pick it up and destroy it. The default is 60 days, as I've mentioned, but you can set it higher than 60 days, or as low as 2 days.

You can modify one or both of these settings using the **LDP.EXE** utility in the Windows 2000 Resource Kit, or the Windows Server 2003 Support Tools. **LDP.EXE** is a powerful utility that allows you to modify the Active Directory schema and configuration through a GUI interface, as well as add and delete Active Directory objects and containers. LDP comes with a lengthy white paper that is required reading before using this utility in a production environment, since you are directly modifying the configuration of Active Directory and might otherwise make inadvertent changes that could cripple your AD configuration.

So what happens when you restore an object with a lower USN than the one that exists in the production database? And what happens when you need to restore a deleted object? You have a few different options in performing AD restores that will help you address both of these points, which we'll discuss next.

Nonauthoritative Restores

The default Active Directory restore type is a nonauthoritative restore. In a nonauthoritative restore, you're restoring Active Directory onto a domain controller in an existing AD network, and then allowing the other DCs in the domain to replicate any changes that have been made since the backup was performed. Let's look at an example of a nonauthoritative restore to clarify this a bit.

Say that you have an Active Directory domain with three domain controllers: DC1, DC2, and DC3. You've configured an Active Directory backup to run on each machine on a nightly basis, with the .BKF files stored on a remote server in another location. You come into the office one morning to find that the rather unimaginatively named DC3 has suffered a disk failure, and it takes until the next morning to have a replacement drive shipped from your vendor. You're in luck in this situation because you still have DC1 and DC2 performing authentication requests for your network clients, and you've also modified a number of users accounts while DC3 was down. So when you perform a restore of Active Directory on DC3, the Update Sequence Numbers of the restored accounts will be lower than the ones held by DC1 and DC2. In this case, you actually *want* those newer updates to be replicated to DC3 after it's been restored. (We'll get into some situations in the next section where you might not necessarily want this to happen.) So you'll perform a nonauthoritative restore on DC3, so that any updated information will be replicated from DC1 and DC2 to bring DC3 up to date.

To perform a nonauthoritative restore using Windows **Backup**, you'll follow these steps:

1. Reboot the domain controller into Directory Services Restore Mode by pressing F8 at the initial startup screen. When prompted, enter the Directory Services Restore Mode password.

■**Caution** Remember that this is different from your domain account password. Keep this password stored in a secure location if you think you will forget it, since the only way to change it is to boot the server normally and run **ndtsutil** with the **set dsrm password** option in Windows Server 2003, or the **setpwd** utility in Windows 2000. If you're unable to boot into Normal Mode, this becomes one big chicken-and-egg game, which is best avoided if at all possible.

---

2. Open the Windows **Backup** utility from **Start ➤ All Programs ➤ Accessories ➤ System Tools ➤ Backup**.

3. Select **Tools ➤ Restore Wizard**. Click **Next** to bypass the initial **Welcome** screen.

4. Click the radio button next to **Restore files and settings**, then click **Next**.

5. Browse to the file or tape that contains the Active Directory data you want to restore, and drill down to the check box next to **System State**. Click **Next** when you're ready to continue.

6. From here, you can simply click **Finish** to begin the restore process. The **Advanced** button will allow you to specify several additional configuration options for a restore operation such as restoring files to an alternate location, and whether or not to overwrite any existing information. However, these will only apply to any data that you're recovering in addition to the system state. The system state data must be restored to its original location, and must overwrite any existing files.

7. Once the restore has finished, reboot the domain controller normally. Once the machine has rebooted, check the Directory Services log in the Event Viewer to verify that replication has taken place.

Caution A nonauthoritative restore depends on the existence of another domain controller with a known-good copy of the Active Directory database that the restored DC can receive updates from. If you're restoring the first domain controller in a test or disaster recovery environment, any changes that have been made since your most recent backup will be lost.

Authoritative Restores

As you can probably guess, you'll use an authoritative restore when you *don't* want to have any updates that have taken place since a particular backup to be replicated back to a restored server. The most common use for this is in recovering deleted objects within Active Directory, since a nonauthoritative restore won't do you any good in this situation. Why not, you ask? Because of the Update Sequence Numbers and tombstone identifiers that we talked about at the beginning of this section. Let's go back to our example environment with three domain controllers. We'll say that you accidentally delete a user object from one of your DCs, and the deletion gets replicated to the other two domain controllers so that this user object has been tombstoned throughout Active Directory. Now you need to restore this object, so you perform a nonauthoritative restore of the AD database on DC3. But the first thing that will happen after the restore is that DC1 and DC2 will replicate their Active Directory updates back to DC3. But one of those updates is actually the *deletion* of the user object in question, so DC3 will just redelete the object that you just tried to restore. Why? Because the USN of the tombstoned user object is higher than the USN of the restored object, so DC3 updates its copy of the AD database accordingly.

So how do you avoid this game of the re-re-re-disappearing user account? By telling Active Directory that the data you're restoring to DC3 is the most current copy of Active Directory that's available on the network, and that any subsequent updates that any other domain controllers have essentially don't count. An authoritative restore does this by incrementing the USN of any restored objects by 100,000 for each day since the backup was made, which should be more than enough for even the busiest AD network. This way, the restored objects appear to the other DCs in your environment to be the newest versions available. In this example, performing an authoritative restore on DC3 will cause DC1 and DC2 to take their updates *from* DC3, rather than replicating information *to* the restored DC.

You'll perform an authoritative restore by following the steps for a nonauthoritative restore in the previous section. To mark the restore as authoritative, follow the steps outlined in the previous section, then take these steps before rebooting the server into normal mode:

1. Open a command prompt and type **ntdsutil**.

2. Type **authoritative restore** and press Enter.

3. To authoritatively restore the entire Active Directory database from your backup media, type **restore database** and press Enter. Windows will throw up a warning that you are about to mark the restored data as authoritative, which will overwrite any changes you've made to Active Directory since the time of the backup. Click **Yes** to confirm.

4. Type **quit** until you return to the command prompt, and then reboot the server normally. Check the Event Viewer to confirm that the restore completed successfully and that replication is taking place the way you expect.

Luckily, ntdsutil has several optional switches that will allow you to fine-tune what information you're actually marking as authoritative within a particular restore. ntdsutil offers you the following command-line options when marking a restore as authoritative:

- restore database: This is the command you already saw that will mark the entire restored database as authoritative. All other domain controllers in your environment will use the restored DC as the authoritative source of information for Active Directory, and will update their own records and Update Sequence Numbers accordingly. Only use this option if you are 100% certain that you haven't made any changes to Active Directory since the last backup that you might miss, since you're about to lose all of them.

- `restore database verinc %d`: This command will let you control how the USN gets incremented for authoritatively restored objects, where *%d* is some whole number that `ntdsutil` will use instead of the standard 100,000/day. This will come in handy if you need to perform an authoritative restore on top of another one: you restored Active Directory from a backup tape created on Friday afternoon, only to figure out later that you need to do another restore from a backup tape created on Friday morning. You'll want to authoritatively restore Active Directory using a higher increment number, like 300,000, to ensure that the other DCs in your domain will regard the authoritative data from the second restore as more recent than the first one.

- `restore %s subtree`: This will restore a specific container or subtree within the AD structure, as well as any child objects underneath that subtree. We'll talk about this extensively in the next section.

- `restore subtree %s verinc %d`: This will control the USN increment when restoring a single object or subtree using the `restore subtree` command.

■**Caution** The Active Directory schema cannot be authoritatively restored. If the schema of your production environment has become corrupted, you'll need to rebuild your Active Directory environment from scratch, using a primary restore from media created before the offending schema modifications occurred. For this reason, you should always test schema changes in a lab environment before implementing them on your production network.

Restoring Individual Objects

Now, the steps I just outlined might be a bit too much of a sledgehammer approach for some situations: you may only need to restore a single object or container and don't want to overwrite the entire Active Directory database. To do this, you'll use the `restore subtree` command within `ntdsutil`. This will allow you to restore as much or as little information as you need, down to a single object within the directory tree. In order to do this, you'll need to provide `ntdsutil` with the precise distinguished name of the object or container that you want to restore. So to restore an Organizational Unit called Marketing in the example.com domain, you'll issue the following command:

```
restore subtree "ou=Marketing,dc=mycompany, dc=com"
```

To restore a single user object, you'll do something like this:

```
restore subtree "cn=Joanna Smythe,ou=Finance,dc=example, dc=com"
```

You can see how the restore subtree command will take that sledge-hammer and replace it with a small chisel, allowing you to authoritatively restore a single object or container without overwriting other important changes to the rest of your Active Directory database.

Now here's a bit of a quandary that might not occur to you until it actually happens: a junior administrator on your network inadvertently blows away an OU containing a few hundred user accounts, as well as group memberships for those user accounts. So you perform an authoritative restore of the OU, and all is right with the world. At least it is until you notice that the group objects contained in the restored OU are missing, incomplete, or some combination of the two. Why did this happen? When a user object is deleted, it's also removed from the Member list of any group or groups that it used to belong to, and restoring the user and group objects simultaneously can create a "chicken-and-egg" problem where your group memberships don't get restored correctly. So you need to perform the restore *twice*: once to restore the user objects, and a second time to restore the group objects after the users have been re-created. Your other option is to perform a single restore to re-create the user accounts, and then manually re-create your group memberships. You'll need to decide which option is a more efficient use of your time, based on the size and complexity of your Active Directory environment.

Using Primary Restores

Windows Server 2003 introduces another restore type that you can use in specific disaster recovery situations. If the machine that you're restoring is the first domain controller that you're bringing back online, you can perform a primary restore to designate the data as the first replica that exists on your "new" network. To perform a primary restore, you'll perform the steps listed for a nonauthoritative restore, except that you'll click the **Advanced** button after you've selected your backup media. In the final Advanced Options screen, you'll place a check mark next to **When restoring replicated data sets, mark the restored data as the primary data for all replicas**. Remember to leave the other advanced options alone, so that you're restoring Active Directory to its default location and overwriting existing files.

You can also use a primary restore if you have application data partitions configured on your network. (You'll remember from Chapter 6 that application data partitions are used to control the replication of certain application data, like DNS data, across domain controllers in a Windows Server 2003 network.) If you're restoring the first replica set of a particular application partition, you can mark that restore as a primary restore as well.

Restoring to Dissimilar Hardware

System state data is highly machine-specific: each computer's Registry and system files are uniquely based on the hardware that's installed and drivers that have been loaded. How about when you need to restore Active Directory from your production environment onto a server that has completely dissimilar hardware specifications? Your production servers are all Compaqs, but you're in the middle of a disaster and only have Dell or IBM machines available to get your network back up and running. So what happens when you try to restore your system state onto this completely different hardware?

I'm not going to lie to you and tell you that it's pretty: it's not. But it's doable if you follow certain steps to minimize the hardware conflicts that you're going to run into by restoring the system state of one machine onto another. To restore system state data onto new hardware, follow these steps:

1. Install the Windows operating system with similarly configured disk partitions. Give the recovery machine the same NetBIOS and DNS name as the server whose system state data you'll be restoring.

2. Boot into Directory Services Restore Mode.

3. Open Device Manager. Disable any network interface cards that are installed on the machine that you aren't actually using to perform the restore.

4. Take a backup copy of the boot.ini file so that the new server will be able to boot to the correct ARC path.

5. For the first domain controller in your restore process, perform a nonauthoritative (for Windows 2000) or a primary (for Windows Server 2003) restore from your backup media.

6. Before rebooting, go back to Device Manager. Uninstall all NIC cards that are present in the Device Manager, as well as any display adapters. Since these are usually plug-and-play devices, your new hardware will redetect the correct hardware and install the appropriate drivers on the next reboot.

7. Restore the boot.ini file that you made a backup copy of in step 3.

8. Reboot the server normally.

Even after you follow these steps, you might still run into a situation where your new hardware is unwilling to boot once the system state has been restored. Typically, the OS will hang interminably at the **Preparing Network Connections** or **Applying Computer Settings** screen, though you might see the dreaded Blue Screen of Death, as well. Your next step, if this happens, is to perform a repair installation of the server operating system. This will rescan all the hardware in your system and refresh the contents of the *%systemroot*\Repair directory. If you're still out of luck at this point, you can try for a full-scale in-place upgrade of the operating system.

Another common error I've run into when doing Active Directory restores (though not on 2003; the primary restore function seems to solve this problem pretty nicely) is that I'll be unable to create any new objects in the directory once the system state data has been restored. This happens because the replication links between domain controllers get seriously confused when they're trying to replicate with other servers that don't exist anymore. To correct this, you'll first seize the five Flexible Single Master Operations (FSMO) roles to the restored server—remember that these are the domain- and forest-wide role holders present in an Active Directory forest. Then perform a metadata cleanup of the Active Directory database to remove references to any nonexistent servers in your disaster recovery environment. To seize the five FSMO roles to your restored server, do the following:

1. Open ntdsutil and type **roles** to connect to the Roles menu on the recovery server.

2. Type **connections** and press Enter.

3. From the connections menu, type **connect to server *servername***, where *servername* is the server you've just restored.

4. Type **seize *role*** for each of the five FSMO roles, as follows:

   - **seize rid master**
   - **seize infrastructure master**
   - **seize schema master**
   - **seize domain naming master**
   - **seize pdc**

5. Type **quit** until you return to the command prompt.

Once you've seized the operations master roles to the new server, you'll perform a metadata cleanup to remove references to the old domain controllers within Active Directory:

1. Open a command prompt. Type **ntdsutil** and press Enter.

2. Type **metadata cleanup** and press Enter.

3. Type **connections** and **connect to server *servername*** to open a connection to the recovery server. Then type **quit** to return to the Roles menu.

4. Type **quit** to return to the Metadata Cleanup menu. Type **select operation target** and press Enter.

5. Type **list domains** and press Enter. Each domain in your environment will be listed with a number next to the domain name.

6. Type **select domain** *number*, where *number* is the number of the domain you're cleaning up.

7. Type **list sites** and press Enter. Just like the domains, each site will be listed with a corresponding number. Type **select site** *number* using the number of the site containing the server you've just restored.

8. Type **list servers in site** and press Enter. Each server configured in Active Directory will be listed with a corresponding number.

9. Type **select server** *number*, where *number* is the number of the server you want to remove. (You can only remove one server at a time.)

10. Type **quit** to return to the Metadata Cleanup menu.

11. Type **remove selected server** to remove the server's information from the Active Directory database.

12. Type **quit** until you've returned to the command prompt.

You'll repeat these steps for each extraneous server you need to remove. You should also remove the server's CNAME record in the _msdcs. zone of your DNS server, if it exists. Once you've removed the metadata references to any other servers, you'll also need to remove the replication connections from Active Directory Sites & Services. From the command prompt, type **repadmin /showreps**. You'll see output similar to the following:

```
CN=Schema,CN=Configuration,DC=example,
    DC=comDefault-First-Site-Name\DC1 via RPC
    objectGuid: 477d627a5-7452-1ad5-6921-f216135ba623
    Last attempt @ 2004-12-21 08:25.43 was successful.

CN=Configuration,DC=example,DC=com
    Default-First-Site-Name\DC1 via RPC
    objectGuid: 477d627a5-7452-1ad5-6921-f216135ba623
    Last attempt @ 2004-12-21 08:25.42 was successful.

DC=example,DC=com Default-First-Site-Name\DC1
    via RPC objectGuid: 477d627a5-7452-1ad5-6921-f216135ba623
    Last attempt @ 2004-12-21 08:25.42 was successful.
```

From here, you'll type **repadmin /delete**, followed by the naming context and the objectGUID listed when you used the /showreps command. (Copy and paste is your friend here, trust me.) So in this example, you'd type the following:

```
repadmin /delete CN=Schema,CN=Configuration,
    DC=example,DC=comDefault-First-Site-Name\DC1
    via RPC objectGuid: 477d627a5-7452-1ad5-6921-f216135ba623

repadmin /delete CN=Configuration,DC=example,DC=com
    Default-First-Site-Name\DC1 via RPC
    objectGuid: 477d627a5-7452-1ad5-6921-f216135ba623

repadmin /delete DC=example,DC=com
    Default-First-Site-Name\DC1 via RPC
    objectGuid: 477d627a5-7452-1ad5-6921-f216135ba623
```

By this point, you should be one final reboot away from a well-functioning domain controller. What I like to do at this point is to bring up a fresh installation of Windows 2000 or Windows Server 2003 on a second machine, and then run **dcpromo** to create a "clean" copy of Active Directory. I'll then transfer the FSMO roles over to this second server, and then run **dcpromo** on the original restored server to remove it from Active Directory. This final sequence is one that you can potentially skip if you're pressed for time, but I find that it removes any lingering weirdness from working with a restored copy of a different server's system state.

Note I've also found that some third-party backup utilities can get rather ornery when restoring Active Directory onto different hardware. As another level of backup protection, consider scheduling a Windows **Backup** job to create a .BKF file of your system state, and then include that .BKF file as part of the regular data backups you perform, in addition to backing up the system state with your third-party utility. It creates an extra step in the backup process, but for something as important as your system state data, it's worth the extra effort.

I'll leave you with one final recommendation for your backup and restore strategies for Active Directory, as well as the rest of your network data. It all boils down to one word: test. Test your backups, test your restores, and then test them again. It's not enough to assume that your backups are working properly just because you're getting a confirmation message from your backup software at the end of each job. Are you certain that your critical files are being backed up every night? Have you tried restoring a single file? An entire application? A single Active Directory object? Your entire directory? Even though no one really has time to do disaster recovery drills, it's the kind of thing that you should really *make* time for. Because the last thing you want to find out after a server has failed . . . is that you're unable to restore the data that was stored on it.

Creating a Test Network

Before you even get as far as disaster recovery, you should first be concerned with disaster avoidance, since the best way to fix a problem is to prevent it from being a problem in the first place. And the only way to safely implement changes to an Active Directory network is to test them first. This is especially true of anything that makes changes to the Active Directory schema, since schema changes can't be easily rolled back without rebuilding the entire AD configuration from scratch. And I don't know about you, but for me that doesn't sound like a lot of fun.

Because the Active Directory schema is shared by an entire forest, the best configuration for a test network is that of a completely separate forest. This way you'll be able to implement changes in your test environment without having any impact on your production servers and clients. Windows 2000 and 2003 offer a number of built-in tools that can help you create a test environment that mirrors your production environment as closely as possible. You can also use additional applications like Virtual PC and Virtual Server to mimic any number of server installations, even when your spare hardware is limited to only one or two machines.

THERE ARE TEST LABS, AND THEN THERE ARE TEST LABS

Unfortunately, the only way to create a truly realistic replica of your Active Directory configuration on a test machine is to do a system state restore from a production server. I say "unfortunately" because most of us aren't going to have the luxury of going out and buying a second $30,000 server to mimic the one we have in our production environment. (Although if you can justify it to the bean counters, by all means do so.) So restoring the system state onto a test server usually means going back to the task of restoring Active Directory onto dissimilar hardware, which we've already discussed at great length. The important thing to keep in mind here is that, if you're going to restore your production system state data onto a test server, you need to be certain that your test lab is physically isolated from the rest of your production network. Otherwise you'll be performing FSMO role seizures and Active Directory metadata cleanup on your *production* environment instead of your test environment, which is a situation that simply cannot end well.

The advantage of creating a test lab in this way is that it gives you a truly accurate assessment of your Active Directory forest and how it will react to software installations and security updates. Too often, the thing that jumps up and bites you in a software install is that it interferes with some small-yet-critical administration script or other piece of software that you just didn't think to include in your test environment. The disadvantage, obviously, is that it's a lot of work to set up and maintain, especially since it requires physical connectivity isolation so that it doesn't interfere with your production environment.

The first of these built-in tools is the Group Policy Management Console, which we discussed at length in Chapter 4. While the GPMC has a few functions that can only be used with Windows 2003 and XP, you can still use it to manage Windows 2000 Active Directory domains. (Things like WMI filtering, which are new to Windows XP and 2003, won't be available when you're managing a Windows 2000 domain.) But the features that are the most useful in creating a test network are applicable to both 2000 and 2003 networks. GPMC comes with a number of predefined scripts that allow you to copy or import Group Policy Objects from one domain or forest to another, which you can use to re-create your Group Policy configurations inside of a test environment. You'll only be able to copy GPOs between your test and production forests if they have physical connectivity and a trust relationship configured between them. If your test environment exists in physical isolation, you'll need to use the Import function.

GPMC makes the process of synchronizing your test and production environments incredibly simple by introducing the following two scripts, installed in the Program Files\GPMC\Scripts directory when you install the Group Policy Management Console:

- CreateXMLFromEnvironment.wsf
- CreateEnvironmentFromXML.wsf

The CreateXMLFromEnvironment script will examine your live Active Directory environment, including any OUs, GPOs, GPO links, etc., and create an XML file that represents your production environment. The syntax and command-line switches for CreateXMLFromEnvironment are as follows:

```
createxmlfromenvironment.wsf OutputFile [/Domain:value]
    [/DC:value] [/TemplatePath:value] [/StartingOU:value]
    [/ExcludePermissions] [/IncludeAllGroups] [/IncludeUsers]
```

- Outputfile: Represents the name of the XML file being created. Be sure to give the output file an .XML file extension.
- Domain: Represents the DNS name of your Active Directory domain.
- DC: Specifies a particular domain controller to query for the information.
- TemplatePath: Indicates the directory where the script will back up your Group Policy Objects. This directory needs to be created before the script runs or you'll get an error when it tries to back up your GPOs.
- StartingOU: Lets you create an environment based on a single OU instead of using the entire domain. The script will process the OU you designate, as well as any child OUs nested within it.
- ExcludePermissions: Prevents the script from recording the ACLs attached to your Group Policy Objects.
- IncludeAllGroups: Includes any groups contained in the Users container, as well as any that are contained in Organizational Units.
- IncludeUsers: Includes individual user accounts as well as group objects.

So a simple script to create an .XML file based on an entire domain would use the following syntax:

```
cscript createxmlfromenvironment.wsf output.xml
    /includeallgroups /includeusers /templatepath:c:\gpotemplates
```

The .XML file created by the script will look like the output shown in Listing 8-1. Notice the two sample sections of code that describe an Organizational Unit as well as a Group Policy Object, including the path to the GPO backup in the c:\gpotemplates directory.

Listing 8-1. *XML Output Created by GPMC Script*

```
<?xml version="1.0" encoding="UTF-16" ?>
- <OU Name="Domain Controllers" Description=
    "Default container for new Windows 2000 domain controllers"
    BlockInheritance="false">
- <LinkGPOPermissions Exclusive="True">
  <Permission>Domain Admins</Permission>
  <Permission>SYSTEM</Permission>
  <Permission Inheritable="True">Administrators</Permission>
  <Permission Inheritable="True">Enterprise Admins</Permission>
  </LinkGPOPermissions>
  <GPOLink GPOName="Default Domain Controllers Policy"
    Enabled="true" Enforced="false" />
  </OU>
- <GPO Name="Testing SCA" Enabled="True"
    TemplatePath="c:\gpotemplates"
    Template="{0BAF8B3F-5411-4296-9E79-40F0259EB84E}">
- <ApplyPermissions Exclusive="True">
  <Permission>Authenticated Users</Permission>
  </ApplyPermissions>
- <ReadPermissions Exclusive="True">
  <Permission>ENTERPRISE DOMAIN CONTROLLERS</Permission>
  </ReadPermissions>
- <EditSecurityPermissions Exclusive="True">
  <Permission>Domain Admins</Permission>
  <Permission>Enterprise Admins</Permission>
  <Permission>SYSTEM</Permission>
  </EditSecurityPermissions>
  </GPO>
```

Once you've captured your production environment in an .XML file,
you'll then run the CreateEnvironmentFromXML script in your test environment, using as input the .XML file you just created. The syntax for the
CreateEnvironmentFromXML script is as follows:

```
Usage: createenvironmentfromxml.wsf /XML:value [/Undo]
       [/Domain:value] [/DC:value] [/ExcludeSettings]
       [/ExcludePermissions] [/CreateUsersEnabled]
       [/PasswordForUsers:value] [/MigrationTable:value]
       [/ImportDefaultGPOs] [/Q]
```

- XML: Specifies the .XML file to use as input.

- UNDO: Deletes the objects specified in the .XML file instead of creating them.

- DOMAIN: Specifies the DNS name of the domain the objects are being imported into.

- DC: Names a specific domain controller to perform the import on.

- ExcludeSettings: Ignores any GPO settings in the template files listed in the .XML input file.

- ExcludePermissions: Ignores any Access Control Lists set on Group Policy Objects.

- CreateUsersEnabled: Creates any user objects as enabled, instead of the default setting where all new user objects are initially disabled.

- PasswordForUsers: Sets an initial password for any user object whose password isn't embedded in the .XML file.

- MigrationTable: Specifies a table to use to map UNC settings between the source and the destination domain. For example, you can use this to change all users' home directory from \\SRV1\home\%*username*% to \\SRV2\home\%*username*%.

- ImportDefaultGPOs: Imports any settings defined in the .XML file into the Default Domain GPO and the Default Domain Controller GPO.

- Q: Indicates Quiet Mode; nothing will be displayed onscreen when the script runs.

Note Take a look at Chapter 7 for detailed instructions on creating a Migration Table.

Once you've created a test environment that provides a good representation of your production network, you should use it to test any new software installations or security patches before deploying them to your production network. This way, you can minimize the impact of any upgrades or changes by weeding out any errors or problems before they disrupt your users' ability to access the resources that they need. By combining stringent testing with a well-thought-out disaster recovery plan, you'll actually be able to leave for the occasional four-day weekend without worrying that your network is going to fall to pieces while you're gone. So leave your pager at home and enjoy your vacation next time!

Summary

While I'm tempted to say that it's never too late to start creating a disaster recovery plan, I'm forced to admit that there actually is a time when that's not the case . . . this is, of course, about five minutes after you realize that you need one and don't have one. Because this critical component of administering an Active Directory network is often overlooked, this chapter focused on the key steps necessary in formulating a disaster recovery strategy and restoring a Windows 2000 or Windows Server 2003 server that has suffered hardware failure or data corruption. This chapter covered the steps needed to back up and restore the Active Directory database in a variety of situations, using the built-in Windows **Backup** utility. We also looked at different ways to troubleshoot a failed Windows 2000 or Windows Server 2003 installation, including using alternate startup modes and the Recovery Console. By using the information presented in this chapter, you'll be well on your way to setting up a disaster recovery plan that will help you sleep better at night, knowing that your Active Directory database is protected from any of the bad things that can (and usually do) go wrong.

In the final chapter, we'll finish things up by talking about the Active Directory schema: what it is and how to manage and update it without needing to be a hardcore Windows programmer. We'll also have some fun with a quick introduction to getting started with the Windows scripting technologies that I've mentioned throughout the guide. For those of you who haven't wanted to try any of the scripts I've included thus far because you haven't broken into the world of scripting yet, this will provide a painless introduction that will send you on your way to integrating scripting wizardry into your "network administrator bag of tricks."

Additional Resources

Active Directory for Microsoft Windows Server 2003 Technical Reference, by Stan Reimer and Mike Mulcare. Microsoft Press. ISBN 0-7356-1577-2 —In-depth analyses of Active Directory replication, installation, and domain controller configuration, straight from the folks at Microsoft. Like the title indicates, this is more of a reference than something you'll read from cover to cover, but it's densely packed with useful and hard-to-find facts.

"Best Practices for Backup": http://www.microsoft.com/resources/documentation/WindowsServ/2003/standard/proddocs/en-us/Default.asp?url=/resources/documentation/WindowsServ/2003/standard/proddocs/en-us/sag_backconcepts_03.asp—If this link changes, just enter the title of the article in your search engine of choice.

CHAPTER 9

■ ■ ■

Scripting and Schem(a)ing

Now that we've looked at most of the administrative tasks you'll perform on an Active Directory network, it's time to actually take a peek "under the hood" of AD, to see exactly how the underpinnings of the directory service work and how you can manage and modify them. Now I don't know about you, but I have a tendency to start tuning out when people start talking about schemas, metadata, auxiliary classes, and the like. As administrators and consultants, we're often less concerned with the detailed schematics of how a clock works, and instead are far more focused on how to make the clock display the correct time. So I'll be keeping this discussion of the schema as functional as possible, showing you what you can *do* with the schema to improve your Active Directory infrastructure.

We'll close things out with a more detailed look at using scripting technologies to automate your administrative tasks. A good understanding of scripting and automation can often spell the difference between a good administrator and a great one, so I'll go over some of the basic concepts behind using VBScripting to help you get started. I've also included a number of code samples that will show you how to use scripting to connect to anything from an Active Directory tree to the file system of a local or remote computer.

In this chapter, you'll learn how to do the following:

- Configure a domain controller to allow schema modifications.
- Include a schema attribute in the Global Catalog.
- Index an Active Directory attribute.
- Activate and deactivate a schema class or attribute.
- Extend the Active Directory schema.
- Install Active Directory Application Mode (AD/AM).
- Configure an instance of AD/AM.
- Connect to WMI, ADSI, and the file system using scripts.
- Create a basic VBScript to automate network administration.

So What's This Schema Business (and Why Do I Care)?

Okay, I know I promised not to put you to sleep by giving you 30 pages of background on how the schema is constructed. But if you're going to be working with Active Directory, it's helpful to have at least a reasonable understanding of what the schema is and how it interacts with the Active Directory objects that you administer on a daily basis. So I'll spend a bit of time here giving you an overview of how the schema is structured and how it makes up the underpinnings of Active Directory as a whole.

The schema's role in Active Directory is to define what objects look like and what they can contain. In other words, the schema enforces the rules that govern both the structure and the content of Active Directory. This takes a step back from how individual objects are defined and instead is concerned with objects as a *class*—the characteristics that all objects of a particular type will have in common. Let's take user objects as an example. The jsmith object in an Active Directory domain has the following characteristics:

- A first name of Joan
- A last name of Smith
- A logon profile of \\fs1\share\jsmith
- Logon hours of 8 a.m. to 5 p.m., Monday through Friday

The classUser *class*, on the other hand, defines the characteristics that all users will possess within an Active Directory forest. Each individual user object will have their own information listed for each of these values—the purpose of the user class is to define *what* values should be configurable for each object. Every object is an *instance* of a particular object class. For example, the User *class* will define characteristics like these:

- Last name
- First name
- Profile name
- Logon hours

In addition to object classes, the schema also defines Active Directory *attributes*. Attributes are values that are shared among different object types. For example, the Description attribute appears in multiple object classes, but it is only defined *once* within the schema. This means that every object that uses a Description will have the same definition for that attribute. Each object class is made of a specific collection of attributes—a list of attributes that the object *must* have defined (mustContain), as well as a list of optional attributes that the object *may* have defined (mayContain). Attributes can contain single values or can be multivalued.

When you install Active Directory, you'll have a certain number of default classes and attributes predefined for you. Active Directory–aware applications such as Microsoft Exchange will *extend* the schema to add their own classes and attributes, or you can add your own using VBScript or another programming language. Every domain controller in an entire forest will share a single schema; any changes you make to the schema will be replicated to your entire organization. The schema is stored in its own container within the AD database, with a distinguished name of CN=Schema, CN=Configuration, *DC=ForestRoot_DomainName*. This container is the topmost object in the *schema directory partition,* which contains all of the classes and attribute definitions that are required to locate objects within AD, as well as to create new ones. So the schema for the mycompany.com forest would be located at CN=Schema, CN=Configuration, DC=mycompany, DC=com.

The Active Directory schema is organized into a *tree* hierarchy called the Directory Information Tree (DIT). The DIT is similar to the Windows file system, where classes that are further up the tree are *superclasses* of objects lower down in the hierarchy. (Another way of saying this is that classes lower in the tree are *derived* from the classes above them.) So you can derive a new class of user object from the default user class—this new class would have all of the attributes that the default user class has, as well as any new ones that you define. Any class that you can actually use to create Active Directory objects is referred to as a *structural* class. Superclasses can be structural classes, or they can be *abstract* classes that are only used to provide the basis for their child classes.

You can also define *auxiliary* classes that will provide attributes for multiple classes. An auxiliary class might contain a set of six attributes, and you can apply that auxiliary class to many different classes that should *all* contain those six attributes. This makes creating new object classes much more efficient because you can use a single auxiliary class to define multiple attributes rather than needing to add in one attribute at a time. You can extend the schema by creating a subclass from an existing class, by adding new attributes to an existing class, or by creating a brand new class from scratch.

■**Note** If you've ever worked with Java or another object-oriented programming language, this structure should seem pretty familiar, where classes lower in the tree *extend* their superclasses and auxiliary classes correspond pretty closely to *interfaces*.

As an administrator, you need to be aware of the impact of extending the schema. As I've already mentioned, schema changes are universal and affect every domain controller in the forest. Extending the schema is also a one-way operation: once you add a new class or attribute to the schema, there's no way to delete it. Windows Server 2003 will allow you to *deactivate* a new object you've added to the schema, but you still won't be able to delete anything outright. (Deactivated classes and attributes will remain in the schema, but you won't be able to create any new objects using them unless you reactivate the class or attribute.) Because of this, you should only extend the schema when it's absolutely necessary; that is, if no existing object class will meet the requirements of your application.

You also need to understand the security implications of modifying the schema, since this is something that Active Directory sets a number of limitations on. Because modifying the schema is not something that you should really be doing on a regular basis, Active Directory contains a special security group to control which users can perform schema modifications. The Schema Admins group is created when you install the first domain tree in an Active Directory forest, and only exists in the forest root domain. In order to perform any modifications to the schema, including installing any applications that require schema extensions, you need to be a member of the Schema Admins group.

■Caution When you first install Active Directory, only the Administrator account belongs to the Schema Admins group. You'll need to manually add any other user or group objects that should have the ability to manage the schema.

The MMC console that you'll use to manage the schema isn't even registered by default when you install the Active Directory Administration tools. In order to use the Active Directory Schema administration tool, you'll need to do the following:

1. Go to the command prompt and type **regsvr32 schmmgmt.dll**. This will register the DLL needed to run the MMC snap-in.

2. Select **Start ➤ Run**, and type **mmc /a** to open a blank MMC console in Author mode.

3. Select **File ➤ Add/Remove Snap-in**. Click **Add**, and then scroll to the **Active Directory Schema** snap-in. Click **Add** and then **Close**, and then click **OK**.

4. To save the Schema Admin console for future use, click **File ➤ Save As**, and save it as an .MSC file in the *Systemroot*\System32 directory. Create a shortcut to the new .MSC file in the Administrative Tools folder.

In addition, only one domain controller can perform write operations against the schema at any time—the *Schema Master* is one of the two forest-wide Flexible Single Master Operations (FSMO) role holders in your Active Directory forest. To identify the current Schema Master, open up the Active Directory Schema MMC console, right-click the topmost node of the MMC, and select **Operations Master**. You'll see the current FSMO role holder listed under **Current Schema Master (online)**. By default, this will be the first domain controller that was installed in your Active Directory forest. To improve performance, however, you'll want the Schema Master FSMO to reside on a DC in the same site as the server that houses the application that requires the schema extensions. You can transfer the Schema Master to another DC by doing the following:

1. Right-click the topmost node of the Active Directory Schema snap-in and select **Change Domain Controller**.

2. Click **Specify Name** and select the domain controller that should hold the FSMO role. You can also select **Any DC** to connect to the first available domain controller if necessary. However, the Schema Master role holder should be chosen with care, so I don't recommend transferring the role to an arbitrary DC like this.

3. Right-click the Active Directory Schema node again and select **Operations Master**. The name of the new DC should be listed under the **Current Schema Master (online)** heading.

4. Select **Change** to transfer the Schema Master to the new DC.

Caution You can also *seize* the Schema Master to another domain controller in your forest by using the **ntdsutil** utility. Be careful with this, however, since the DC that originally held the Schema Master role can never return to your production network without completely reinstalling the operating system. Seizing the Schema Master is a drastic step that you should take only if the current role holder will never be available again in your production network.

There's one final step that you need to take before you can actually make any changes to the schema. Even if you're a member of the Schema Admins group and working on the Schema Master FSMO, you still need to manually configure the controller to allow the schema to be updated. Just right-click the Active Directory Schema node and select **Operations Master** again. To allow changes to the schema, place a check mark next to **The Schema may be modified on this Domain Controller** and click **OK**. This change doesn't require a restart.

■Note You can also make this change by creating the following Registry key: HKLM\ System\CurrentControlSet\Services\NTDS\Parameters\Schema Update Allowed. To enable schema updates, this key should have a value of **1**. Otherwise it should be set to **0**.

Managing the Schema

Once you've installed the Active Directory Schema snap-in, you can perform a few simple tasks relating to the schema. To view a particular class or attribute, just right-click the object you want and select **Properties**. Figure 9-1 show the properties of the User class. You can also work from this attribute list to add new attributes to the Global Catalog. By default, only certain attributes are included within Global Catalog servers to be replicated throughout the Active Directory forest. You can add additional attributes to the Global Catalog using the Active Directory Schema snap-in. Just right-click the attribute you want to include and select **Replicate this attribute to the Global Catalog**.

■Caution If your forest functional level is set lower than **Windows Server 2003**, adding a new attribute to the Global Catalog will cause a full synchronization of all objects stored in the Global Catalog. The Windows Server 2003 forest functional level improves on this by replicating only the attribute that was added to the GC.

You can also *index* an attribute within Active Directory to improve the performance of any queries that you need to perform against it. When you index an attribute, the attribute gets indexed for every class that uses the attribute—this has a performance impact on replication and creating new objects, so it's important not to overdo it. To index an attribute, select the **Index this attribute in the Active Directory** option from the attribute's **Properties** sheet.

Because each domain controller holds a copy of the schema, Active Directory uses schema *caching* to improve performance, which means that each domain controller holds a copy of the schema in memory as well as on the local hard drive. This cached copy will update a few minutes after any schema modifications are made, or else you can manually prompt a particular DC to reload its cache by right-clicking the MMC node and selecting **Reload the schema**.

Finally, you can active and deactivate a class or attribute using the Active Directory schema snap-in by placing or removing the check mark next to **Class is active** or **Attribute is active**, as appropriate.

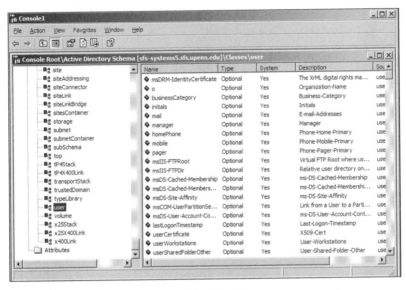

Figure 9-1. *Viewing the properties of the User class*

USING OBJECT IDENTIFIERS

When you create a new object within the schema, you'll also need to create a new Object Identifier (OID) for that object. The schema uses OID numbers to ensure that all objects in the same class are created from the same object in the schema—so that you don't click **New ➤ User** in Active Directory Users & Computers and wind up with a computer object instead. Now, if you're doing major software development, you'll want to apply for your own OID namespace from an issuing authority such as the International Organization for Standardization (ISO), and assign your OID numbers from there, but here I'm assuming that you're just adding information to the schema for your own administrative use. The quickest way to create an OID for your new class or attribute is to use the **oidgen.exe** utility from the Windows 2000 or 2003 Resource Kit, which will create a (very, *very* long) OID using the list of OIDs available for Microsoft products.

Manually Extending the Schema

So let's work through an example of how to manually extend the schema for an Active Directory forest. Let's say that you have an accounting application that uses a cost center ID number to track employee expense reports. Because this is a minor change to the User class, you can simply add an additional attribute to the existing class and extend the User class to include the new attribute. To create new attribute to add to the User class, follow these steps:

1. Open the Active Directory Schema console. Right-click the Attributes node and select **Create Attribute**.

2. You'll see a warning message indicating that you won't be able to delete an attribute from the schema once it's been created, shown in Figure 9-2. Click **Continue** to begin creating the new attribute.

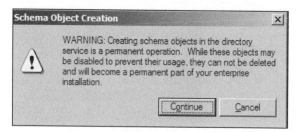

Figure 9-2. *Extending the schema is a one-way operation—we really mean it.*

3. From here, you'll see the Create New Attribute dialog box, shown in Figure 9-3. To create a new attribute, enter the following values:

Text Field	Value
Common Name	MyCompany-Cost-Center
LDAP Display Name	MyCompany-Cost-Center
Unique X500 Object ID	Create an OID using oidgen.exe
Description	Cost Center
Syntax	Case Insensitive String

■**Note** To help you keep track of changes you make to the schema, use a standard prefix to name any new attributes or classes you create. In the example here, we've prefaced the new attribute with the string "MyCompany". If we preface all new classes and attributes with this text, they will be easy to search for later.

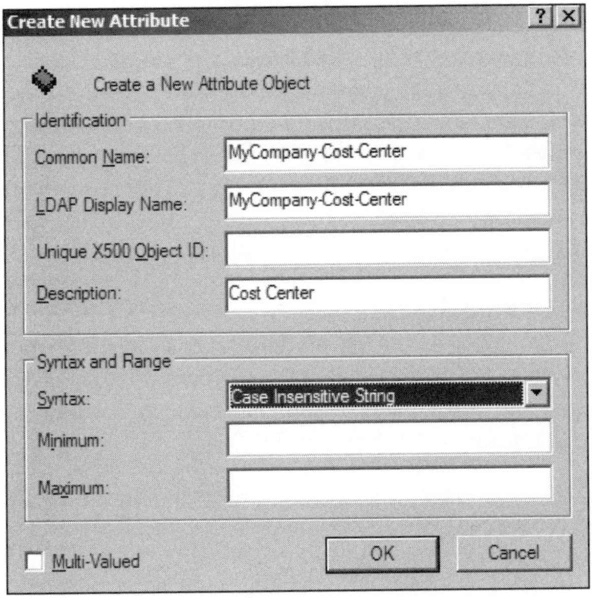

Figure 9-3. *Creating a new schema attribute*

Now that you've created the MyCompany-Cost-Center attribute, you need to modify the User class so that it includes the new attribute. To extend the classUser class, do the following:

1. Open the Classes node in the Active Directory Schema snap-in. Scroll down to the User class. Right-click the class and select **Properties**.

2. Go to the **Attributes** tab and select the **Add** button.

3. Browse to the MyCompany-Cost-Center attribute you just created, then click **OK**.

■**Caution** Be careful when selecting new attributes to add to the schema. Every few months, the topic of "How do I add user photos to Active Directory?" comes up in an e-mail or on one of the newsgroups. Invariably, the answer I give is something along the lines of "Please don't do that. You'll thank me, your servers will thank me, and your users will thank me." Remember that these new attributes will need to be replicated to every domain controller in your forest, and replicating even a 100K graphics file will bring your bandwidth utilization to a screeching halt when that's multiplied by a thousand users.

Using LDIF to Modify the Schema

You can also modify the schema using scripts and programming languages like C++. For those of us who aren't programmers by trade, we can still get by using LDIF files, which are largely readable (and even writable!) by nonprogrammers. LDIF stands for the LDAP Data Interchange Format, which is a file format supported by most major manufacturers of directory services. Because LDIF files are so widely used, you can use them to exchange information between different directory services in addition to modifying the Active Directory schema.

LDIF files follow a standard format that's actually pretty simple once you stare at it for awhile. Each line of an LDIF file consists of an **attribute name**, followed by a colon, followed by the **value** of the attribute. So to create a new Active Directory attribute, you'd open up a simple text file in Notepad, and start by specifying the distinguished name of the object:

```
dn: cn=mycompany-Cost-Center,cn=schema,cn=configuration,
    dc=mycompany,dc=com
```

Once you've specified the object you're dealing with, you'll need to follow this up with an instruction telling Active Directory what to do with it. Since this is a new attribute, we'll specify add; for an existing attribute we could specify modify or delete: changetype: add.

The remainder of an LDIF file will configure the rest of the properties of the new attribute, including the object class, the LDAP display name, and the description field. Once you've set up the new object's configuration in the text file, save it with an .LDF extension. You can import the file into Active Directory using the ldifde command, using the following syntax:

```
ldifde -i -f filename.ldf -s dc1.mycompany.com
```

■**Note** -i instructs LDIFDE to use *import* mode. -f specifies the file name to be imported, and -s is the name of the domain controller that should perform the import operation.

Once you've imported the new attribute into the schema, you need to instruct your domain controller to update the schema cache that is still in memory. To update the schema cache, use the following code in your .LDF file:

```
dn:
changetype: modify
add: schemaUpdateNow
schemaUpdateNow: 1
-
```

Documenting Changes to the Schema

When you add your own extensions to the Active Directory schema, either manually or programmatically, it's always helpful to document the changes you've made. This will help you with any future changes that need to be made, and creates a record of what was done when you need to perform any troubleshooting. Microsoft has made this a relatively painless process by creating a downloadable Schema Documentation program, available at http://www.microsoft.com/downloads/details.aspx?FamilyId=BEF87B1D-D2F1-➥4795-88C5-CA66CFC3AB29&displaylang=en. This free utility allows you to document any extensions you've made to the Active Directory schema by creating an .XML file describing any new classes or attributes you've created. This works by searching for classes and attributes based on a specified prefix, which should be easy to set up if you've used a standard naming convention for your schema extensions. To document changes you've made to the schema, follow these steps:

1. Unpack all files stored in the **schemadocfile.exe** installer. Before you run the Schema Documentation program, you first need to register a .DLL file that's necessary for the utility to run. Just copy the xmlschema.dll file to the ~\System32 directory, and then run **regsvr32 xmlschema.dll**.

2. Double-click the **schemadoc.exe** file or launch it from the command line; you'll see the screen shown in Figure 9-4. By default, the utility will search the default schema container of LDAP://CN=Schema,CN=Configuration,DC=<*Forest Root*> for whatever text you include in the **Naming Prefix** field. You also need to specify logon credentials, or else the utility will connect to the schema anonymously. Click **Next** when you're ready to continue. Finally, enter the path and name of the .XML file that you want the utility to produce as output.

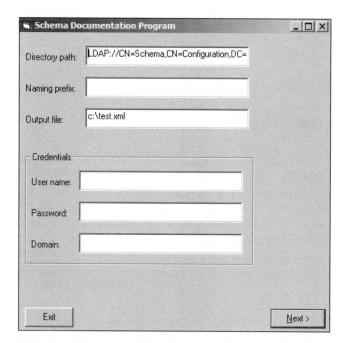

Figure 9-4. *Using the Schema Documentation utility*

3. You'll then be prompted to enter contact information for your company, including the company name, address, telephone number, and an e-mail address to use for support requests. Click **Next**.

4. The next screen you'll see is the **Product Information** screen, shown in Figure 9-5. Here you'll enter the name of the application that the schema extensions are being used for, as well as a description. Even for small-scale changes, you can use this information to go back and understand why the schema was extended.

■**Note** You can find some Best Practices for managing the schema at http://www. microsoft.com/technet/prodtechnol/windows2000serv/technologies/activedirectory/plan/ bpaddsgn.mspx.

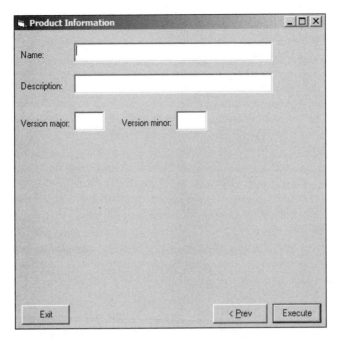

Figure 9-5. *Entering product information for the schema extension*

5. When you're ready to produce the output file, click **Execute**. The Schema Documentation utility will produce an XML file; you can leave it as-is, or use style sheets to modify the way it's formatted in your browser as shown in Figure 9-6.

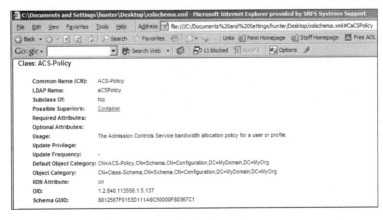

Figure 9-6. *Viewing the output of the Schema Documentation utility*

Using Active Directory Application Mode

As you've probably gathered by now, the Active Directory schema can be a pretty harrowing place to "play around" in, since you only get one for your entire forest, and rolling back from any changes ranges from annoying to impossible. Prior to Windows Server 2003, you were quite limited in terms of how you could test applications that needed to make schema modifications, since you were pretty much locked into creating a separate forest for testing purposes and hoping that your test environment sufficiently mimicked your production AD. What many administrators have been wishing for (really since the schema made its first appearance) is the ability to interact with the schema in a less invasive manner. We've wanted to be able to make allowances for Active Directory–aware applications while still being able to change our minds, to be able to roll back from any mistakes, or just plain remove a piece of software that we decided we didn't want to use anymore. Windows Server 2003 has addressed these issues rather nicely with the introduction of Active Directory Application Mode, or AD/AM, which is available as a free download from http://www.microsoft.com/adam.

AD/AM is a service that sits on top of the Windows operating system, and acts as a kind of go-between that creates a simplified instance of the AD directory service and schema for use by individual applications. It does this by providing you with a Lightweight Directory Access Protocol (LDAP) directory service that runs as a user service, rather than as a system service within Active Directory. Because AD/AM sits on top of the OS and isn't tied into Active Directory, you can have multiple instances of it running on one or more computers, you can configure each AD/AM instance independently of any other instances, and you can add and remove AD/AM instances at will.

So if you have an application that needs to extend the Active Directory schema, you can instead point the app to an instance of AD/AM, and the application will add the schema modifications to this localized instance of Active Directory. This means that your domain controllers as a whole won't need to be aware of the change, since the actual schema itself was left untouched by any changes that the application made. When the application needs to access Active Directory information, it goes to the AD/AM instance that has the necessary changes. AD/AM will then pass through any requests that require user authentication from the AD user database itself. This feature is an application developer's dream, because it allows developers to try out their applications within a working Active Directory forest without needing to worry about cluttering up the schema with changes that can't be undone. They can also bring AD/AM instances on and offline without affecting the stability of the Active Directory infrastructure—you can even host an instance of AD/AM on a developer's local workstation. So developers could save a known-good instance of AD/AM before making a change to the application; if the change doesn't work, they can roll back to the other AD/AM instance much more easily than if they needed to perform surgery on the schema. You can modify the AD/AM schema using tools you're already familiar with: **ldifde**, the Active Directory Schema snap-in, and the AD/AM ADSI Edit tool.

AD/AM also incorporates the new application directory partition functionality that's available in Windows Server 2003. Maybe you have an Active Directory–enabled application that creates extremely volatile data, like an intranet portal that personalizes web content for each user and stores that personalization information within the directory itself. But if this application is only being used by a subset of your userbase, deploying it to Active Directory itself would increase replication traffic for every domain controller in your domain whether they needed access to the information or not. By using an AD/AM instance to host this application, you can restrict replication of the application data only to the server or servers that require it. Just like in the previous example, the intranet would query Active Directory for user authentication, but store the application-specific data within AD/AM. Continuing to use Active Directory for authentication prevents you from requiring your users to remember another set of logon credentials for any new applications that you host on an instance of AD/AM.

■**Note** You can install instances of AD/AM on machines running Windows XP Professional and Windows Server 2003 Standard, Enterprise, and Datacenter Edition. AD/AM will work and play well with Windows 2000 Active Directory and even NT 4.0 domains, but it will still need to be installed on an XP or 2003 machine.

Active Directory Application Mode uses a pretty standard Windows installer routine. Once you've downloaded the installer from the Microsoft homepage (http://www.microsoft.com/downloads/details.aspx?FamilyID= 9688f8b9-1034-4ef6-a3e5-2a2a57b5c8e4&displaylang=en), just double-click to launch it and click **Next** to skip the initial **Welcome** screen. After that, the installation process will go something like this:

1. Select the radio button to accept the End User License Agreement (EULA) and click **Next**.

2. On the next screen, select the option to install both AD/AM and the AD/AM administrative tools, and click **Next**.

3. On the **Setup Options** screen, select the option to create a unique instance of AD/AM. This will create a brand new instance of AD/AM with its own configuration and schema, but that will not be able to replicate with any existing AD/AM instances on your network. Click **Next** to continue.

4. On the **Instance Name** screen, enter a name that will identify this AD/AM instance on the local computer. For instance, if you call it webportal, it will be displayed as ADAM_webportal. Click **Next** to continue.

5. On the **Ports** screen, enter the port numbers that AD/AM should use to transmit LDAP and encrypted LDAP (LDAPS) traffic. If the computer hosting the AD/AM instance is *not* a domain controller, you can leave these at the defaults of 389 and 636, respectively. If you've installed AD/AM onto a DC, change these from their default values to ports in the 1025–65535 range. Click **Next** to continue.

6. Next, you'll select whether you want to create an Application Directory Partition within Active Directory. If you're working with a commercial application that creates its own directory partition, you can click **No** here and allow the application installer to create the partition later. Otherwise, click **Yes** and specify the naming context of the new partition. Remember that the naming context of an Application Directory Partition can be any name that doesn't already exist in your AD namespace—this can be a child of an existing domain, or a brand new tree within the AD forest. So you can create a directory partition named webportal within your domain, and its distinguished name would be CN=webportal,DC= mycompany,DC=com. Click **Next** when you're ready to continue.

7. On the **File Locations** screen, you'll specify where AD/AM should store its data and recovery files. "Recovery" files here are analogous to the Active Directory log files, so this screen should look quite familiar if you've run **dcpromo** even once. The default location is under C:\Program Files\Microsoft ADAM*InstanceName*\data, but you can easily shunt them off to other drives or directories. Click **Next** to continue.

8. On the next screen, you'll specify whether AD/AM should run under the security context of a specific Active Directory user, or default to the Network Service Account. Click **Next** once you've configured the credentials the AD/AM should use to access AD.

■**Note** The Network Service Account is a new security feature in Windows Server 2003. It allows Windows services that need access to network resources to run in the security context of a member of the Users group, which limits the risks posed by service accounts running as Domain Admins or other administrative users.

9. Next, you'll assign an Active Directory user or group administrative rights to this instance of AD/AM. This setting defaults to the currently logged-on user, or you can specify another AD user or group object. Click **Next** to continue.

10. On the **Importing LDIF files** screen, you can select one or more LDIF files to import into this instance of AD/AM. You can import the Active Directory schema definitions for the user object class, the InetOrgPerson class, the UserProxy class, or the AZMan (Authorization Manager) class. This step is necessary if the applications installed on this instance of AD/AM need to extend any of these object classes. Select **Import the selected LDIF files for this instance of ADAM**, and click **Add** to add one or more of the available LDIF files. Click **Next** to continue.

11. Click **Next** and then **Finish** to complete the AD/AM installation and start the AD/AM service on the local computer.

Once you've installed an AD/AM instance, you can view its settings using the AD/AM ADSI Editor from the **Program Files** menu. When you first open the AD/AM ADSI Editor, it'll look quite similar to the Active Directory ADSI Editor: all you'll see is a blank MMC console with the AD/AM ADSI Edit node in the left-hand pane. To browse this AD/AM instance, right-click the AD/AM ADSI Edit node and select **Connect To**. You'll see the screen shown in Figure 9-7. To connect to an AD/AM instance, you'll need to specify the following:

- A friendly name for the connection.
- The name of the server hosting the AD/AM instance—this can be **localhost** if you're on the same computer.
- The port number to connect with. This defaults to 389, the default LDAP port. If you specified an alternate port when you installed AD/AM, enter that number here.
- The context that you want to connect to, either **Configuration**, **RootDSE**, or **Schema**. You can also specify the distinguished name of an Application Directory Partition here.
- The credentials that you want to connect with. You can choose between the currently logged-on user, or an alternate set of credentials.

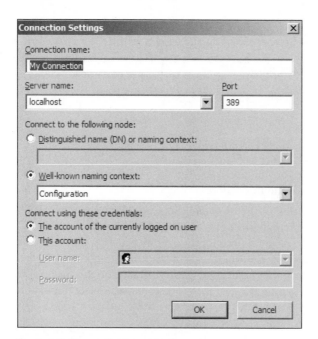

Figure 9-7. *The AD/AM ADSI Edit utility*

Once you've entered all the necessary information, you'll see a screen similar to Figure 9-8—once again, this looks remarkably similar to the Active Directory ADSI Edit console. You can also view the AD/AM schema by opening up a blank MMC console and adding the AD/AM Schema snap-in. Here you can see the list of classes and attributes available in this instance of AD/AM, most of which carry directly over from the AD Schema Management MMC.

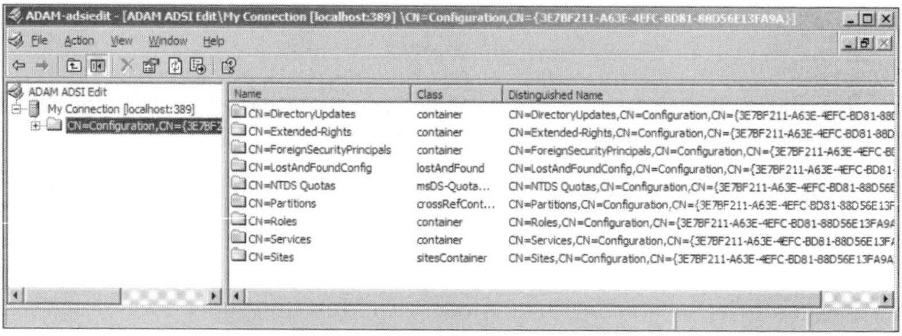

Figure 9-8. *Connecting to ADSI Edit*

A Scripting Primer

To close things out, I'll use the next several pages as an introduction to using scripting to automate your administrative chores. I've made many references to scripting throughout this book while discussing other topics, but here you'll get a 30-minute crash course in scripting and only scripting. Now, I'm not going to try to turn you into the Ultimate Scripting Champion in the space of ten pages, but this will give you an introduction to the tools and concepts that you'll need to start incorporating scripting into your arsenal of tools and tricks. It can be pretty intimidating to get started with scripting because there seems to be so much to it, and it all seems to be written in some strange, cryptic language. But you'll find as you read through these examples that it's not all that intimidating, and that scripting all follows a very logical flow from one command to the next. Having this understanding of scripting basics under your belt will also enable you to make better use of the many free scripting samples that you can find on the Microsoft website, as well as many other sites around the Internet.

Getting Started

One of the major stumbling blocks to the new scripter is probably the fact that there are so many languages to choose from. Trying to decide whether you're going to learn VBScript, JScript, Perl, or Python can be stressful enough when they're all brand new to you, and it gets even harder if you come across any programming "zealots" who insist that only their chosen language could possibly be the sensible choice. But I'll let you in on a little secret: *it really doesn't matter* which language you pick. After all, what are you trying to do with your scripts? Maybe create user objects, start or stop a service, or send an e-mail alert to an administrator based on information in your event logs. And, at the end of the day, any one of these languages will be able to accomplish these tasks. The reason for this is that any scripting language you use is going to *connect* to Active Directory or your local computer to work their magic; the actual commands and syntax that they use to get there is really a matter of personal preference. For example, if you want to display the running processes on a Windows XP workstation using VBScript, your syntax will look like the following code snippet (I've placed the code that is connecting the script to the local computer in bold):

```
On Error Resume Next

strComputer = "."

Set objWMIService = GetObject("winmgmts:\\" &
    strComputer & "\root\CIMV2")
```

```
Set colItems = objWMIService.ExecQuery
    ("SELECT * FROM Win32_Process", "WQL", _
    wbemFlagReturnImmediately + wbemFlagForwardOnly)

For Each objItem In colItems
    WScript.Echo "Caption: " & objItem.Caption
    WScript.Echo "CommandLine: " & objItem.CommandLine
    WScript.Echo
Next
```

Even if you don't speak any VBScript at all, you can probably guess the purpose of the SELECT * FROM Win32_Process item, as well as the WScript.Echo commands. Producing the same output using Perl would require this syntax:

```
use strict;
use Win32::OLE('in');

 my $objWMIService = Win32::OLE->GetObject
   ("winmgmts:\\\\.\\root\\CIMV2") or die "WMI connection failed.\n";
    my $colItems = $objWMIService->ExecQuery
   ("SELECT * FROM Win32_Process","WQL",wbemFlagReturnImmediately |
wbemFlagForwardOnly);

 foreach my $objItem (in $colItems) {
    print "Caption: $objItem->{Caption}\n";
    print "CommandLine: $objItem->{CommandLine}\n";
 }
```

Even though these are two different languages with completely different syntaxes, you can see the similarity in the way that they connect to the local computer and output information, where Set objWMIService becomes my $objWMIService and WScript.Echo becomes print. So if you already have a background in Java, Perl, or Python and want to use one of these languages in your scripting, go right ahead. The code examples in this section all use VBScript, since I think it's the easiest for a beginning scripter to pick up quickly. VBScript also has the advantage of being supported by most Windows operating systems out of the box; there's no compiler or other software that you need to install.

Running a Script

If you have a premade script that you need to run, you'll use one of two commands followed by the name of the script:

- cscript
- wscript

cscript will send your script output to the command line, while wscript will create a pop-up window containing a line of output. Each of these methods has their place: cscript is useful for scripts that produce a large amount of output, while wscript is more useful to pop up a single message to get an administrator's attention. You should be careful using wscript for longer scripts, since it can pop up hundreds of windows that each need to be closed individually. The default script processor for Windows is wscript, but you can change this to cscript by entering the following at the command line:

cscript //H:cscript //s

Using Windows Management Instrumentation

As an administrator, you'll probably spend as much time writing scripts that interact with your servers and client workstations as you'll spend working with the Active Directory database. To help you with this, you'll use Windows Management Instrumentation (WMI) to interact with your Windows-based computers in a systemized fashion. It uses a common framework to allow you to access and update information about different components of a Windows-based computer, including installed hardware, software, disk drive information, and more. You can use WMI in almost any Windows-based script or application. WMI is supported by default on Windows Server 2003, Windows XP, and Windows ME computers, and on Windows 2000 computers that have at least Service Pack 2 installed. If you're still supporting NT 4.0 or Windows 9*x* clients, you can download software to support WMI from http://www.microsoft.com/downloads. Once installed, WMI runs as a service that you can start and stop like any other Windows service. There's also a WMI Control MMC snap-in that you can use to manage the WMI service on a local or remote computer.

Probably the easiest way to think of WMI is as a "doorway" to information about a particular computer. Much like the Active Directory schema, WMI is made up of a series of *classes* that define how this information gets displayed. You can query WMI for information about particular *instances* of these classes, which are similar to the objects in Active Directory. For example, WMI provides a class called Win32_OperatingSystem that contains some of the following *properties*:

- BootDevice
- BuildNumber
- BuildType
- CountryCode
- CreationClassName
- CSCreationClassName
- CSDVersion
- CSName
- CurrentTimeZone
- DataExecutionPrevention_32BitApplications
- Description
- FreeVirtualMemory
- Manufacturer

When you query a particular computer, you'll receive information about the *instances* of this class that are present on a computer. In the case of the Win32_OperatingSystem, you'll receive information like this:

```
BootDevice: \Device\HarddiskVolume1
BuildNumber: 2600
BuildType: Uniprocessor Free
Caption: Microsoft Windows XP Professional
CodeSet: 1252
CountryCode: 1
CreationClassName: Win32_OperatingSystem
CSCreationClassName: Win32_ComputerSystem
CurrentTimeZone: -300
DataExecutionPrevention_32BitApplications: False
Description:
FreeVirtualMemory: 2056112
Manufacturer: Microsoft Corporation
```

As you can see, a particular computer will return whatever information it has regarding each of these fields, though not every field will necessary contain any information (like the Description field in the previous example).

In order for your script to view information about the different WMI classes, it must connect to the WMI service that's running on the target computer. You'll do this with a line of code similar to this one:

```
set objWMIService = GetObject("winmgmts:\\.\root\CIMV2")
```

Let's break this down one step at a time so that you understand what it all means:

- `set objWMIService`: Here you're creating a variable to hold a reference to the WMI instance on a particular computer. I know, I know, I sound like a programmer and your eyes are glazing over. Here's what this means. Remember how I said that WMI is basically a doorway to information on the local computer? To be able to refer to this doorway in our script, we need to be able to call it something to be able to do anything with it. So whenever we use the `objWMIService` name in our script, we're referring to the "doorway" to WMI on the local computer. You use the `set` command because this reference is considered an *object*, rather than a simple number like 5 or a string like "Hello".

- `GetObject`: This is a VBScript command to create the WMI reference that the `objWMIService` variable will refer to.

- `winmgmts`: This is the beginning of the WMI *moniker*, or connection string, that will create the actual instance of WMI.

- `\\.`: This is the computer name and WMI *namespace* that you're connecting to. In this case, the computer name is represented by the `.`, which is shorthand for `localhost`. The `.` shorthand is useful if you're looping through a large number of computers, since it essentially translates to "Whichever computer we're on right now, tell it to run the commands in this script." (More on loops in the next section.) You can also specify a particular computer name, like `\\workstation1\root\CIMV2`. In this case, the computer name looks much more like the UNC naming convention that you're already familiar with.

- `\root\CIMV2`: So what about the `root\CIMV2` part? This is the name of the WMI *namespace* that holds the information you're trying to get at. For 99% of the scripting you'll do, you can leave this at this setting.

■**Caution** There's also a `root\default` namespace that you can work with, but this isn't the namespace you'll use to access most of the information you're interested in, despite the misleading name.

So how do you know what kind of information is out there in the WMI universe? The simple answer is, of course, "practice." But you also have a few utilities available to help you explore the available classes in the Windows Management Instrumentation. The most useful one is probably **Script-O-Matic**, which is a free download available from the Microsoft Scripting Center at http://www.microsoft.com/technet/scriptcenter/tools/scripto2.mspx. Version 2 of **Script-O-Matic** was just released in January of 2005, and is much improved over the first incarnation of the tool. **Script-O-Matic** provides a GUI interface that will generate code to list the different fields of each WMI class. As you can see in Figure 9-9, you can generate code in VBScript, JScript, Perl, or Python. **Script-O-Matic** will generate output to the command prompt, or will pipe the results of a script to Notepad, Excel, or to your web browser in XML or HTML format. You can also specify one or more computers to run the script against, and you can run the script right from within **Script-O-Matic** using the **Run** button. **Script-O-Matic** provides an easy way to look around the different WMI classes, as well as providing you with instant code that you can learn from and modify to your heart's content.

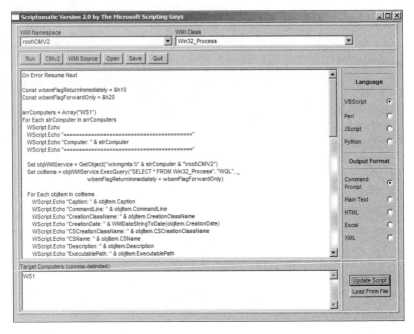

Figure 9-9. *Generating code with Script-O-Matic*

You can also use the **wbemtest** utility to take an even more in-depth look at WMI classes. When you type **wbemtest** at the Run line, you'll first need to click **Connect** to connect to the root\CIMV2 namespace. This defaults to root\default so change it to **root\CIMV2** and click **Connect** again. To view the available WMI classes, do the following:

1. Click **Enum classes**. You'll see the screen in Figure 9-10.

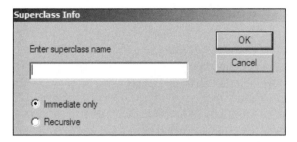

Figure 9-10. *Enumerating WMI classes with wbemtest*

2. Leave the **Enter superclass name** field blank. Change the radio button to point to **Recursive**, and click **OK**. This will present you with a list of all of the classes in the root\CIMV2 namespace, nearly a thousand of them.

3. To view a particular class, scroll to the class name and double-click it. For the Win32_Process class, as an example, you'll see the screen shown in Figure 9-11.

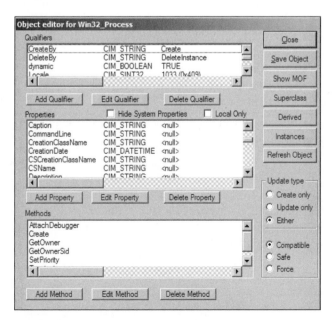

Figure 9-11. *Viewing the properties of a class in wbemtest*

Querying WMI

So now that you've got an idea of what kind of information you can gather from WMI, how do you go about retrieving that information through a script? Take another look at the example script from the beginning of this section, paying attention to the code in boldface:

```
strComputer = "."

Set objWMIService = GetObject("winmgmts:\\" & _
    strComputer & "\root\CIMV2")
Set colItems = objWMIService.ExecQuery("SELECT * " & _
    "FROM Win32_Process", "WQL", _
    wbemFlagReturnImmediately + wbemFlagForwardOnly)

For Each obj In colItems
  WScript.Echo obj.Name
Next
```

We've already discussed the fact that objWMIService refers to the "doorway" into WMI. The next command, ExecQuery, means exactly what you might think. We're asking the script to *execute* a WMI *query*: to request information from the WMI service running on the local computer. So once you've opened the door, you need to be able to ask WMI for information in a language that it can understand. In this case, it's the WMI Query Language, or WQL. Now, if you've ever done any work in Microsoft SQL or another database product, the query syntax itself should look really familiar:

- SELECT is just another way of saying "Return" or "Give me . . . "
- The * is a wildcard indicating "all information," so SELECT * will return all fields for a particular class.
- FROM Win32_Process, as you might guess, instructs WQL to retrieve information from the Win32_Process class.

So far you've only seen the most basic examples of WQL syntax. If you only want your query to retrieve certain fields, for example, you could restrict that portion of the query by specifying something like SELECT Caption, CommandLine, ExecutablePath instead of SELECT *. Now, WQL is only a subset of SQL, and so isn't nearly as fully featured in terms of the kinds of queries it can generate. The basic syntax of WQL looks like this:

```
SELECT <SOMETHING> FROM <SOME CLASS> WHERE <SOME CONDITION IS TRUE>
```

LINE BREAKS AND CONCATENATION (GESUNDHEIT!)

You may have noticed the underscore character in a few of the code examples we've used so far. In a VBScript, you need to type one command on each line or the *compiler* will return an error. (The compiler is the piece of software that translates the VBScript commands that you can read into commands that the operating system can actually follow.) You'll use the underscore to break up a long line of code into more manageable chunks; so if the VBScript compiler finds a _ character, it will continue reading the next line of code as if it were written on the same line. As an example, the following code:

```
For Each objItem _
  In colItems
```

will look to the operating system as though it were all written on one line, like this:

```
For Each objItem In ColItems
```

The only exception is that the underscore will be ignored if it happens within double-quotes, like this:

```
strTestString = "This will _
  produce an error"
```

You've probably noticed that when I create a line of code that goes across two lines like this, I indent the second line of code. This is a trick that will make your code more readable, since it's more visually apparent that the second line of code "belongs" to the first.

You may have also seen that the name of a variable can be offset by ampersands, like this:

```
Set objWMIService = GetObject("winmgmts:\\" & strComputer & _
    "\root\CIMV2")
```

This is called *concatenation*, where the variable is combined with the code around it. Whenever VBScript encounters the & character, it will take whatever appears after the ampersand and add it to whatever came before it. Since strComputer is defined as ., VBScript will make the following substitution when it finds the first &:

```
Set objWMIService = GetObject("winmgmts:\\." & "\root\CIMV2")
```

When VBScript runs into the next &, it will concatenate the rest of the line into a single line of code:

```
Set objWMIService = GetObject("winmgmts:\\.\root\CIMV2")
```

Concatenation is an easy way to insert variables into your code. Whenever VBScript encounters ampersands surrounding a variable, it will look up the current value of the variable, and insert it into the line of code.

You've already seen the <SOMETHING> and <SOME CLASS> syntax in action. The WHERE clause will restrict the information that's returned by the query to match specific criteria. Say that you have a new application that you want to roll out to your clients that requires Windows XP Professional. You can create a WMI query that will return only Windows XP computers by using a WHERE clause like this one:

```
SELECT * FROM Win32_OperatingSystem WHERE Caption =
    "Microsoft Windows XP Professional".
```

■**Note** You can find the full syntax of WQL on the Microsoft MDSN website, at http://msdn. microsoft.com/library/default.asp?url=/library/en-us/wmisdk/wmi/querying_with_wql.asp at the time of this writing.

Interacting with ADSI

In addition to connecting to the WMI service on a particular server or workstation, you can also connect to the Active Directory Services Interface, or ADSI, to automate Active Directory management tasks. You can use ADSI to perform any number of operations against your AD database, including the following:

- *Creating objects*: This includes user objects, computer objects, printers, and more.

- *Modifying objects*: For example, you can add a telephone number to a user object or change the description of every computer object in an OU.

- *Reading information*: This is pretty similar to performing a query against WMI—you can query Active Directory for information about particular objects contained within it.

- *Deleting objects*: This could obviously be a pretty dangerous function if used carelessly, but you can connect to ADSI to perform bulk deletions of Active Directory objects, or create a query to delete only objects that meet certain criteria.

One of the most convenient things about interacting with ADSI is that the syntax you'll use for each of these operations doesn't really change when you're dealing with different types of objects. So a script to create 1,000 user objects would look almost identical to a script used to create 1,000 computer objects, which wouldn't look all that different from a script that created 1,000 printers. Scripting with ADSI consists of three steps:

1. Connect to the Directory Service. This is also called *binding* to ADSI.

2. Perform the operation.

3. Save (or *commit*) any changes you've made to the AD database.

We'll focus on the first of these tasks here, since you'll likely find it to be the most confusing because you'll use a different syntax depending on what you're trying to do. The basic syntax involves using the GetObject command just like with WMI. To connect to the root of the mycompany.com Active Directory domain, for example, you would use the following syntax:

```
Set objADSI = GetObject("LDAP://dc=mycompany, dc=com")
```

To connect to a particular OU within the mycompany.com domain, you'll just change the distinguished name that you use after the "LDAP://" string:

```
Set objADSI = GetObject("LDAP://ou=finance, dc=mycompany, dc=com")
```

You can even bind to an individual object by using the distinguished name of an object instead of a container, like this:

```
Set objADSI = GetObject("LDAP://cn=jsmith, ou=hr," & _
    dc=mycompany, dc=com")
```

So the question really becomes, how do you know which object to *bind* to? And that all depends on what you're trying to do, as you can see in Table 9-1.

Table 9-1. *Binding to ADSI to Perform Different Functions*

If You Want To . . .	Bind To . . .
Read or modify the properties of an object.	The individual object.
Create or delete an object.	The *parent container* of the object you want to delete.
Delete a container object that holds other objects (like an OU)	The object itself so that you can delete the objects it contains. *Then* connect to the parent container of the object to delete the container.

Talking to the File System

Another common task that you'll probably run across is the need to connect to the file system of a local or a remote computer. To do this, you can use the FileSystemObject that's included in the Windows Scripting Host (WSH). WSH is installed by default on any Windows 2000, 2003, or XP machine, or you can download it from the Microsoft website (http://www.microsoft.com/downloads/details.aspx?FamilyID=c717d943-7e4b-4622-86eb-95a22b832➡caa&DisplayLang=en) to access the FileSystemObject on earlier operating systems. You can use the FileSystemObject to work with local files and folders, as well as using UNC paths (*servername**sharename*) to work with remote files and folders. Connecting to the FileSystemObject will look quite familiar now that you've seen how to connect to WMI and ADSI, since it uses an almost identical syntax:

```
set objFSO = CreateObject("Scripting.FileSystemObject")
```

Once you've created this doorway or *reference* to the FileSystemObject, you can use it to create and delete folders and files, as well as read and write data to a text file. As an Active Directory administrator, you'll find that your most frequent use of the FileSystemObject will be in creating output files to store the results of WQL queries and to record information from your servers and clients. For example, you can configure a logon script that will query each computer that logs on to your network to see if it is running a particular service. If that service is found, you can use the WriteLine method to record that information to a central text file that you can view later.

More Scripting Tricks to Make Your Life Better

So now that I've given you some background, we'll look some more at the actual mechanics of creating a script, including the most frequently used syntax in VBScript. When it comes to creating a script from scratch, you really don't need anything more than a text editor. There are more fully featured development tools out there like Visual Studio, but you can use something as simple as Notepad or Wordpad to get started. This is especially true because you can't save your scripts with any formatting information, only the plain text.

■**Caution** VBScript uses the .VBS file extension. You'll need to enclose the filename in double-quotes when you save a file to keep Notepad from appending a .TXT extension to the end of it.

Creating a Variable

You've already seen a few examples of creating a variable in a script file. A variable in VBScript is a lot like the ones you learned about in high school algebra: you can set a equal to 5, and anytime you see a later in the program, the compiler will say, "Oh, I know what this is, it's really a 5." A variable can hold a number like 5, a string like "Hello", or a reference to something like WMI, ADSI, or a file system object. Variables are useful to make your script more readable, and to hold information to perform equations and other operations against it. So if you have two lines of code that read as follows:

```
NumberOfServers = 10
NumberOfWorkstations = 20
```

it makes it quite simple later in the program to say something like this:

```
TotalComputers = NumberOfServers + NumberOfWorkstations
WScript.Echo("Total Computers = ") & TotalComputers
```

You should also remember earlier examples of using a variable to represent a *reference* to WMI. In this case, you'll need to precede the name of the variable with the set command, like this:

```
set objWMIService = GetObject("winmgmts:\\.\root\CIMV2")
```

So why do you need to use set here, when you can just say a = 5 to represent the number 5? In programmer-speak, this is because a variable that's referring to WMI or ADSI is pointing to an *object* instead of a *primitive* like a number or a text string. The easiest way to remember it is this: if your variable is referring to something that's creating a "doorway" to WMI, ADSI, or the file system, you need to use set when you create the variable. You can change the value of any variable during your script simply by assigning it a new value.

If you have a programming background, you might be complaining that I didn't tell you to *declare* a variable before you used it. Quite simply, declaring a variable means that you create the variable before you assign a value to it. In VBScript this is not a required step: you can create variables on the fly. But declaring a variable before you use it can be helpful when (not if) you need to troubleshoot or modify your scripts. In fact, you can include the line Option Explicit at the beginning of your script, and that will tell the compiler to complain if you use a variable that you haven't declared.

Why is Option Explicit helpful? Let's look at a simple code example in which variables aren't declared before they're used:

```
NumberOfServers = 10
NumberOfWorkstations = 20

TotalComputers = NumberServers + NumberWorkstations
```

Now, it's pretty obvious in this example that the wrong names have been used for the variables in that third line. But unless you use Option Explicit, VBScript won't complain when you try to run this VBScript and will run using the incorrect variable names. Because a value was never given to NumberServers and NumberWorkstations, you'll just end up getting an incorrect value for TotalComputers. In a long script, it can be infuriating to track down troubles like this. Here's the same code, using the Option Explicit instruction:

```
Option Explicit
Dim NumberOfServers
Dim NumberOfWorkstations

NumberOfServers = 10
NumberOfWorkstations = 20

TotalComputers = NumberServers + NumberWorkstations
```

In this case, you'll receive an error when you try to run this script, because NumberServers and NumberWorkstations haven't been declared yet. Though it adds a few lines of code to your scripts, it's a really good practice to use Option Explicit, since it forces you to be more careful about how you create and use variables.

Using Constants

Constants are pretty similar to variables, in that they create a name for something that you can reuse throughout your script. Unlike variables, though, you can't change what a constant stands for once you've created it—it's a read-only value. In almost all cases, you'll use constants to make your scripts more readable and easier to troubleshoot. As an example, the VBScript command that writes text to a file will take a few different parameters, including a numeric parameter specifying how the file should be opened. To see the value of a constant, see if you can tell what the following code does:

```
Set objFile = FSO.OpenTextFile("c:\scripts\log.txt", 2, true)
```

It obviously has something to do with opening a text file, but what's that 2 about? Now try the same code, using a constant:

```
Const FOR_WRITING = 2
Set objFile = FSO.OpenTextFile("c:\scripts\log.txt", _
    FOR_WRITING, true)
```

Even though it took an extra line of code, it's a lot easier to tell what this code is doing, isn't it? In a long, complex script, using constants will make it much simpler to decipher what your code is supposed to be doing, especially if you need to edit it many months after you first wrote it.

Using Collections

When you run a WQL query, WMI returns zero or more records that match the query. You can think of this as information that you might see in a table, where each field corresponds to a column, and each record corresponds to a row in the table. So you can visualize the results of a WQL query like the information in Table 9-2.

Table 9-2. *Results of a WQL Query on the Win32_Process Class*

Caption	CommandLine	ExecutablePath
winlogon.exe	winlogon.exe	C:\WINDOWS\system32\winlogon.exe
services.exe	services.exe	C:\WINDOWS\system32\services.exe
lsass.exe	lsass.exe	C:\WINDOWS\system32\lsass.exe

As you can see, you receive multiple results back from many queries, which VBScript refers to as a *collection*. Your script will need to *loop* through each item in a collection to take any actions, whether it's just to print out the results or to call any kind of a method. To take a particular action against each item within a collection, you'll use a For...Each loop. This essentially translates to "For each item in the collection that was returned by this query, do *something*." After the command, you'll use the Next command to tell VBScript to move to the next item in the collection. To print out the name of each running process on a particular computer, for example, you could use the following code:

```
For Each objService in colServiceList
    WScript.Echo "Caption: " & objService.Caption
Next
```

But what happens if you run a query that only returns one row in the "table"? Is it still a collection? Absolutely, and you can still use the For...Each loop to cycle through the items in the collection. It just means that the loop will only run *once* for the single item in the collection. (If a query returns *no* results, then the For...Each loop won't run at all.)

Using Methods

In addition to the different attributes that you can view, many WMI and ADSI classes also have *methods*. You can think of an attribute as something that a class *has*, like a name or a description. A method, on the other hand, is something that a class can *do*, like starting or stopping a service. (You can also think of a method as another word for a *command*, if that's helpful.)

You'll tell your scripts to perform a method by specifying the name of the object, followed by a ., followed by the name of the method. To stop the Spooler service on a particular computer, for example, you would use the following code (the code that's performing the method is listed in bold):

```
strComputer = "."
Set objWMIService = GetObject("winmgmts:" &
    "{impersonationLevel=impersonate}!\\" &
    strComputer & "\root\cimv2")

Set colServiceList = objWMIService.ExecQuery _
  ("Select * from Win32_Service where Name='Spooler'")

For Each objService in colServiceList
    errReturn = objService.StopService()
Next
```

■Note Remember that this code needs to loop through the *collection* of services returned by the WQL query, even though the collection only has a single item in it.

You'll also use methods when interacting with ADSI, to Create, Modify, or Delete an object, or else to Read information about it. ADSI methods use the same "dot notation" that you just saw with WMI methods. To create a user within an AD domain, for example, you'll use the following code:

```
Set objDomain = GetObject("LDAP://dc=mycompany, dc=com")
Set objUser = objDomain.Create("user", cn="kmanderville")
objUser.put "sAMAccountName", "kmanderville"
objUser.setInfo
```

As you can see, there's quite a bit going on here. So let's break this code down line by line:

- `Set objDomain = GetObject("LDAP://dc=mycompany, dc=com")`: This line creates a connection to the mycompany.com domain, and creates the `objDomain` variable as a reference to that connection.

- `Set objUser = objDomain.Create("user", cn="kmanderville")`: This line creates a new variable called `objUser`. It then instructs `objDomain` to perform the `Create` method, to create a new object in the `"user"` class with the CN of `"kmanderville"`. The `objUser` variable is set as a reference to this newly created user.

- `objUser.put "sAMAccountName", "kmanderville"`: This line instructs the `objUser` variable to perform the `put` method, which puts the value of `"kmanderville"` into the `"sAMAccountName"` attribute of the new user object.

- `objUser.setInfo`: This command will save, or *commit*, the changes you just made to the Active Directory database. Any time that you add, modify, or delete information with an ADSI script, you need to use this `setInfo` command at the end to save your changes.

Making Choices

There will probably also be instances where you need your script to display some sort of decision-making abilities, where it will perform different actions based on the value of a variable or the result of a query. The simplest kind of choice your script can make is an `If...Then` statement. Basically, this translates to "If *this thing* is true, then do *this thing*." The syntax of the `If...Then` statement looks like this:

```
Option Explicit
Dim x

x = 2
y = 2
If x + y = 4 Then
  Wscript.Echo "2 + 2 = 4"
End If
```

For a more complex decision-making structure, you can add one or more ElseIf statements, translating to "If *this thing* is true, then do *this thing*. Or if *this other thing* is true, then do *this other thing*." You can have as many ElseIf statements as you want, but the final statement needs to be an Else and not an ElseIf—this is the script's way of saying "As your final choice, to this last thing here." The full syntax will look like this:

```
Option Explicit
Dim x

x = 2
y = 2
If x + y = 4 Then
  WScript.Echo "2 + 2 = 4"
Else If x + y = 5 Then
  WScript.Echo "The computer has forgotten how to add."
Else
  WScript.Echo "Something has gone terribly wrong in the universe."
End If
```

For even more complex decision-making routines, you might want to move from an If...Else statement to a Case statement. Say you have a variable that can have a value between 1 and 10, and you need your script to take a different action depending on the value of that variable. Now, you could use ten If...Else statements, but this makes for some ugly-looking code. A cleaner option would be to use a Case statement that looks like this:

```
switch (NumOfRunningProcesses)
  case 1 :
    WScript.Echo("One running process.")
    break;
  case 2 :
    WScript.Echo("Two running processes.")
    break;
  ...
  case 10 :
    WScript.Echo("Ten running processes.")
    break;
  default : WScript.Echo("Each case needs a default clause.")
```

As you can see, you need to finish up Case statements with that default clause. The default clause is basically a catchall—it's the thing that the Case statement should do if *none* of the cases matches the item specified in the opening switch.

Summary

I wrap things up in this chapter with a look at two topics that can really take your AD administrative skills to the next level. All of the objects that you work with in AD are ultimately based on the Active Directory schema, which defines how objects like user and group objects are created and what types of information they can contain. Since each Active Directory forest shares a single schema, editing this schema is a delicate operation and one that you need to plan carefully so as not to adversely affect the rest of your AD network. To help mitigate the risks associated with editing the Active Directory schema, Windows Server 2003 has created Active Directory Application Mode (AD/AM), which creates an isolated incidence of the AD database that developers can modify without these edits affecting the entirety of the network. If you find that you need to edit or extend the actual AD schema at any point, you'll need to know how to work with the Schema Master FSMO role holder, and how to enable this server to allow schema edits.

As a final treat, you also hold in your hands a primer to get you started with writing scripts to help to automate your administrative tasks. Scripting languages such as VBScript, JScript, Perl, and Python are freely available, and allow you to automate tasks such as creating and modifying user objects, as well as interact with workstation and server properties like services, processes, and the Windows file system. We looked at such fundamental tasks as creating variables, making decisions using `If...Else` and `Switch` constructs. We also looked at the powerful Windows Management Instrumentation tool that allows you to retrieve information about many aspects of the Windows operating system by performing SQL-like queries in the WMI Query Language. By integrating script automation into your administrator's arsenal, you'll save time and become a better and more efficient Active Directory administrator.

Additional Resources

Active Directory Schema Technical Reference: http://www.microsoft.com/resources/documentation/WindowsServ/2003/all/techref/en-us/Default.asp?url=/Resources/Documentation/windowsserv/2003/all/techref/en-us/W2K3TR_schem_intro.asp—Everything you ever wanted to know about the schema, from the people who know it best.

Active Directory Programmer's Guide: http://msdn.microsoft.com/library/default.asp?url=/library/en-us/ad/ad/active_directory.asp—Provides sample code to help you automate administrative tasks and manage the schema.

Active Directory Programming, by Gil Kirkpatrick. Sams. ISBN 0-672-31587-4 —This book was published in 2000 and is now out of print, but you can still find it from eBay or another reseller if you look for it. It's a great introduction to working with ADSI and the schema.

Microsoft Scripting Center: http://www.microsoft.com/technet/ scriptcenter/default.mspx—This is a free resource available on the Microsoft website that includes tutorials and webcasts about using scripting for system administration, as well as hundreds of ready-made scripts that you can easily customize to your own environment. This site is a goldmine for new and seasoned scripters alike.

Index

■W

well-connected, description, 14, 205
Windows Application Compatibility
    Toolkit, 228
Windows Catalog (Hardware
    Compatibility List), 223
Windows Management
    Instrumentation (WMI) filters,
    customizing inheritance
    policies, 122, 124–25
Windows Network Monitor, 150
Windows Server 2003
    anonymous access, 175
    application directory partitions, 213
    Automated System Recovery (ASR),
        260–69
    bridgehead server, 209
    changes, Active Directory security,
        163–64
    deactivation, schema or attributes,
        91
    delegation preconfigured tasks, 93
    dsmod tool, 84
    EFS disable, 110
    external trusts, 194
    forest trust, 197–98
    functional levels, new, 98, 199
    GPMC installation, 114
    GPO default permissions, 123
    GPO network access
        recommendations, 175
    group membership caching, 97
    Install application at logon option,
        144
    IP filter list options, new, 156
    IPSec features, new, 161
    Lan Manager authentication, 174
    Last Known Good Configuration,
        254
    logon event logging, Active
        Directory security, 179

migration scenario, NT, 240–49
netsh utility, 157
offline file configuration, 104
offline file synchronization, 107
primary restore, 270
registry settings, incompatible with
    Server 2000, 176
repadmin tool, 214
Secure-Only default, 55
software restriction options, 128
software restriction policies, 127, 128
supported domain controllers, 231
supported upgrade paths, 221–22
TCP/IP stack security, 163
Universal group membership
    caching, 212
user rights configuration, 169
Windows server upgrade paths, 221, 223
WINS integration into DNS, 48–49
WINS support, 68–70
    burst handling, 70
    client options, 71
    configuring replication, 72, 74
    database backup, 70
    database verification, 70
    extinction interval, 69
    extinction timeout, 69
    and NETBIOS, 68–73
    overview, 69
    renew interval, 69
    restoring the database, 71
WMI (Windows Management
    Instrumentation) filters,
    customizing inheritance
    policies, 122, 124–25
Write lockoutTime, Windows 2000, 191

■Z

Zone rules, Group Policy deployment,
    130